A Field Guide to the

CASCADES & OLYMPICS

Stephen R. Whitney

The Mountaineers • Seattle

THE MOUNTAINEERS: Organized 1906
". . . to explore and study the mountains,
forests, and watercourses of the Northwest."

Published by The Mountaineers
1001 S.W. Klickitat Way, Suite 201, Seattle WA 98134

Published simultaneously in Canada by Douglas & McIntyre, Ltd.
1615 Venables Street, Vancouver, British Columbia V5L 2H1

Published simultaneously in Great Britain by Cordee
3a DeMontfort St., Leicester, England LE1 7HD

Printed in Korea

Edited by Barbara Chasan
Book design by Elizabeth Watson
All illustrations by the author. Color plates rendered in acrylics
    on cold pressed illustration board.

Library of Congress Cataloging in Publication Data

Whitney, Stephen, 1942–
    A field guide to the Cascades & Olympics.

    Bibliography: p.
    Includes index.
    I. National history – Washington (State) – Olympic
Mountains.   2. Natural history – Cascade Range.
I. Title.   II. Title: Cascades & Olympics.
III. Title: Cascades and Olympics.
QH105.W2W47   1983   508.795   83-13121
ISBN 0-89886-077-6

09876

10987

CONTENTS

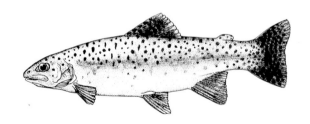

ACKNOWLEDGEMENTS

The author would like to thank the following people for their assistance in the preparation of this book: Bill Kemsley for generously supporting the project from its inception; members of The Mountaineers Editorial Review Committee for their helpful comments and criticisms; William F. Dengler and William Swift of the National Park Service for reviewing the manuscript; Jeffrey Schaffer for improving the sections on geology; Barbara Chasan for catching the little errors and inconsistencies that I overlooked; Betty Watson for her lovely design; and to my wife Vandana and son Aaron for tacitly consenting to tolerate my seemingly neverending stints in the study during the writing and illustration of this book.

Stephen Whitney
Seattle, Washington

INTRODUCTION

This guidebook is for readers who want to identify the common plants and animals of the Cascade Range and coastal ranges of southwestern British Columbia and the Pacific Northwest. Part I is an overview of the mountain ranges covered in this guide, with separate chapters devoted to physiography, geology, climate, and plant and animal distribution. Part II consists of separate field guides to ferns, wildflowers, shrubs, and trees. Part III provides similar guides to butterflies, trout and salmon, amphibians, reptiles, birds, and mammals. So this book is essentially 10 field guides rolled into one. It allows the mountain traveler to identify a wide variety of plants and animals without having to lug about a small library of specialized guidebooks.

Altogether this field guide contains accounts and illustrations of approximately 600 species of plants and animals. Important groups of organisms, such as mushrooms and insects, were omitted in order to keep this volume to a convenient, manageable size for use in the field. Other groups, such as grasses, lichens, mosses, aquatic plants, and most invertebrate animals, were omitted both for reasons of space and because they are either difficult to distinguish by species or are of relatively little interest to most casual observers.

GEOGRAPHIC SCOPE

The area covered by this guidebook includes all of the Cascade Range — from southern British Columbia to northern California — the Coast Mountains of British Columbia north to the Bella Coola River, the Vancouver Island Range, and the Olympic Mountains. Along the eastern flank of the Coast Mountains and Cascade Range, the area extends to the lower limit of the continuous forest. The book will also prove useful in the forested lowlands of southwestern British Columbia and western Washington and in the Oregon-Washington coast ranges (which should be distinguished from the Coast Mountains of British Columbia). Plants and animals of Oregon's drier interior valleys—the Willamette, Umpqua, and Rogue—are not included unless they also occur in the Cascades.

HOW TO USE THIS BOOK

Each chapter in parts I and II consists of an introduction followed by species accounts and corresponding illustrations. The latter are grouped on 90 plates, of which 36 are in color. Each plate depicts from six to twelve species either in paintings or line drawings. The corresponding species accounts are found on the page facing each plate, thereby eliminating the need to flip back and forth in the book when attempting to identify a plant or animal.

The format of the species accounts is more or less consistent throughout the book. Each account includes a common name, scientific name, description of important features, habitat and geographic range, and, in some cases, brief accounts of similar species. Since this guidebook is intended primarily for the observer untrained in the natural sciences, the species accounts employ a minimum of technical jargon. A few technical terms have been retained, however, particularly in the plant descriptions, because accurate or convenient vernacular substitutes do not exist. These terms are defined in the introduction to the chapters on ferns and flowering plants.

Common and Scientific Names. A common (English) name and a scientific (Latinate) name are provided for each species described in this book. Where more than one common name exists for a single species, alternatives are presented in parentheses. Sources of both common and scientific names are listed in the chapter introductions.

The concept of species is fundamental to the study of plants and animals, in particular to the practice of identifying and naming types. When we wish to know what "kind" of, say, bird we have seen, we are really asking what species it belongs to. Taxonomists—the biologists who specialize in the naming and classifications of organisms—commonly define a species as a population of actually or potentially interbreeding organisms that share a common gene pool. For example, all house cats belong to the same species because they are capable of producing offspring, whether they do in fact or not. The house cat and the mountain lion, however, though both are clearly cats, belong to different species because they are incapable of producing offspring under normal conditions. Two different species that are clearly related, as are those two, are assigned to the same genus, in this case *Felis*, which designates the "true" or typical cats.

Each scientific name has two parts. The first name, which is always capitalized, specifies the genus; the second name indicates the species. Thus the mountain lion is *Felis concolor*, the bobcat is *Felis rufus,* and the lynx is *Felis lynx.* Similarly, the western white pine is *Pinus monticola* and the ponderosa pine is *Pinus ponderosa.*

Two separate species may be so similar that they cannot be distinguished safely on the basis of outward appearance alone. Still other species include individual populations that differ markedly in appearance. Such distinctive populations are often designated as subspecies or varieties, a practice not followed by all biologists. In this guidebook subspecies and varieties are indicated only for populations that are consistently and dramatically different in appearance from other populations of the same species occurring in a region.

Above the generic level, taxonomists have grouped organisms in progressively more inclusive groups—families, orders, classes, phyla or divisions, and kingdoms—that express increasingly distant degrees of relationship among their members. This book groups plants and animals by family for purposes of discussion, but categories above the family level are not indicated.

Scientific names have three principal advantages over common, or English, names. First, scientific names not only designate the particular species but, by including the genus, indicate its relationship to other, similar species. Second, scientific names are unambiguous, each referring to one, and only one, species. Common names, on the other hand, may obscure an organism's relationship to other organisms. For example, Douglas-fir, *Pseudotsuga menziesii,* is not a true fir of the genus *Abies,* but a member of an entirely different genus of conifers. For a second example, *Montia sibirica* and *Claytonia lanceolata* are both sometimes called western spring beauty, even though they belong to entirely different genera. Finally, scientific names are recognized internationally, while common names often change from place to place or person to person.

Descriptions of Important Features. Following the names of each species is a brief description of the critical features (field marks) by which it can be identified. The emphasis is on those features that best distinguish the species from similar ones and that are readily apparent to an ordinary observer. In attempting to identify a specimen, readers are urged to use the species descriptions along with the illustrations because either may be insufficient by itself.

All measurements are given in feet and inches, but a table of metric conversions will be found on page 13 and rules marked in both inches and centimeters are printed on the last page of this guide. Measurements are included in the species accounts merely to give a general idea of size, not as a means for absolutely distinguishing one species from another.

Habitat and Geographic Range. Habitat expresses the ecological distribution of a species; range, the geographic distribution. In many instances similar species can be separated, at least tentatively, on the basis of different habitats or ranges. The various habitats in our mountains are discussed in chapter 4, "Plant and Animal Distribution." The range given for each species includes both its local distribution and its general occurrence worldwide. The phrases "in our area," "in our region," and "in our mountains" are synonymous and indicate the presence of a species in all the mountain ranges covered by this book.

Similar Species. Many species accounts include brief descriptions of similar species. This is usually the case either when a genus contains more local species than there is room in this guide to treat separately or when related species are so similar that a separate illustration is not warranted. In some cases a single genus containing numerous, very similar species is represented by only one species or a few more or less typical and common ones.

Illustrations. Paintings and line drawings are employed in this guidebook because they often show critical field marks more clearly than photographs. In most cases figures on a single plate are drawn to the same scale. Where two or more scales are used, each is indicated by a multiplication sign ($\times$) followed by a fraction. For example, $\times \frac{1}{2}$ means that a figure is shown one-half its actual size.

ON BEHALF OF THE MOUNTAINS

Those of us who love and frequent the mountains of our region should always leave an area and its inhabitants as little disturbed by our passage as possible so that what attracted us to the place will remain intact for others to enjoy in their turn. Certain habitats by their very nature are extremely fragile and deserve our special care. These include: wet or boggy places, where just a few bootprints can turn an emerald garden to black muck; dry, rocky places, where plants cling precariously to existence, and revegetation is a long, difficult, often chancy prospect; and subalpine and alpine habitats, where a combination of short growing seasons, low temperatures, reduced insolation, and poor soil conditions has produced extremely harsh conditions for plant growth. Alpine and subalpine plants are able to occupy their habitats through the evolution of a variety of ingenious anatomical, physiological, and behavioral features. Growth rates are so slow at such high elevations, however, that once disturbed, some communities may take many decades to fully recover. It is therefore important wherever possible that we stick to established trails, avoid trampling vegetation, and refrain from tramping across or camping in especially fragile wet meadows. It is also important not to cut across switchbacks, as the resulting erosion not only destroys the trail, but also the plants alongside.

We should also avoid taking specimens in our zeal to identify species. Collecting plants and animals is expressly forbidden in a number of preserves both in Canada and the United States, but the conscientious naturalist will refrain from the practice even where it is permitted. This guidebook concentrates on external field marks that can be ascertained readily without resort to hand-held specimens. Species that cannot be thus distinguished are treated generically and are best identified by genus or family alone. To molest or destroy an organism simply to learn its name is inexcusable under most conditions.

Wild animals present a special problem. Many people seem to lose all sense in their presence, insisting on behaving toward them as if they were house pets or lovable transplants from children's stories. The importance of leaving all wild animals alone cannot be overstressed. By encouraging campground animals to approach us or to take handouts of food, we degrade their dignity, disrupt their diets and behavior—on which their survival ultimately depends—and increase the danger of injury to ourselves by causing the animals to overcome their innate distrust of humans. The potential danger posed by large, unpredictable mammals such as bears should be apparent to anyone—though it demonstrably is not—but even cute little chipmunks and squirrels can and do inflict painful bites on the hands that feed them. It is also important not to handle young animals. Either you may injure them, or their parents, in the case of large animals such as bears, deer, and hawks, may injure you in the attempt to protect their young.

Many people have discovered and will continue to discover that a trip to the mountains, whether for camping, hiking, climbing, skiing, fishing, or hunting, becomes a richer, more enjoyable experience when they are able to identify the plants and animals they encounter. When we name a plant or animal, we have formally made its acquaintance, and when we encounter it again, we will greet it as a familiar companion. In this way we can begin to experience the mountains more intimately and thereby perhaps come a step closer to understanding them better. Upon such an understanding of the natural world, the future of our species, *Homo sapiens,* may ultimately depend.

ABBREVIATIONS

The wish to keep all species accounts on the page facing their corresponding illustrations required the extensive use of abbreviations. Most should be self-evident. In any case, all are listed below. In addition, when the name of a genus or species occurs more than once in a single paragraph, it is first written out completely, then indicated in subsequent citations only by its initial letter. For example:

Grand Fir, *Abies grandis*

Red Fir, *A. magnifica* = *Abies magnifica*

Shasta Fir, *A. m.* var *shastensis* = *Abies magnifica* variety *shastensis*

abun	*abundant*	cf	*refer to*
Alas	*Alaska*	CMtns	*Coast Mountains of*
Albta	*Alberta*		*British Columbia*
alp	*alpine, alpine zone*	Colo	*Colorado*
alt	*alternate*	com	*common*
Apr	*April*	conif	*conifer(ous)*
Amer	*America*	CRGorge	*Columbia River*
Ariz	*Arizona*		*Gorge*
Atl	*Atlantic*		
Aug	*August*		
		diam	*diameter*
Baja	*Baja California*	dk	*dark*
BC	*British Columbia*		
		e(E)	*east(ern, ward)*
ca	*approximately*	ea	*each*
Cal	*California*	E Cas	*eastern Cascades*
Can	*Canada*	E CMtns	*eastern Coast*
Cas	*Cascade Range*		*Mountains*
cen	*central*	el	*elevation*
Cen Amer	*Central America*	esp	*especially*

F	*female*	OMtns	*Olympic Mountains*
flr(s)	*flower(s)*	OPen	*Olympic Peninsula*
FW	*forewing (butterflies)*	opp	*opposite*
		Ore	*Oregon*
gen	*generally*		
		Pac	*Pacific*
H/B	*head and body length*		
	in mammals	R	*River*
hemis	*hemisphere*	reg	*regular*
ht (Ht)	*height*	res	*resident; birds*
HW	*hindwing (butterflies)*		*(present year-around)*
		RM	*Rocky Mountains*
inflor	*inflorescence*		
irreg	*irregular*	s (S)	*south(ern, ward)*
		S Amer	*South America*
L	*length*	sbsp	*subspecies*
lb(s)	*pound(s)*	se	*southeast(ern, ward)*
lf	*leaf*	segm	*segment(s)*
lfless	*leafless*	Sept	*September*
lflet	*leaflet*	SNev	*Sierra Nevada*
lowl	*lowland(s)*	sp	*species (singular)*
lvd	*leaved*	spp	*species (plural)*
lvs	*leaves*	spr	*spring*
		subalp	*subalpine, subalpine*
M	*male*		*zone*
mdw(s)	*meadow(s)*	sum	*summer*
mid	*middle*	sum res	*summer resident;*
migr	*migrant*		*birds (nests in our*
Minn	*Minnesota*		*region in the*
Mont	*Montana*		*summer; absent in*
mont	*montane*		*winter)*
mtn(s)	*mountain(s)*	sw	*southwest(ern, ward)*
n (N)	*north(ern, ward)*	T	*tail length for*
N Amer	*North America*		*mammals*
NCas	*North Cascades*		
NDak	*North Dakota*	uncom	*uncommon*
ne	*northeast(ern, ward)*	US	*United States*
NEng	*New England*		*exclusive of Alaska*
Nev	*Nevada*		*and Hawaii*
NMex	*New Mexico*	usu	*usually*
n Mex	*northern Mexico*		
		Vanc I	*Vancouver Island*
occas	*occasional(ly)*	var	*variety*
Oct	*October*	vis	*visitor*
oft	*often*	Vt	*Vermont*

w (W)	west(ern, ward)	×	times, as in 2× =
W Cas	western Cascades		two times and × ½ =
W CMtns	western Coast		times one-half
	Mountains	+	or more, as in 2+ =
win	winter		two or more
Wn	Washington	±	more or less
WS	wingspan (butterflies)		
wt (Wt)	weight		

METRIC CONVERSION TABLE

1 inch = 2.54 centimeters
1 foot = .3048 meters
1 mile = 1.6 kilometers
F° = 9/5 C° + 32

Part I

THE MOUNTAIN ENVIRONMENT

THE MOUNTAINS

Two great parallel mountain systems form the North American Cordillera: the Rocky Mountain System on the east and the Pacific Mountain System on the west. Separating them is a series of high plateaus, including the Interior Plateau of British Columbia, the Columbia Plateau of Washington and northern Oregon, and the Great Basin, which stretches from southern Oregon to southern Nevada. In Alaska the Pacific Mountain System includes the Aleutian Islands, the great arc of the Alaska Range, and the lofty Wrangell and St. Elias ranges. The latter merge in southeastern Alaska with the Coast Mountains of British Columbia, which extend the length of the province. West of the Coast Mountains, beyond the Hecate Depression and Strait of Georgia — southern legs in the famed Inside Passage to Alaska — rises the Insular Range, which consists of the Queen Charlotte Islands to the north and Vancouver Island to the south. In southern British Columbia the Coast Mountains merge with the Cascade Range, which extends southward to northern California, where it merges in turn with the Sierra Nevada. West of the Cascade-Sierra axis rise the parallel Coast Ranges of Washington, Oregon, and California, which culminate in the Olympic Mountains of northwestern Washington. In southwestern Oregon and northwestern California the rugged Klamath Mountains interrupt the Coast Ranges, forming a bridge between them and the southern Cascades. The southernmost section of the Pacific Mountain System consists of the Transverse and Peninsular ranges of southern California, the latter extending southward into Mexico to become the backbone of Baja California.

THE CASCADE RANGE

The Cascade Range extends from the Fraser River in southern British Columbia to just south of Lassen Peak in northern California. The range is

Figure 1. Mountain ranges covered by this book.

approximately 700 miles long and varies in width from 30 miles in southern Oregon and British Columbia to 120 miles along the international boundary, where it merges on the east with the Okanogan (Okanagan) Highlands. A series of lowlands borders the Cascades on the west: the Puget Lowland of western Washington and southwestern British Columbia; the Willamette, Umpqua, and Rogue river valleys of Oregon; and the northernmost portion of the Sacramento Valley in California. East of the Cascades lie the Thompson Plateau of British Columbia, the Columbia Plateau of Washington and northern Oregon, and the Basin and Range plateaus of southern Oregon and northeastern California.

From Lassen Peak to central Washington the Cascade Range is a broad highland of modest elevation surmounted at intervals by volcanoes from 8000 feet to more than 14,000 feet in height. This portion of the range—hereinafter referred to as the southern Cascades—is made up almost entirely of volcanic rocks, primarily andesite, as old as 40 million years and as young as the recent eruptions of Mt. St. Helens. From Snoqualmie Pass, east of Seattle, north to the Fraser River, the nature of the range changes dramatically. Although two large volcanoes crown this section as well, they rise above a maze of spectacular alpine ridges, some of which nearly approach the great cones in height. This section of the range, known as the North Cascades, consists primarily of metamorphic rocks—mostly gneiss, schist, and phyllite—between 100 million and more than 1 billion years old and granitic rocks—mostly quartz diorite and granodiorite—18 to 90 million years old. In topography and geology the North Cascades are more closely allied to the Coast Mountains of British Columbia, with which they merge, than they are to the southern Cascades.

The great Cascade volcanoes are the most distinctive feature of the range and, since the 1980 eruption of Mt. St. Helens, the most notorious as well. From north to south they are as follows:

Mt. Baker	10,778 feet	Washington
Glacier Peak	10,541 feet	Washington
Mt. Rainier	14,410 feet	Washington
Mt. Adams	12,307 feet	Washington
Mt. St. Helens	ca. 8400 feet	Washington
Mt. Hood	11,235 feet	Oregon
Mt. Jefferson	10,497 feet	Oregon
Three Sisters		
North Sister	10,085 feet	Oregon
Middle Sister	10,047 feet	Oregon
South Sister	10,358 feet	Oregon
"Mt. Mazama"	8156 feet	Oregon
(Crater Lake)		
Mt.McLoughlin	9495 feet	Oregon
Mt. Shasta	14,162 feet	California
Lassen Peak	10,457 feet	California

In addition to these major volcanoes, countless smaller cones are scattered throughout the length of the range.

The undisputed monarch of the Cascades is Mt. Rainier, which rises 8000 feet above its neighboring ridges and nearly three miles above the Puget Lowland at its base. Few other mountains so completely dominate their surroundings. The most massive of the Cascade volcanoes, however, is Mt. Shasta, which is nearly as high as Rainier and covers more than 300 square miles. It features a secondary summit, Shastina, that is the third highest peak in the range, after Rainier and Shasta itself. All of the Cascade volcanoes are magnificent, nearly symmetrical cones that rise an average of one mile above the surrounding mountains. Most are stratovolcanoes consisting of alternating layers of lava and volcanic rock debris (pyroclastics). Lassen Peak, however, is a giant lava dome flanked by volcanic talus slopes.*

From the Three Sisters, in central Oregon, northward, all the major Cascade volcanoes but Mt. St. Helens have alpine glaciers on their flanks. Ice covering 20 square miles almost completely mantles Mt. Baker, in the North Cascades. Mt. Rainier, owing to its far greater bulk, is less icebound but nevertheless supports the largest single glacier system in the contiguous United States, with 26 named glaciers covering 34 square miles. Mt. Adams, Mt. Hood, and Glacier Peak also bear significant amounts of ice. Mt. Shasta's five summit glacierets, though small, form the largest assemblage in California.

The North Cascades are a deeply dissected mountain range in which countless icy crags rise abruptly from river valleys of remarkably low elevation. Although summit elevations are modest by Cordilleran standards — about 6500 to 9500 feet for nonvolcanic peaks — local relief is awesome. Ridges commonly rise 5000 to 7000 feet in the space of three miles, starting from valley floors that often lie at only 1000 to 2000 feet deep within the heart of the range. Among the higher nonvolcanic peaks are Bonanza Peak (9511 feet), Mt. Stuart (9415 feet), Mt. Fernow (9249 feet), and Mt. Shuksan (9127 feet), all in Washington. In the Cascades of British Columbia the highest peaks are Lakeview Mountain (8622 feet), Mt. Grimface (8600+ feet), and Cathedral Peak (8601 feet).

The rugged topography of the North Cascades is the product of stream cutting followed by profound glacial scouring during the Ice Age. Today, the higher ridges west of the crest, less commonly to the east, bear alpine glaciers and perennial snow fields. The largest concentrations of ice occur on Glacier Peak, Mt. Baker, Mt. Shuksan, the Picket Range, the El Dorado massif, and near Dome Peak. There are some 750 glaciers in the American North Cascades, covering 104.3 square miles — about half the area covered by all other glaciers in the contiguous United States combined.

The Columbia River and its tributaries comprise the principal river system of the Cascade Range, draining the entire chain northward from central Oregon to Mt. Rainier on the western flank and British Columbia on the eastern flank. Rising in the Canadian Rockies, the Columbia River flows 1200 miles to the Pacific Ocean, enroute ploughing through the Cascades in a spectacular gorge bounded by lava cliffs. The river's present course through the gorge predates uplift of the range. As the mountains arched upward, the river eroded its channel faster, thereby entrenching itself in the young range. Great arches and sags in the piled lava flows that make up the walls of the gorge record the folding and crumpling that accompanied uplift.

Other important Cascade rivers include: tributaries of the Fraser River in British Columbia; the Skagit River of the North Cascades; the Ashnola, Okanogan, Cowlitz, Deschutes, and Willamette rivers, all tributaries of the Columbia; the Umpqua, Rogue, and Klamath rivers in southern Oregon; and the Sacramento River in northern California.

Lovely mountain lakes abound in the Cascade Range, particularly near timberline, where they lie in glacially quarried rock basins. Glacial lakes are most abundant in the North Cascades but also occur southward in the range. One of the most remarkable bodies of water in the Cascades is Lake Chelan, a slender finger lake about 50 miles long and one mile across. It occupies most of the Stehekin Valley on the eastern flank of the North Cascades. The lake is dammed at the mouth of the valley behind a ridge of glacial drift that was deposited by the Okanogan Lobe of the Cordilleran Ice Sheet during its advance into the Columbia Basin about 15,000 years ago. Bounded by mountains on each side, Lake Chelan resembles nothing so much as a land-locked fiord.

Some of the lakes in the southern Cascades are the results of volcanic activity rather than glacial processes. Most of these lakes lie behind dams of lava or volcanic mud, but Crater Lake, at an elevation of 6176 feet, occupies the collapsed summit, or caldera, of Mt. Mazama, which erupted violently about 6900 years ago. The lake's level remains nearly constant, representing a balance between current precipitation and seepage. Crater Lake is roughly circular in outline, about 5 miles across, nearly 2000 feet deep, and encircled by cliffs up to about 2000 feet tall. Its great depth, exceeding that of any other lake in North America, is responsible for the deep, inky blue color of the water. Crater Lake is the supreme gem among the lakes of the Cascade Range.

THE COAST MOUNTAINS

The Coast Mountains of British Columbia extend northward from the North Cascades to the Yukon. The range is about 1000 miles long and 30 to 100 miles wide. On the west it rises abruptly from the Inside Passage, its flanks deeply indented by spectacular fiords up to 60 miles long, 2 miles wide, and 2000 feet deep. The steep walls of the fiords, laced with waterfalls, rise precipitously to 6000- to 8000-foot glaciated peaks. Summit elevations increase considerably toward the center of the range, where numerous peaks top

9000 feet and in some areas exceed 10,000 to 13,000 feet. The range is bordered on the east by the Interior Plateau and its associated highlands.

The Coast Mountains consist of three sections, each roughly 300 miles long: the Boundary Ranges on the north, the Kitimat Ranges in the center, and the Pacific Ranges on the south. This guidebook is concerned only with the Pacific Ranges, which extend from the Fraser River north to the Bella Coola River. The Pacific Ranges constitute the highest section of the Coast Mountains, culminating in 13,177-foot Mt. Waddington, which sits at the head of Knight Inlet, about 200 miles north of the city of Vancouver. A number of other peaks rise above 10,000 feet, including Monarch Mountain (11,590 feet) and Mt. Tidemann (12,800 feet).

As indicated earlier, the Coast Mountains are remarkably like the North Cascades in both topography and geology, a relationship obscured by their historical division into two separate ranges along the boundary of the Fraser River. The Pacific Ranges feature the same spectacular alpine scenery as the North Cascades, except on an even grander scale. High craggy summits abound, their upper flanks mantled in ice, their sides plunging to deep glacial valleys. The Pacific Ranges, owing to their more northerly position and therefore cooler, wetter summers, boast the most numerous and extensive ice fields found in any of the mountains covered by this book. Located in the central portion of the ranges, in areas around Mt. Silverthrone, Mt. Waddington, Mt. Grenville, Mt. Gilbert, and the headwaters of the Lillooet River, these vast ice fields dwarf anything found in the North Cascades.

During the Ice Age, most of British Columbia lay at various times beneath thousands of feet of ice. The Pacific Ranges were one of the principal accumulation centers for the Cordilleran Ice Sheet, which pushed westward to Vancouver Island and southward into the Puget Lowland, North Cascades, and Columbia Basin. Glaciation began with the formation of alpine glaciers; these coalesced to form ice caps and spawned valley glaciers that pushed into the lowlands. Eventually the ice became so thick that it overrode all but the highest peaks and formed a continuous cap, the surface of which stood at 5000 to 8000 feet above sea level.

The Pacific Ranges consist of the same types of rocks as the North Cascades, but the proportions are reversed. The North Cascades feature large expanses of metamorphic rocks interrupted by intrusions of granitic rocks, whereas the Pacific Ranges consist almost entirely of granitic and related crystalline rocks in which older metamorphic rocks persist mainly as isolated caps or as slices sandwiched among the granites. The rocks of the Coast Mountains Crystalline Complex, one of the most extensive fields of granite in the world, originated as magma, or molten rock, deep within the earth. These rocks were later uplifted and exposed by erosion. The most extensive metamorphic outcrops occur along the eastern margin of the Pacific Ranges, notably in the Chilcotin Mountains, a prominent subsidiary range. Most of the granites and gneisses of the Coast Mountains Crystalline Complex formed between 50 and 125 million years ago, with individual intrusions ranging in age from 20 million to 220 million years.

Volcanoes of types and ages comparable to the younger cones of the Cascade Range occur in three belts in the Coast Mountains. The southern belt extends northward from Vancouver and includes Mt. Garibaldi (8787 feet), a stratovolcano. The Coast Mountains volcanoes, however, are nowhere near as numerous, as tall, or as grand as those of the Cascade Range.

One of the remarkable features of the Coast Mountains is the large number of rivers that originate east of the range but cut directly across it in deep gorges en route to the Pacific Ocean. In the Pacific Ranges such rivers include the Fraser, Klinaklini, Bella Coola, and Homathko. They, like the Columbia River through the Cascades, were able to maintain their courses across a rising mountain range. Among the principal westbound rivers of the Pacific Ranges, only the Lillooet, a tributary of the Fraser, rises within the mountains rather than on the Fraser Plateau to the east.

The lower reaches of the river valleys were scoured by glaciers well below the present sea level and are now flooded by salt water. These are the famous fiords of British Columbia's west coast, which rival in size and magnificence those of Norway, New Zealand, and Chile.

THE OLYMPIC MOUNTAINS

The Olympic Mountains rise from coastal plains and salt-water shores to culminate in icy crags nearly 8000 feet high. They form the wilderness core of Washington's Olympic Peninsula, a square thumb of land about 85 miles across with an area of some 6500 square miles. The peninsula is bounded on the west by the Pacific Ocean, on the north by the Strait of Juan de Fuca, which separates it from Vancouver Island, and on the east by the fiordlike Hood Canal, an arm of the inland sea. No peak in the Olympics is farther than 30 miles from salt water.

The Olympics form a roughly circular mountain complex about 55 miles across and some 3000 square miles in area, with ridges and valleys running every which way in apparent topographic confusion. The loftiest peaks are less than 8000 feet high, and most prominent summits are in the 5500- to 7000-foot range. Nevertheless, these mountains are dramatic in their isolation and bold, craggy architecture. Mt. Olympus (7965 feet), the highest peak in the range, is a massive, multi-summited mountain rising about 6500 feet above adjacent valleys. The Olympus massif, which includes several peaks over 7000 feet high, is located in the west-central Olympics. Other "7000-footers" occur in the eastern half of the range. Local relief in the Olympics often equals and sometimes exceeds 5000 feet in three miles.

The Olympics were repeatedly glaciated during the Ice Age. The nearly 60 glaciers now found in the range, however, are of more recent origin. The greatest concentration of ice occurs on the Olympus massif, where 6 major glaciers cover some 15 square miles. The Hoh and Blue glaciers extend down their respective valleys for nearly 3 miles to elevations near 4000 feet. Smaller glaciers occur on the Bailey Range, the Valhallas, the peaks flanking Low Divide, the Mt. Anderson massif, and in the northeastern corner of the Olympics.

The Olympic Mountains are composed of marine basalts, sandstones, and shales that were slightly metamorphosed during the course of mountain building. Although many Olympic peaks are composed of basalt, a highly fluid lava of the type produced by the famous Hawaiian volcanoes, none of the peaks are themselves volcanoes. Instead, they are the eroded remnants of a huge pile of basalt that accumulated 30 to 55 million years ago on the sea floor as a consequence of recurrent submarine volcanic activity during that period. Later, the lavas and their associated sedimentary rocks were uplifted, folded, metamorphosed, and deeply eroded to produce the mountains we see today. The underwater origin of the Olympic basalts is indicated by their globular "pillow" structure, which is so evident in numerous outcrops. The lava flows that formed these rocks piled up to depths of many thousands of feet, eventually breaking the ocean surface to form a chain of islands. Evidence for these islands exists in the uppermost flows, which show features, such as columnar jointing, that do not occur in submarine lavas. The Olympic sandstones and shales originated as deposits of sand and mud that were carried to the sea by rivers draining the adjacent continent.

Drainage in the Olympics is radial, with streams flowing down all sides of the range. The Quinault, Queets, Hoh, Bogachiel, and Soleduck rivers flow westward to the Pacific Ocean; the Elwha and Dungeness rivers, northward to the Strait of Juan de Fuca; the Quilcene, Dosewallips, Duckabush, Hamma Hamma, and Skokomish rivers, eastward to the Hood Canal; and the Wynoochee and Humptulips rivers, southward to the Chehalis River and Grays Harbor respectively. All the streams head in glacial cirques, where they are nourished year around by glaciers or snowmelt. They flow down abandoned glacial valleys into which they have cut precipitous inner gorges 100 feet deep or more. Although the eastern streams have short, steep courses, those on the west have relatively gentle gradients for most of their length. Valley floors commonly lie below 1500 feet within less than 10 miles of the headwater basins.

THE VANCOUVER ISLAND RANGE

Vancouver Island and the Queen Charlotte Islands to the north are part of the mostly submerged Insular Range, an offshore chain that is separated from the Coast Mountains of the British Columbia mainland by the Hecate Depression and the Strait of Georgia. West of the Insular Range lies the open water of the northern Pacific Ocean.

The Vancouver Island Range forms the rocky backbone of that island, running nearly its entire length but reaching greatest elevation in the north-central section. The highest peaks—Golden Hinde (7219 feet), Elkhorn (7190 feet), and Victoria Peak (7095 feet)—are all found in this area, north and south of which ridge elevations decrease to 4000 to 5000 feet or less.

During the Ice Age, Vancouver Island was covered at elevations above 4000 feet by alpine glaciers and below 4000 feet by the Cordilleran Ice Sheet. As one would expect, glacial sculpting has produced in these mountains the same general type of spectacular alpine scenery that characterizes the other ranges included in this book. Today, there are 219 small glaciers in the range, some extending to an elevation as low as 2200 feet. An extensive, gentle upland surface is a distinctive feature of the range in the Nanaimo Lakes region of Strathcona Provincial Park. Numerous peaks rise above this surface. The west side of Vancouver Island is deeply indented by fiords, though none is as spectacular as those of the mainland, and countless glacial lakes, both large and small, occur from the lowlands to the high country.

Although the Vancouver Island Range resembles the Olympics in its general ruggedness and vegetation, the two ranges are geologically unrelated. The oldest rocks in the Olympics date back only about 50 million years, but those in the Vancouver Island Range are mainly 65 to 225 million years old. They consist of a heterogeneous group of sedimentary and volcanic rocks intruded by numerous bodies of granite. The rocks of the Queen Charlotte Islands are of similar age and type. The Insular Range probably was uplifted during the same general period of mountain building that produced the Coast Mountains on the mainland.

2

THE GEOLOGIC STORY

Most geologists now agree that mountain ranges form along the boundaries of huge, slowly moving plates that make up the earth's crust. New crustal material is generated as upwelling basalt along mid-ocean ridges. Plates move out from the ridges and are consumed along the continental margins, where they meet and dive beneath plates bearing the continents.

In the process—called plate subduction—marine sedimentary and volcanic rocks resting on the sea floor may be folded and metamorphosed as they are compressed against the continents. Metamorphosis involves the chemical and physical alteration of rocks as a result of enormous heat and pressure of the sort commonly experienced during the course of mountain building. When rocks are folded, sheared, buried at great depth, or intruded by large bodies of magma, old minerals may break down and new ones form in their place, even though the rocks remain all the while in their original solid state. Granite is thus altered to form gneiss, shale to form slate, limestone to form marble, and volcanic rocks to form schist or greenstone. Other types of metamorphic rocks in our mountains include phyllite, quartzite, and hornfels.

As an oceanic plate dives beneath a continent, slices of sea floor may be scraped off on the continental lip or thrust up and outward along nearly horizontal faults. In the North Cascades, for example, great sheets of rocks were displaced for miles along such thrust faults. Associated with those faults are granitic gneisses of the Yellow Aster Complex, which date back well over one billion years and are the oldest rocks found in any of the mountain ranges discussed in this book.

When diving plates reach sufficient depth, tens of miles beneath the earth's surface, heat and pressure become so intense that the rocks begin to melt, forming plumes of magma that rise buoyantly into the overlying rocks. In the process, the rising magma melts and incorporates a portion of the overlying rocks and, along its periphery, metamorphoses adjacent rock formations. As the magma slowly cools, insulated by the thick roof of older rocks, various types of large mineral crystals—primarily quartz, feldspars, and mica—precipitate out of solution and bond together to form granite and related rocks. Large fields of granitic, or intrusive, rocks are called *batholiths,* meaning deep rocks. These may be eventually brought to near the earth's surface by uplift and then ultimately exposed through erosion of the overlying rocks. The Coast Mountains Crystalline Complex consists of numerous batholiths of various composition. A number of relatively small batholiths outcrop on Vancouver Island and in the North Cascades.

Perhaps 100 million years ago, plate subduction along the northern Pacific margin began to deform and metamorphose the marine volcanic and sedimentary rocks that now outcrop so conspicuously in the North Cascades and to a lesser extent in the Coast Mountains and Vancouver Island Range. These rocks were folded, faulted, and metamorphosed to schists, slates, phyllites, and other metamorphic rocks. Granites of comparable age were metamorphosed to gneiss, which together with schist forms the core of the North Cascades. After deformation subsided, about 80 million years ago, large batholiths began to intrude into the metamorphic roof, a process that continued at least until about 15 million years ago and may be continuing unseen today. This early phase of mountain building in our region culminated in the formation of sizeable mountain ranges, precursors to those of today, but by 40 million years ago they had been eroded to ranges of hills.

During the emplacement of batholiths, significant amounts of magma typically rise to the earth's surface by way of faults and fissures in the overlying rocks. Upon reaching the surface the magma erupts from volcanic vents in the form of lava. Volcanic rocks are therefore identical in source and mineral composition to granitic rocks, differing mainly in texture. Volcanic rocks are typically fine grained because, in the lower temperatures near and at the earth's surface, they cool too rapidly for large crystals to form. Andesite, the most common type of volcanic rock in the Cascade Range, is the volcanic equivalent of quartz diorite, the most common type of granitic rock in those mountains.

Volcanism is most evident and widespread in the southern Cascades, where the oldest rocks are lavas and pyroclastics about 55 million years old. They outcrop notably near Mt. Rainier, which is much younger, and in the Western Cascades of Oregon. Over the following 10 to 15 million years, volcanoes continued to erupt enormous amounts of material. Then, about 18 million years ago the Cascades were again uplifted, folded, and intruded by granite, only to be reduced once again to low hills. About 15 million years ago, basalts flooded from fissures east of the Cascades to bury most of eastern Washington—as well as adjacent parts of British Columbia, Oregon, and western Washington—to depths of 2000 feet in the Columbia River Gorge and more than 5000 feet in parts of the Columbia Basin.

The modern Cascade Range was uplifted 5 to 6 million years ago, and the

Coast Mountains and Vancouver Island Range are of comparable age. Uplift in the Cascades was approximately 8000 feet in the North Cascades, diminishing to about 3000 feet at the Columbia River and steadily less southward into Oregon. Uplift was minor in southern Oregon and northern California, where subsequent accumulations of volcanic material are primarily responsible for current elevations. The Cascade Range probably reached its present height about 3 million years ago. Uplift in the Coast Mountains is probably continuing today.

The Olympic Mountains present one of the clearest, most straightforward examples of a mountain range forming as a result of plate subduction along a continental margin. Between 30 and 55 million years ago, submarine basalts piled up on the sea floor, and continental sediments were deposited on both the seaward and landward sides of the pile. About 30 million years ago, the Juan de Fuca Plate began to plunge beneath the continent. The basalts and landward sediments were scraped off against the continental margin and folded in the process. The seaward sediments were folded more severely, faulted, and thrust by the diving plate beneath the basalt pile. Plate movement ceased about 12 million years ago, and the sedimentary rocks, being lighter than the sea floor crust, bobbed upward, in the process upending the basalt flows. As uplift continued, streams poured down all sides of the resulting dome, incising the radial pattern of ridges and valleys that exists today.

The rugged and spectacular alpine topography of the North Cascades, Coast Mountains, Olympic Mountains, and Vancouver Island Range is the product of glacial erosion in terrain already deeply cut by streams. Alpine glaciers form when the amounts of snow that fall in successive winters exceed the amounts that melt during the intervening summers. The accumulated snow becomes compacted and gradually changes to ice. When a body of ice becomes large enough, it begins to flow plastically downslope in response to gravity. In the process it quarries huge amounts of rock from the confining walls and floors of its valley and transports these materials downslope, eventually depositing the rubble in ridges called moraines. In their retreat, glaciers litter their beds with stranded boulders—called erratics—which they earlier had plucked from upstream quarries and transported downslope. As a result, erratics may be entirely different types of rocks than those upon which they finally come to rest.

Glaciers strip the land of vegetation and soil and polish the underlying rock to a high sheen. Remnants of glacial polish persisting from the Ice Age exist throughout our mountains. Rock materials embedded in the bottom of a glacier also cut shallow, parallel grooves, or striations, into the rock, and by examining the grooves, geologists can determine which direction a glacier was flowing.

Glaciated mountain ranges exhibit concave or scooped-out landforms resulting from glacial quarrying. Mountainsides are scalloped with cirques—large ice-carved amphitheaters located at the heads of glacial valleys.

Cirque development around the perimeter of a mountain produces a pyramidal peak, or matterhorn. Cirque formation on opposite sides of the same ridge reduces it to a knife-edged arête. Glaciated valleys are typically U-shaped troughs produced as ice streams steepened, widened, and straightened what were formerly V-shaped river canyons. Smaller, tributary glaciers, unable to quarry as deeply as the trunk glaciers, produced hanging valleys that intersect the main valleys high above their floors. In addition, glacial valleys often feature a series of giant steps—flat areas—and risers—cliffs—along their courses. Giant staircases of this kind, which are so familiar to backpackers trudging up a mountain valley, result from differential erosion as a glacier moves downslope.

Within the past 600,000 years, more or less, all our mountains have experienced at least four major glaciations. These were separated by long interglacial periods in which the climate was as warm or warmer than it is today.* Our knowledge of the earlier glacial advances is scanty because the most recent one destroyed most of the evidence. This latest advance began about 21,000 years ago with the growth of alpine glaciers throughout our mountains. Ice accumulation was greatest in the Coast Mountains, where glaciers coalesced to form a vast ice sheet that buried the range to a depth of 8000 feet and pushed southward into Washington and westward to Vancouver Island. At its maximum advance, about 15,000 years ago, the Cordilleran Ice Sheet had pushed as far south as Olympia and as far west as the Pacific Ocean. In the Columbia Basin another lobe for a time displaced the Columbia River southward from its present channel, causing the river to erode the now abandoned Grand Coulee of eastern Washington.

The Cordilleran Ice Sheet was about 8000 feet thick in northern Washington, 3000 feet thick at Seattle, and 1000 feet thick at Olympia. It buried the North Cascades as far south as Darrington and banked up against the western front of the range—as well as the eastern and northern fronts of the Olympics—as far south as Mt. Rainier. During this period, alpine glaciers in the Cascades and Olympics had retreated to their accumulation basins, and large lakes formed behind the lowland ice that dammed the mouth of each valley. About 13,500 years ago, as the Cordilleran ice was in retreat, alpine glaciers began to advance once again, but by 10,000 years ago they too were on the wane. Present-day glaciers in our region developed during periods of cooling that have occurred within the last 3000 to 5000 years.

The major Cascade volcanoes are among the youngest geologic features in our mountains, having formed within the last 700,000 years atop a range that had already reached its present height. The relative symmetry and great height of these cones, despite the repeated assaults of Ice Age glaciers, suggests that the volcanoes continued to erupt during that period, repairing

---

* Many climatologists and glaciologists believe that the Ice Age is not yet over and that the present era of relatively warmer climate, which began about 10,000 years ago, is but one more interglacial period.

eroded slopes with new lava. The mudflows resulting as lava poured over the ice fields must have been prodigious indeed.

Evidence of numerous violent eruptions over the past several thousand years persists in the form of volcanic ash (minute particles of volcanic rock) and pumice, a porous volcanic glass. Both are typically products of explosive eruptions of the type that recently occurred at Mt. St. Helens. Pumice blankets large areas throughout the Cascades, particularly east of Crater Lake. Much of the pumice was produced about 6900 years ago during the final eruption of Mt. Mazama, the most violent thus far experienced by any of the recent Cascade volcanoes. Mt. Mazama expelled more than 12 cubic miles of pyroclastic debris, much of it pumice, over an area of 350,000 square miles. The summit of the then 12,000-foot volcano collapsed into the void created by the emptying of its magma chamber, producing the enormous caldera—improperly called a crater—that now holds Crater Lake.

Mts. Hood, Rainier, Baker, St. Helens, Shasta, and Lassen Peak have all experienced eruptions of varying magnitude over the past two centuries. Lassen Peak, which was active from 1914 to 1917, is the only Cascade volcano other than Mt. St. Helens to have erupted in this century. St. Helens, though relatively quiet after its massive explosion of 1980, has not yet subsided into dormancy. Moreover, it is entirely possible that other volcanoes in the range could awaken in our lifetimes. Clearly, the forces that made the mountains have yet to complete their work.

3

THE CLIMATE

Two major factors govern weather and climate in British Columbia and the Pacific Northwest. One is the interplay of two atmospheric pressure cells over the northern Pacific Ocean. The other is the position of the Coast Mountains and Cascade Range across the track of the prevailing westerlies, which creates a sharp contrast in climate between coastal and interior regions.

The abundant rainfall for which the region is notorious results from its proximity to a great storm factory situated in the Gulf of Alaska. In both the mountains and the lowlands, the greatest amounts of precipitation (75 to 85 percent of a year's total in the Puget-Willamette lowlands) fall from October 31 through March 31. Winter storms are generated by an enormous center of rising air called the Aleutian Low, which sits over the Gulf of Alaska during that season. Winds associated with these storms circulate in a counter-clockwise direction, causing them to strike the coast from the southwest.

As spring progresses, however, the low is gradually displaced northward by the North Pacific High, a large fair-weather system centered between Hawaii and North America. Winds radiate from the high in a clockwise direction and cover most of the northern Pacific, diverting most low-pressure systems northward and thereby bringing drier weather to the west coast of North America. The winds strike the coast from the northwest and pass over frigid coastal waters. As a result the air is cooled and much of its water vapor condenses to form fogs that blanket the coast for prolonged periods in summer. The warmest, driest periods in our region occur when high pressure systems develop to the east of the mountains, causing warm, dry winds from the interior to blow toward the coast.

Mountain ranges create their own climates by forcing incoming air masses upward. In the process the air cools at an average rate of 3.5°F per 1000 feet. The actual rate for any given time and place varies considerably from this mean. By-products of this cooling are cloud formation and increased precipitation. A volume of air can hold only so much water vapor—an invisible gas—and the amount it can hold decreases as the air becomes cooler. When air ascending a mountain slope is cooled to its saturation point, excess water vapor condenses to form clouds. That is why mountain ranges are often cloud capped even when adjacent lowlands bask under clear skies. Further cooling of the air may produce rain or—if air temperatures aloft are below freezing—snow. On the leeward side of a mountain range, however, the process is the reverse. As the air grows warmer in its descent, precipitation declines sharply and eventually ceases; clouds begin to dissipate and may disappear entirely. As a result, regions downwind from a mountain range receive considerably less precipitation than its other side and are therefore said to lie in its "rain shadow."

The Cascade Range, by virtue of its great height and extent, is responsible for the sharp contrast in climate between the coastal and interior portions of Oregon and Washington. The Coast Mountains affect the regional climates of British Columbia in a similar fashion. The region west of the Coast Mountains-Cascades barrier has a maritime climate characterized by mild, rainy winters and cool, relatively dry summers. Annual precipitation exceeds 15 inches at even the driest stations, with most receiving at least two or three times that amount. Along the coast, above-freezing temperatures are recorded 240 to 300 days a year. The coldest periods occur during outbreaks of frigid polar air, which enter the region from the interior of British Columbia.

The climate of eastern Washington and Oregon results from a blend of marine and continental influences, with the latter predominating. Winters are moderately cold and dry; summers, hot and very dry. Annual precipitation, except in mountainous areas, is less than 15 inches a year at all stations, with true desert conditions occurring in southeastern Oregon. Interior British Columbia is significantly colder during the winter than eastern Washington and Oregon and cooler and more humid during the summer. By intercepting most of the moisture from incoming storms and inhibiting the flow of marine air into the interior, the Cascade Range and Coast Mountains are responsible for the more severe climates of these rain-shadow lands.

The Olympic Mountains and Vancouver Island Range also cast rain shadows, albeit not so extensively as the Cascades and Coast Mountains. The sunniest, driest region in western Washington lies northeast of the Olympic Mountains. Although mean annual precipitation on the southwestern flank of the Olympics exceeds 120 inches, it drops on the northeastern side of the mountains to as little as 17 inches, the lowest total in western Washington. The San Juan Islands and southernmost Vancouver Island also lie within the Olympic rain shadow, and Victoria averages only 27 inches of rain a year. The northeastern shore of Vancouver Island and the southwestern shore of the British Columbia mainland (known locally as the "Sunshine Coast") lie in the rain shadow of the Vancouver Island Range and enjoy much drier, sunnier weather than the southwestern side of the island.

OLYMPIC MOUNTAINS AND VANCOUVER ISLAND

Exposed to the open ocean on the west, the Olympic Mountains and Vancouver Island Range receive the full brunt of incoming storms, with resulting high winds and heavy precipitation. At higher elevations in the mountains, winds over 100 miles per hour occur every winter. Annual precipitation in the Olympics ranges from 70 to 100 inches along the western coastal plain and exceeds 150 inches on the slopes of Mt. Olympus. The greatest amount ever recorded in the contiguous United States was 184 inches in the rain forest at Wynoochee Oxbow (at 600 feet), on the southwestern flank of the range. Winter snowfall is 10 to 30 inches at lower elevations, increasing to 250 to 500 inches or more on the higher slopes. Above 4500 feet nearly all precipitation is in the form of snow. The winter snow line usually lies at 1500 to 2000 feet, with depths seldom surpassing 15 inches at that elevation. Higher ridges are snow covered from November through early July, and snow remains in sheltered places throughout the summer.

The western flank of Vancouver Island is even wetter than the western Olympics. Henderson Lake averaged 262 inches of rain a year over a 14-year period. Zeballos averages 250 inches a year. These figures are exceptional, however, with most stations recording amounts only somewhat greater than those from the Olympics. Snowfall in the higher mountains is comparable both in amount and duration, but the regional snow line is somewhat lower owing to the island's more northerly latitude.

Thanks to the moderating influence of marine air, the Olympic Mountains and Vancouver Island Range are warmer in winter and cooler in summer than mountain ranges of comparable altitude and latitude at inland locations. Daily temperature ranges and seasonal fluctuations are also less than in continental mountain ranges. At higher elevations, temperatures during the summer range from the mid-thirties at night to 55° to 65°F during the day, occasionally reaching the low seventies during warmer periods. Subfreezing temperatures are rare in summer, though snow can fall any month of the year. During the winter, temperatures in the higher mountains usually range from the mid-teens at night to the mid-twenties during the day—hardly shirtsleeve weather, but downright balmy compared to the subzero temperatures of British Columbia's northern interior.

Overcast skies are the rule over the western sections of Vancouver Island and the Olympic Peninsula. Along the coast, there are normally only two or three clear or partly cloudy days a month from October through June and only about seven such days per month from July through September. During the summer, fog commonly blankets the coastal areas, but with cloud tops at 2000 to 3000 feet, the higher mountains are often clear.

THE CASCADE RANGE
AND COAST MOUNTAINS

The climate along the west side of the Cascades and the Coast Mountains is similar to that of the Olympic Mountains and Vancouver Island Range respectively. Winters are cold and wet, with only a few, usually brief periods of clear weather. Summers are cool and relatively dry, with over-cast skies on about 40 percent of the days in the Washington Cascades and somewhat more often in the Coast Mountains. Fogs are common in the valleys below 2000 to 3000 feet, particularly during the morning hours. From July through September, rain falls on an average of about 9 days a month in the Washington Cascades and 14 to 17 days in the Coast Mountains. In some summers, however, there may be periods of clear or mostly clear skies lasting up to several weeks.

Winter temperatures in the western Cascades of Washington are moderate for a range of its height and latitude. At lower elevations, January tempera-tures usually range from 30°F at night to 40°F during the day. At 5500 feet, the average minimum and maximum temperatures for the month are about ten degrees lower. Minima from 0° to −17°F have been recorded at higher elevations. In July, daily temperatures usually range from 40° to 75°F at lower elevations and from the 30s to the 60s above 3000 feet. Subfreezing temperatures are possible at higher elevations anytime during the summer months.

Winters are much colder in the southern Coast Mountains than in the Cas-cades, with average January temperatures of 5° to 14°F. In July, mean daily temperatures are less than 60°F.

Annual precipitation along the west side of the Washington Cascades is typically 60 to 100 inches at mid-elevations, increasing perhaps to well over 150 inches on the higher ridges. Precipitation is comparable in the Coast Mountains. Most precipitation occurs during the winter as snow, with amounts ranging from 50 to 75 inches below 3000-foot elevations to 400 to 600 inches above the 4000-foot level. Maximum amounts probably occur near 7000 feet, but there are no recording stations at that elevation, so it is impossible to know for sure. In the winter of 1971–1972, Paradise Ranger Station (at 5450 feet on the south slope of Mt. Rainier) received an incred-ible 1122 inches of snow. More than 1000 inches of snow also fell at Para-dise in the winters of 1955–1956 and 1970–1971. In March of 1956 the snowpack was 367 inches deep—more than 30 feet!

Snowfall begins at higher elevations in September and moves down to about 1000 to 2000 feet in midwinter (lower in the Coast Mountains than in the Cascades). Some snowfall occurs, however, down to sea level nearly every winter, the frequency and amounts increasing with latitude. The snowpack reaches a maximum depth of about 10 to 25 feet during the first half of March, after which snow begins to melt faster than it accumulates. Above 5000 feet in the Washington Cascades and somewhat lower in the southern Coast Mountains, snow remains on the ground through late June or early July, and in cool, shady sites it commonly persists through the entire summer.

Moderate wintertime temperatures and proximity to the ocean make the snow of our mountains wet and heavy. Combined with great snowpack depths and precipitous slopes, this presents a severe avalanche hazard. In fact, the great majority of avalanche accidents in the United States occurs in the Washington Cascades. The worst American avalanche accident on record happened near Stevens Pass, east of Seattle, in 1910, when two stalled trains filled with passengers were swept off the tracks into a canyon and 92 people were killed.

The eastern sides of the Coast Mountains and the Cascades are significantly drier than the western flanks and experience warmer summers, colder winters, and longer periods of clear weather throughout the year. Precipitation declines steadily as elevation drops and distance increases from the crests of the ranges. In the central Washington Cascades, for example, average annual precipitation in the Yakima River valley declines from 92 inches at Stampede Pass (3958 feet) at the crest of the range, to 22 inches at the town of Cle Elum (1920 feet), only 20 miles to the east. Another 25 miles farther east yet, the town of Ellensburg (1726 feet), located at the foot of the mountains, averages only 9 inches a year. Average snowfall declines from about 450 inches at Stampede Pass to 86 inches at Cle Elum and only a trace at Ellensburg.

Snowfall in the eastern Washington Cascades begins in October at higher elevations, but snow does not begin to stick until November. By the first of March, the pack is commonly 10 to 20 feet deep at elevations above 4000 feet. Below 3000 feet, midwinter snow depth is usually 2 to 5 feet. Snow disappears from the east side of the mountains as much as a month earlier than it does from comparable sites on the western flank. Rarely does it persist through the summer, even on the coldest, shadiest slopes.

January air temperatures in the eastern Washington Cascades average 15° to 25°F at night and 25° to 35°F during the day. Minimum temperatures of 0° to −15°F are recorded almost every winter, and they sometimes reach −30°F in the colder valleys. Summertime highs average 70° to 85°F, depending on elevation. At lower stations the maximum daytime temperature often exceeds 90°F for 15 to 20 days each summer. Highs of 100° to 105°F are not unusual on at least a few days. At higher elevations daytime highs in the 80s are recorded most summers. Nighttime lows during the season are commonly 45° to 50°F, with subfreezing temperatures occurring during any month of the year.

The extension of the Cascade Range over some 10 degrees of latitude results in marked climatic differences between the northern and southern extremities of the range. The mean annual temperature for stations at mid-elevations along the western flank increases from about 40°F at the international border to about 48°F along the Oregon-California boundary. Precipitation decreases from an average of about 100 inches near Mt. Baker to less than 50 inches at Mt. Shasta. Similar gradients in air temperature and precipitation occur along the eastern side of the range. Accompanying these changes southward are a steady increase in hours of sunshine and a progressive tendency for precipitation to be restricted to the winter months. In the North Cascades roughly one-fourth of the total annual precipitation falls between April 1 and September 30, while less than 5 percent falls during the same period at Mt. Shasta. Overcast days decrease from an average of 11 days per month during July and August at Stampede Pass to only 2 per month at Mt. Shasta. Even during the winter only about 50 percent of the days are overcast in the California Cascades, compared to 84 percent in the North Cascades.

4

PLANT & ANIMAL DISTRIBUTION

Plants and animals are neither randomly nor uniformly distributed. Instead, each species is limited to certain habitats within a particular geographic range. Plant habitats are determined mainly by the physical environment: the range of air temperature; the amount, type, and seasonal distribution of precipitation; the physical and chemical characteristics of the soil; and the effect of local topography on climate, soils, and drainage. Animal habitats are governed directly by the kinds of food and cover that are afforded by various types of vegetation and therefore indirectly by all the factors that affect the distribution of plants. Plants and animals that occur together within a particular habitat form a community.

Through photosynthesis, plants use the energy obtained from sunlight to manufacture carbohydrates. Herbivores obtain nourishment (their share of the sun) by consuming the carbohydrates bound up in plants and converting these to proteins. Carnivores receive their share by eating the herbivores. In return, carnivores keep populations of herbivores under control through predation and thereby help maintain the stands of vegetation upon which they both depend.

Animals also perform other functions that are beneficial to plants. The pollinization of flowers by butterflies, bees, and other insects is perhaps the best-known example. Another is the dispersion of seeds, which may ride along in a mammal's fur or a bird's feathers or pass through its digestive tract into feces that are then deposited in a potential growing site. Burrowing animals, such as moles, gophers, and earthworms, aerate the soil, and all animals ultimately enrich it through the contribution of feces and, ultimately, their remains. Microorganisms break down the remains of both plants and animals into humus from which new plants will spring. They also interact with the roots of plants in ways that allow the latter to utilize otherwise unavailable nutrients bound up in the soil. Communities, then, are dynamic systems exhibiting mutual dependence and accommodation among their members. Biologists call them *ecosystems,* from a Greek root meaning household. Ecology is that branch of biology devoted to the study of nature's households.

Although animals are an important element of a community, they are generally less conspicuous than plants and account for a smaller portion of the total mass of organisms. Moreover, because animals are not rooted to a particular spot, they are generally less reliable indicators of the physical environment in any given place. Finally, plants play a much larger role in determining the distribution of animals than the reverse. Therefore, it is customary to identify communities by their dominant plants—the ones that are most conspicuous and that determine the essential character of each community. Dominant species are the ones best adapted to conditions found in their particular habitats. They even alter those habitats in ways that reduce the ability of other plant species to compete. For example, the shade cast by dominant forest trees eliminates plants intolerant of shade from the community.

Ecologists distinguish between climax communities and seral communities. A climax community is one that is so well adapted to its environment that it will persist indefinitely in the absence of disturbance. A seral community is one that occupies a site following natural or human disturbance, such as fire, flood, logging, or cultivation. Under natural conditions, seral vegetation will gradually revert to climax vegetation over a period of years or decades or even longer. This process is called plant succession.

Climate is the most important factor governing the distribution of vegetation over large geographic regions. Each region of more or less uniform climate has its own characteristic vegetation that is climax for that region. In the Puget Lowland, for example, western hemlock forest is the climax vegetation on typical sites. Such an area of distinctive climate and vegetation constitutes a vegetation zone. Vegetation, however, is never entirely uniform, so each zone also includes a number of communities in addition to the climax. These secondary communities generally occupy atypical habitats resulting from local conditions of soil, topography, or climate, or from various types of disturbance.

In mountain ranges, where climatic gradients occur mainly as functions of elevation (see chapter 3), vegetation zones tend to form a sequence of belts on the mountainsides. The transition from one zone to the next is generally gradual, with certain plants increasing in numbers as others gradually drop out. As a rule among both plants and animals, some species are restricted to a single zone, others range across two or three zones, and still others may be found in almost any zone.

In addition, zone boundaries do not follow neat elevational contours. Instead, zones tend to "interfinger" along their shared boundaries, extending upslope or downslope according to local topography, which exerts a profound influence on climate. In the northern hemisphere, for example, the south side of a ridge is generally warmer than the north side because the former faces the sun while the latter faces away. Therefore, zones tend to extend higher on south-facing slopes than they do on those facing north. Similarly, exposed ridges tend to be warmer than adjacent valley bottoms, partly because the ridges receive more sunlight, partly because cold air drains downslope at night into the valleys. As a result, zones tend to range higher on the ridges than in the valleys. The elevational ranges given for mountain vegetation zones are therefore approximate, with upper and lower boundaries varying somewhat according to local conditions.

Various systems of vegetation zones have been applied to our region. The one used here is a simplified version adapted primarily from two sources: *Natural Vegetation of Oregon and Washington* by Jerry F. Franklin and C. T. Dyrness; and "Biogeoclimatic Zones and Classification of British Columbia" by V. J. Krajina in *Ecology of Western North America*, V. J. Krajina, editor. The following summaries are offered to aid readers in (1) recognizing the zones and (2) forecasting the kinds of plants and animals that are likely to inhabit each zone.

I. Coastal Forest Zone. Vancouver Island Range, Olympic Mountains, west slope of the Coast Mountains and Cascades south to Umpqua Divide in southern Oregon, at elevations from sea level to 2000 feet in the north (4000 feet in the eastern Vancouver Island Range and eastern Olympics) and 5000 feet in the south. Lush lowland forests dominated by western hemlock, Douglas-fir, Sitka spruce (near the coast), or western red-cedar (wet sites). The Olympic and Vancouver Island rain forests occur in this zone. Old-growth stands are fairly open, with luxuriant understories. Common plants and animals include:

Trees: western hemlock, Douglas-fir, Sitka spruce, western red-cedar, western white pine, grand fir, silver fir, bigleaf maple, red alder, black cottonwood, madrone.

Shrubs: salal, creambush, Oregon-grape, Pacific rhododendron, vine maple, devil's club, salmonberry, evergreen huckleberry.

Wildflowers and Ferns: sword fern, deer fern, Oregon oxalis, false Solomon's seal, vanilla leaf, queen's cup, twisted-stalks, foamflower, Siberian montia, evergreen violet, Hooker's fairybell.

Butterflies: Clodius parnassian, pine white, Johnson's hairstreak.

Amphibians: rough-skinned newt, northwestern salamander, Pacific giant salamander, red-legged frog, western toad.

Reptiles: northern alligator lizard, rubber boa, garter snakes.

Birds: ruffed grouse, Steller's jay, chestnut-backed chickadee, brown creeper, winter wren, varied thrush, Townsend's warbler, western tanager, rufous-sided towhee, pine siskin, dark-eyed junco.

Mammals: mountain-beaver, Townsend's chipmunk, Douglas' squirrel, deer mouse, coyote, black bear, bobcat, elk (winter), black-tailed deer.

II. Silver Fir Zone. Olympic Mountains, west slope of Cascade Range south to McKenzie Pass, Oregon, at elevations of 2000 to 4300 feet in the north and 3300 to 4900 feet in the south (not recognized as a distinct zone in British Columbia, but as the upper portion of the Coastal Forest Zone). Forests dominated by silver fir are transitional between the coastal forests and subalpine forests. Understories range from sparse to well developed. Common plants and animals include:

Trees: silver fir, western hemlock, noble fir, Douglas-fir, western red-cedar, western white pine, Alaska yellow-cedar, mountain hemlock.

Shrubs: vine maple, salal, Oregon-grape, devil's club, red huckleberry, thinleaf blueberry, Alaska blueberry, bunchberry dogwood.

Wildflowers and Ferns: oak fern, lady's fern, prince's pine, beargrass, vanilla leaf, queen's cup, dwarf bramble, starry Solomon's plume, foam-flower, western trillium.

Butterflies: parnassians, northern blue, western meadow fritillary.

Amphibians: northwestern salamander, long-toed salamander, western toad, Cascades frog.

Reptiles: northern alligator lizard, rubber boa, garter snakes.

Birds: blue grouse, Hammond's flycatcher, gray jay, mountain chickadee, hermit thrush, red-breasted nuthatch, western tanager, pine siskin, dark-eyed junco, evening grosbeak.

Mammals: Townsend's chipmunk, golden-mantled ground squirrel, Douglas' squirrel, northern flying squirrel, porcupine, deer mouse, coyote, pine marten, black bear, mule deer.

III. Sierran Mixed-conifer Zone. West slope of the Cascades south of the Umpqua Divide in southern Oregon, at elevations of 2450 to 4600 feet in Oregon and 2000 to 5250 feet in California (3000 to 6600 feet on east slope of the California Cascades); the upper, white-fir phase of this zone continues northward in Oregon to McKenzie Pass. Forests dominated by Douglas-fir, white fir, incense-cedar, ponderosa pine, and sugar pine in various proportions form a northern continuation of the mixed-conifer forest of California's Sierra Nevada. Understories are typically rather sparse. Along the upper margin of the zone nearly pure stands of white fir are characteristic. Common plants and animals include:

Trees: Douglas-fir, white fir, incense-cedar, ponderosa pine, sugar pine, black oak (California), bigleaf maple, Pacific dogwood, madrone.

Shrubs: golden chinquapin, vine maple, Oregon-grape, mountain lover, snowberries, huckleberries, pinemat manzanita, squaw carpet, deer brush, baldhip rose, salal.

Wildflowers: prince's pine, vanilla leaf, Columbia windflower, trail plant, yerba buena, beargrass, evergreen violet, western trillium.

Butterflies: Clodius parnassian, pine white, Sara's orange-tip, Nelson's hairstreak.

Amphibians: rough-skinned newt, ensatina, western toad, red-legged frog.

Reptiles: western fence lizard, southern alligator lizard, rubber boa, racer, California mountain kingsnake, garter snakes, Pacific rattlesnake.

Birds: common flicker, hairy woodpecker, Steller's jay, mountain chickadee, dark-eyed junco, western wood pewee, olive-sided flycatcher, yellow-rumped warbler, western tanager, pine siskin, chipping sparrow.

Mammals: yellow-pine chipmunk, northern flying squirrel, deer mouse, porcupine, gray fox, coyote, black bear, bobcat, mule deer.

IV. Red Fir Zone. West slope of the Cascades south of the McKenzie River in central Oregon, at elevations of 5200 to 6600 feet in Oregon and up to 8000 feet in the California Cascades; also along the east slope of the Cascades north to near Crater Lake. Nearly pure stands of red fir, *Abies magnifica,* or Shasta fir, *A.m.* var *shastensis,* dominate the zone: red fir in the Sierra Nevada north to Shasta; Shasta fir from Shasta north into Oregon (to distinguish the two varieties of red fir, cf plate 48). Common plants and animals include:

Trees: red or Shasta fir, lodgepole pine, western white pine, mountain hemlock, Jeffrey pine (California).

Shrubs: Pacific blackberry, gooseberries, snowberries, Oregon-grape, huckleberries, pinemat manzanita, greenleaf manzanita, golden chinquapin.

Wildflowers: wild ginger, trail plant, vanilla leaf, American vetch, starry Solomon's plume, white-flowered hawkweed, bedstraws, inside-out flower, western starflower, and wintergreens.

Butterflies: parnassians, short-tailed black swallowtail, fritillaries.

Amphibians: long-toed salamander, western toad, red-legged frog, Cascades frog.

Reptiles: western fence lizard, rubber boa, garter snakes.

Birds: blue grouse, Williamson's sapsucker, Hammond's flycatcher, olive-sided flycatcher, Steller's jay, mountain chickadee, hermit thrush, hermit warbler, western tanager, pine siskin, Cassin's finch, dark-eyed junco, chipping sparrow.

Mammals: snowshoe hare, golden-mantled ground squirrel, Townsend's chipmunk, Douglas' squirrel, northern flying squirrel, deer mouse, voles, porcupine, coyote, black bear, pine marten, mule deer.

V. Subalpine Zone. Vancouver Island, at elevations of 2000 to 3300 feet; Olympic Mountains, 4000 to 5800 feet; Coast Mountains, 2900 to 4900 feet (west slope), 3900 to 7000 feet (east slope); Cascades, 4300 to 5600 feet (western Washington), 4900 to 7000 feet (eastern Washington), 5600 to 6600 feet (southwestern Oregon), 5800 to 7800 feet (southeastern Oregon),

7900 to 10,000 feet (California). Highest forest zone, extending upslope to timberline, which is not a sharp boundary but, rather, a transitional belt in which forest trees gradually give way to meadows and rocky areas in the face of increasing cold, deeper and longer-lying snow, and shorter growing seasons. Three stages mark this transition:

(1) forest line—the upper boundary of the continuous forest;

(2) tree line—the upper limit of erect trees;

(3) scrub line—the upper limit of elfinwood, or krummholz, which consists of timberline trees reduced to prostrate shrubs. Tree limit forms the upper boundary of the subalpine zone, which normally spans an elevation of 1000 to 1500 feet in our region.

The subalpine zone is divided into two distinct parts: a lower, continuous forest zone and an upper, parkland zone where islands of subalpine trees are scattered among extensive meadows.

Continuous Forest. Forests dominated by mountain hemlock are characteristic of the lower subalpine zone on the west slope of the Coast Mountains and Cascade Range, in the Vancouver Island Range, and in the western Olympic Mountains. Forests dominated by subalpine fir occupy the lower subalpine zone along the east slope of the Coast Mountains and Cascades southward to southern Oregon and also in the eastern Olympics. The subalpine forest in the California Cascades is a mixed type in which mountain hemlock, lodgepole pine, red fir, or whitebark pine may be locally dominant. Common plants include:

Trees: mountain hemlock, subalpine fir, Engelmann spruce, lodgepole pine, whitebark pine, silver fir, noble fir, grand fir, red fir, western larch, Alaska yellow-cedar, western white pine.
Shrubs: huckleberries, Cascade azalea, Menziesia, mountain lover, copper bush, mountain-ashes, vine maple, alderleaf buckthorn, Labrador tea, common juniper.
Wildflowers and Ferns: alpine lady fern, mountain wood fern, beargrass, western twayblade, glacier lily, rosy twisted-stalk, queen's cup, violets, dwarf bramble, strawberry bramble, sweet-scented bedstraw, wintergreens, Sitka valerian, heartleaf arnica, groundsels, white-flowered hawkweed, trail plant, asters.

Parklands. Subalpine parklands lie between the continuous forest and the alpine zone. They consist of extensive meadows of various composition and groups of trees scattered over the meadows like islands. Extensive areas of bare or sparsely vegetated rock are also common in parklands. The major types of subalpine meadows are as follows:

(1) heather meadows dominated by red mountain-heather, white mountain-heather, or Cascade blueberry, all mat-forming shrubs;

(2) lush herbaceous meadows dominated by Sitka valerian, green false-hellebore, showy sedge, broadleaf lupine, and common bistort;

(3) subalpine marshes dominated by sedges, rushes, Lewis' monkey-flower, alpine yellow monkeyflower, alpine willow-herb, or marsh-marigolds;

(4) dwarf sedge meadows dominated by black sedge;

(5) subalpine grasslands dominated by green fescue.

Common meadow wildflowers include: partridge-foot, birdsbeak lousewort, glacier lily, avalanche lily, sticky tofieldia, coltsfoot, Gray's lovage, western pasque-flower, magenta paintbrush, fireweed, woolly pussytoes, Brewer's mitrewort, cow parsnip, fanleaf cinquefoil, asters, fleabanes, red willow-herb, white bog-orchid, fringed grass-of-Parnassus, speedwells.

Common plants on rocky or gravelly sites include: Tolmie saxifrage, wild buckwheats, alpine lady fern, common juniper, kinnickinnick, mountain lover, spreading phlox, sibbaldia, mountain sandwort, and stonecrops.

Parkland tree groups commonly include the following species: subalpine fir, mountain hemlock, Alaska yellow-cedar, silver fir, whitebark pine.

Trees occurring at the tree line or scrub line include: subalpine fir, whitebark pine, mountain hemlock, alpine larch, and — less commonly — Engelmann spruce, lodgepole pine, silver fir, red (Shasta) fir, Alaska yellow-cedar.

Common animals of the subalpine zone include:

Butterflies: Phoebus parnassian, Vidler's alpine, Nevada arctic, Hydaspe fritillary, lustrous copper, northern blue, sooty hairstreak, skippers.

Amphibians: western toad, Cascades frog, spotted frog.

Reptiles: northern alligator lizard, western fence lizard, garter snakes.

Birds: northern three-toed woodpecker, rufous hummingbird, calliope hummingbird, Hammond's flycatcher, olive-sided flycatcher, golden-crowned kinglet, gray jay, Clark's nutcracker, mountain chickadee, red-breasted nuthatch, hermit thrush, mountain bluebird, evening grosbeak, Cassin's finch.

Mammals: pika, snowshoe hare, pocket-gophers, golden-mantled ground squirrel, marmots, porcupine, deer mouse, bushy-tailed wood rat, voles, coyote, red fox, pine marten, black bear, elk, mule deer.

VI. Alpine Zone. Vancouver Island Range, Olympic Mountains, and west slope of the Coast Mountains and Washington Cascades at elevations above 4900 to 5900 feet; east slope of the Coast Mountains and Washington Cascades above 6400 to 7900 feet; Oregon Cascades above 5500 to 6500 feet in the north and above 7000 to 8000 feet in the south; California Cascades above 7800 to 9600 feet. The treeless region lying above timberline and below the zone of perennial snow. Vegetation basically consists of two types:

(1) alpine turfs dominated by sedges, grasses, or rushes;

(2) fell-field communities, in which dwarf herbs and shrubs form a sparse cover over areas of bare rock, gravel, or sand.

Snow depth and duration, available moisture, exposure to wind, and soil conditions are the chief factors governing the distribution of alpine communities. The harshest alpine environments are exposed ridges that are swept free of snow by high winds and snowbed areas in which late-lying snow results in cold, poorly drained soils and brief growing seasons. Relatively few species of animals inhabit the alpine zone. Common plants and animals include:

Shrubs: yellow mountain-heather, white mountain-heather, kinnickinnick, crowberry, common juniper, shrubby cinquefoil, elfinwood.

Wildflowers: alpine lupine, coiled-beak lousewort, sandworts, showy sedge, alpine aster, mountain meadow cinquefoil, northern goldenrod, black sedge, yarrow, spreading phlox, Davidson's penstemon, woolly pussytoes, Cusick's speedwell, Tolmie's saxifrage.

Butterflies: western white, arctic sulphur, Chryxus arctic, Milbert's tortoise-shell, checkerspots, Astarte fritillary, American copper, arctic blue, Shasta blue, grizzled checkered skipper.

Birds: white-tailed ptarmigan, horned lark, gray-crowned rosy finch, raven.

Mammals: mountain goat, golden-mantled ground squirrel, deer mouse, heather vole, marmots.

VII. Interior Fir Zone. East slope of the Coast Mountains and Cascades from southern British Columbia to southern Oregon at elevations of 1000 to 4250 feet in the north, 2000 to 4300 feet in northern Oregon, and 5400 to 6600 feet in southern Oregon. Forest composition changes greatly from north to south. Douglas-fir is the dominant tree in British Columbia, grand fir in Washington and northern Oregon, and white fir in southern Oregon. Cool, moist sites in the eastern Cascades of Washington may support forests dominated by western hemlock. Most stands are fairly open, with well-developed understories. Common plants and animals include:

Trees: Douglas-fir, grand fir, white fir, western hemlock, ponderosa pine, lodgepole pine, western larch, and—less commonly—Engelmann spruce, subalpine fir, incense-cedar, sugar pine, western white pine, mountain hemlock, Shasta fir, western red-cedar.

Shrubs: snowberries, wild roses, kinnickinnick, mountain lover, thinleaf blueberry, swamp gooseberry, snow brush, pinemat manzanita, greenleaf manzanita.

Wildflowers: broadleaf arnica, heartleaf arnica, white-flowered hawkweed, queen's cup, wild ginger, broadleaf lupine, dwarf bramble, starry Solomon's plume, trail plant, broad-lipped twayblade, prince's pine.

Butterflies: swallowtails, pine white, Sara's orange-tip, western sulphur, Nevada arctic, Lorquin's admiral, anglewings, greater fritillaries, blues, coppers, skippers.

Amphibians: western toad, spotted frog.

Reptiles: western fence lizard, rubber boa, gopher snake, garter snakes.
Birds: blue grouse, common flicker, yellow-bellied sapsucker, hairy woodpecker, northern three-toed woodpecker, Hammond's flycatcher, olive-
sided flycatcher, gray jay, Steller's jay, red-breasted nuthatch, Townsend's solitaire, yellow-rumped warbler, western tanager, evening grosbeak, Cassin's finch, pine siskin, dark-eyed junco, chipping sparrow.
Mammals: snowshoe hare, yellow-pine chipmunk, golden-mantled ground
squirrel, Douglas' squirrel, northern flying squirrel, porcupine, deer
mouse, coyote, pine marten, black bear, bobcat, mule deer.

VIII. Ponderosa Pine Zone. East slope of the Coast Mountains and Cascades from southern British Columbia to California at elevations of 900 to
2500 feet in British Columbia, 2000 to 4000 feet in Washington, 2900 to
5000 feet in southern Oregon and California; west slope Cascades only near
Lassen Peak at 1600 to 3200 feet. Ponderosa pine forests make up the
lowest forest zone along the east side of the Cascade Range. Along their
lower boundaries they merge more or less gradually with the grassland and
sagebrush steppes of the lowlands or with open woodlands dominated by
western juniper and sagebrush. The forests are open, often parklike, with
well-developed understories of grass or brush. The zone is of intermittent
occurrence in Washington and British Columbia, where it may be replaced
by the interior fir zone. In the pumice region of southern Oregon, east of
Crater Lake, nearly pure stands of lodgepole pine dominate poorly drained
pumice flats, with ponderosa pines relegated to the steeper, better drained
slopes and ridgetops. Common plants and animals include:

Trees: ponderosa pine, lodgepole pine, Jeffrey pine (California), Douglas-
fir, white fir, incense-cedar, western white pine, western larch, black oak
(California), Oregon oak, quaking aspen.
Shrubs: snowberries, spiraeas, wild roses, western serviceberry, common
chokecherry, black hawthorn, creambush, antelope brush, big sagebrush,
snow brush, greenleaf manzanita.
Wildflowers: yarrow, woolly sunflower, arrowleaf balsamroot, dwarf
mountain daisy, varileaf phacelia, spreading dogbane, small-flowered
blue-eyed Mary, violets.
Butterflies: swallowtails, parnassians, Sara's orange-tip, ochre ringlet, satyr
anglewing, Lorquin's admiral, fritillaries, crescents, checkerspots, hairstreaks, coppers, blues, skippers.
Amphibians: western toad, spotted frog.
Reptiles: sagebrush lizard, western fence lizard, southern alligator lizard,
racer, striped whipsnake, gopher snake, garter snakes, Pacific rattlesnake.
Birds: common nighthawk, common flicker, hairy woodpecker, dusky flycatcher, Steller's jay, western bluebird, Townsend's solitaire, western
tanager, chipping sparrow.

Mammals: least chipmunk, yellow-pine chipmunk, porcupine, deer mouse, coyote, raccoon, striped skunk, black bear, bobcat, mule deer.

Part II

THE PLANTS

5

FERNS

Ferns, like flowering plants, have vascular tissue for support and for circulating water and nutrients. Unlike flowering plants, ferns reproduce from spores rather than seeds. Seed-bearing plants, no matter how fernlike their leaves, are not ferns.

Ferns are among the oldest vascular plants in the fossil record, first appearing about 500 million years ago. During the Carboniferous period, about 300 million years ago, they were the dominant land plants. Today, there are about 10,000 species, of which just over 30 occur in our region. Of the 30 species depicted in this guide, 10 occur throughout the northern hemisphere, 9 are endemic to western North America, 5 occur throughout North America, and 4 range throughout Eurasia and western North America, but not east of the Rocky Mountains. The 2 remaining species have curious ranges that are mentioned in the species accounts.

Ferns are an important, highly distinctive element in the humid forests of the Pacific Northwest and British Columbia. They are closely associated with those forests in the popular imagination and, along with mosses and lichens, are largely responsible for their lush, verdant appearance. Sword fern is the most common understory plant in many forest environments, providing a delicate, lacy contrast to the massive solemnity of the dominant trees. Several other species, though less common, are present in large numbers. Bracken is one of the first plants to relieve the devastation of clearcuts and fires. It also grows abundantly along roads and in sunny fields throughout the region, commonly preferring open, disturbed habitats. Other ferns add a touch of green to rocky alpine slopes or combine with mosses and other moisture-loving plants to produce exquisite emerald gardens near seeps and streamlets.

The ferns of our region fall into two broad groups by habitat. One group prefers damp, shaded sites, often in the forest. The other prefers rocky habitats—cliffs, talus, ledges, crevices—which may be sunny or shaded, damp

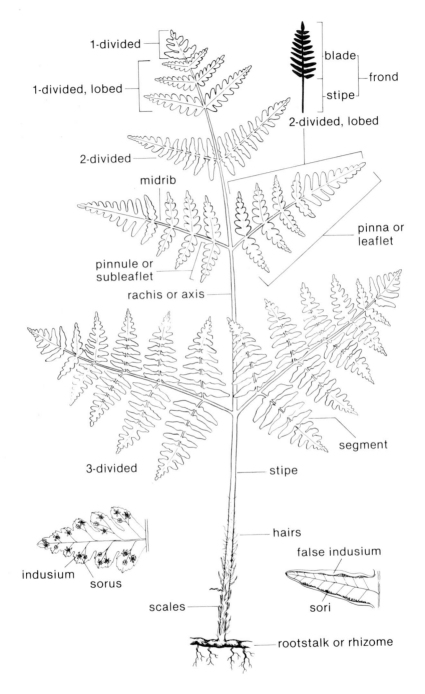

1-divided

1-divided, lobed

blade

frond

stipe

2-divided, lobed

2-divided

midrib

pinna or leaflet

pinnule or subleaflet

rachis or axis

3-divided

segment

stipe

hairs

false indusium

indusium

sorus

scales

sori

rootstalk or rhizome

Figure 2. Anatomy of a fern.

or dry. Ferns of one kind or another may be found nearly anywhere from sea level to above timberline. Some species are extremely local in their distribution, but most are fairly widespread in suitable habitats.

The life cycle of a fern consists of two distinct stages or generations, each represented by a separate plant. The plant we normally call a fern actually represents only the asexual, spore-bearing generation. Spores are produced in minute cases called *sporangia*. Clusters of sporangia form *sori*, which are borne on the underside of fertile leaves. Sori usually appear in summer and in some species are covered by a thin membrane called the *indusium*. In other species, portions of the leaf margin curl under to cover the sori and thereby serve as indusia. Sori may be missing if a plant is immature or if the season or growing conditions are inappropriate.

Upon maturity, sporangia slowly open and then snap shut, in the process slinging out thousands of spores, which are broadcast by the wind. Those landing in suitable habitats germinate to form tiny, simple, heart-shaped plants, each called a *prothallus*. Smaller than a thumbnail, a prothallus is a self-supporting green plant bearing the male and female reproductive cells that, upon uniting, grow into the plant we know as a fern.

When identifying ferns, one must pay special attention to the structure of the leaves and both the location of the sori and the nature of their indusium. If sori are not present, some species may be difficult or impossible to distinguish, though careful attention to other features, as well as habitat and range, will yield results in many cases.

Scientific names conform to those in *Flora of the Pacific Northwest* by C. Leo Hitchcock and Arthur Cronquist. The common names, with some exceptions, are from the same source. For information on the organization and use of the species accounts and illustrations, as well as for a list of the abbreviations used in the accounts, see the Introduction.

PLATE 1

Common Fern Family (Polypodiaceae)

NORTHERN MAIDENHAIR FERN (FIVE-FINGER FERN), *Adiantum pedatum.* Fronds deciduous, to 28″, the stipes shiny black or dk brown, forked to form 2 curved rachises, ea bearing 2–several pinnae with 15–35 pinnules on ea side of midrib. Sori covered by folded marginal lobes. Moist woods, low–mid el, in all our mtns; Alas e across Can, s to Cal, Utah, se US; ne Asia.

PODFERN, *Aspidotis densa.* Fronds evergreen, densely clumped, 4″–8″ long; the sterile ones few or absent, 3-divided, with broad, flat, sharply toothed segm; the fertile ones numerous, 3-divided, with narrow segm having stiff, sharp tips and tightly curled margins covering sori. Moist crevices, talus, esp limestone or serpentine, in all our mtns, s BC to Cal; e to RM and e Can.

MAIDENHAIR SPLEENWORT, *Asplenium trichomanes.* Fronds evergreen, narrow, 1-divided, to 7″ long, with purplish brown stipes and rachises. Pinnae margins slightly toothed. Lvs deciduous but rachises persistent. Sori along veinlets, with thin, flaplike indusia. Moist rock ledges and crevices, oft limestones, in all our mtns; se Alas to e Can, s to Ore, Ariz, se US; Eurasia, Africa, Hawaii. Green Spleenwort, *A. viride,* similar but rachises green.

LADY FERN, *Athyrium filix-femina.* Fronds deciduous, gen 2-divided, 12″–60″ long, broadest in middle, tapering at ea end, tightly clumped amid more numerous dead stipe bases; stipes short, furrowed, straw colored, scaly at base. Sori along veinlets with flaplike but soon deciduous indusia. Com, damp, shaded places, forest, in all our mtns; Alas to e Can and US, s to Cal; Eurasia. Alpine Lady Fern, *A. distentifolium,* similar but fronds gen 3-divided and indusia lacking. Moist, rocky places, streamsides, mont-alp, oft near timberline, in all our mtns; Alas s to Cal, Nev, Colo; e Can, Iceland, Eurasia.

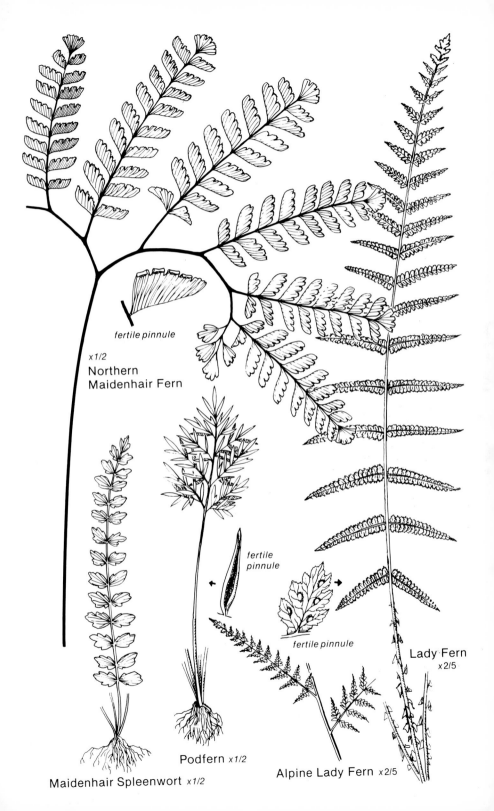

fertile pinnule

x1/2
Northern
Maidenhair Fern

fertile pinnule

fertile pinnule

Lady Fern
x2/5

Maidenhair Spleenwort *x1/2*

Podfern *x1/2*

Alpine Lady Fern *x2/5*

PLATE 2

Common Fern Family (Polypodiaceae)

DEER FERN, *Blechnum spicant*. Fronds evergreen, leathery, tapering toward base, with short brownish stipes; sterile fronds peripheral, erect or spreading, 8″–32″ long, with broad, crowded pinnae; fertile fronds taller, erect from center of plant, with narrow, widely spaced pinnae and sori parallel to midribs, with flaplike indusia attached to margins. Com, damp or wet woods, low–mid el, in all our mtns, mostly W CMtns-Cas, Alas to Cal; Iceland, Eurasia.

LACE FERN, *Cheilanthes gracillima*. Fronds evergreen, 2¾″–8″ long, 2-divided, with usu smooth stipes and scaly rachises and pinna midribs. Pinnae with round or oval pinnules, rolled margins, and dense, woolly, matted brown hairs below. Sori partly covered by curled margins. Rock ledges and crevices, low el-subalp in all our mtns, s to Cal, e to Mont. Lanate Lip-fern, *C. lanosa,* similar but has long, soft hairs on underside of pinnae. In our region found only at one place in OMtns.

ROCK BRAKE, *Cryptogramma crispa*. Fronds evergreen, 3″–6″ long, numerous, densely clustered, hairless, 2- 3-divided, with slender green or straw-colored stipes; fertile fronds stiff, erect, with narrow pinnules, the margins entirely curled to form continuous indusia; sterile fronds more numerous, shorter, with ovate to oblong pinnules, the margins scalloped or sharply lobed. Talus, rocky places, in all our mtns; Alas to e Can, ne US, s to Cal, NMex; Eurasia.

BRITTLE BLADDER FERN, *Cystopteris fragilis*. Fronds to 12″ long, delicate, erect or spreading, gen 2-divided; rachis green; stipe, straw colored or brown; pinnules very thin, sharply lobed. Sori on veinlets, with hoodlike indusia. Com, damp woods, rocky places low el-alp in all our mtns; Alas to e Can, s to Cal, se US; Eurasia; mtns of tropics and s hemis.

WOOD FERN, *Dryopteris austriaca*. Fronds deciduous, to 18″–40″ long, gen 3-divided, the ultimate segm with serrated margins and sharp tips, the stipes brown-scaly, the lowest pinnae asymmetrical. Sori on veins with kidney-shaped indusia. Moist woods, stream banks, in all our mtns; Alas to e Can, ne US, s to Cal, se US; Greenland, Eurasia.

MALE FERN, *Dryopteris filix-mas*. Fronds ± 2-divided, 24″–48″ long, with stipe, rachises, and midribs covered with pale brown, hairlike scales. Sori and indusia similar to those of above sp but confined to upper half of frond. Woods, shaded talus, CMtns, Wn Cas; BC to e Can, s to Cal, e US; Iceland, Eurasia.

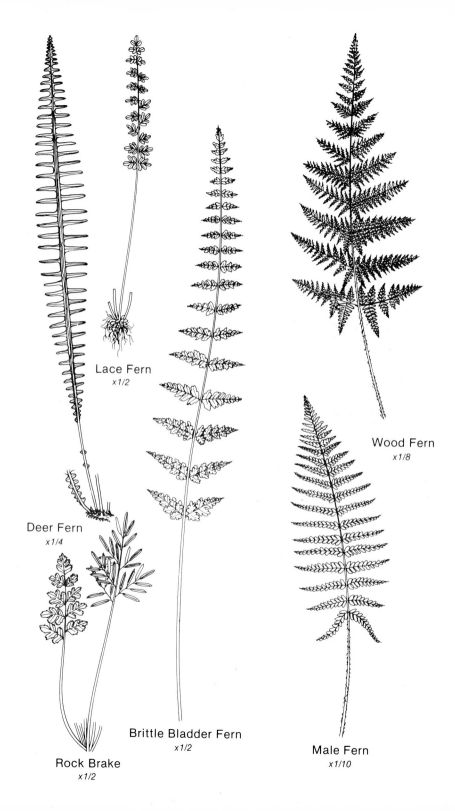

Lace Fern
x1/2

Deer Fern
x1/4

Wood Fern
x1/8

Rock Brake
x1/2

Brittle Bladder Fern
x1/2

Male Fern
x1/10

PLATE 3

Common Fern Family (Polypodiaceae)

OAK FERN, *Gymnocarpium dryopteris.* Fronds deciduous, to 16″ long, few in number, 2- 3-divided, with basal pinnae asymmetrical ea ± as large as rest of blade; stipe smooth, shiny, pale yellow, up to 2× long as blade. Sori on veinlets, no indusia. Damp woods, shaded rocky places, in all our mtns s to n Ore; Alas to e Can, s to Ore, Ariz, NMex, e US; Greenland, Iceland, Eurasia.

BREWER'S CLIFF BRAKE, *Pellaea breweri.* Fronds deciduous, 2″–8½″ long, pinnate, with deeply 2-lobed pinnae; stipes brown, cross-grooved, slightly hairy, old ones persistent and oft more numerous than lvs. Sori partly covered by curled margins. Rocky places, low el-subalp, E Cas, Wn; e to Utah, Wyo, s to Nev, Cal.

SMOOTH CLIFF BRAKE, *Pellaea glabella.* Similar to *P. breweri* but upper pinnae entire or barely lobed and basal ones oft divided again, with 3–5 pinnules; stipes reddish brown, hairless or nearly so, with or without cross-grooves, some persistent but fewer than lvs. Dry rocky places, E Cas, CRGorge, n to s BC; ne Ore and Idaho s to SNev.

GOLD FERN, *Pityrogramma triangularis.* Fronds evergreen, to 14″ long, pinnate near top, 2- 3-divided near base, with yellowish waxy powder beneath; stipe stiff, wiry, dk brown, ca ⅔ length of blade; blade triangular, with asymmetrical basal pinnae much larger than the rest. Sori along veins, no indusia. Rocky places in all our mtns; sw BC to Baja, e to Idaho, Nev, Ariz.

LICORICE FERN, *Polypodium glycyrrhiza.* Plant evergreen. Fronds pinnate, with narrow, pointed, finely toothed pinnae; stipe 2½″–12″ long, stout; blade 6″–20″ long. Sori near veins, no indusia. Com, epiphytic, growing on trees and rocks in shady, damp woods, low el, W CMtns-Cas, Alas to Cal. Western Polypody, *P. hesperum,* similar but pinnae rounded or blunt at tip. Crevices, rocky slopes, Cas, BC to Ore; Alas to Baja, NDak, Ariz, NMex.

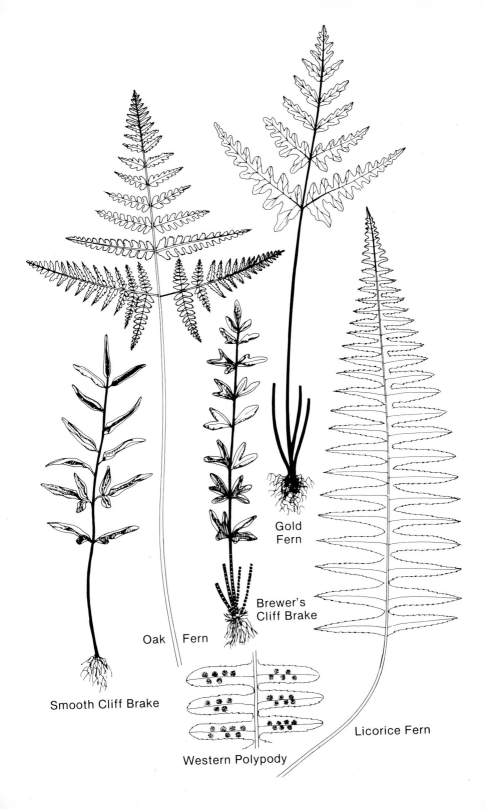

Gold
Fern

Brewer's
Cliff Brake

Oak   Fern

Smooth Cliff Brake

Western Polypody

Licorice Fern

PLATE 4

Common Fern Family (Polypodiaceae)

COMMON SWORD FERN, *Polystichum munitum* var *munitum*. Fronds evergreen, pinnate, 8″–60″ long, swordlike; stipes and rachises densely brown-scaly; pinnae asymmetrical, undivided, with scaly midrib and spinelets along margins and at tip. Sori large, in one or more rows, with shieldlike indusia. Moist forest, low–mid el in all our mtns, Alas to Cal, e to n RM. Imbricate Sword Fern, *P. m.* var *imbricans*, similar but smaller (fronds to 20″), sparsely or not scaled, and prefers drier woods and rocky places, OMtns and Cas s to SNev.

MOUNTAIN HOLLY FERN, *Polystichum lonchitis*. Fronds evergreen, pinnate, 4″–24″ long, with short stipe and slender blade that narrows toward both ends; pinnae leathery, asymmetrical, undivided, with spinelets along margins and at tip. Sori in 2 rows with shieldlike indusia. Rocky places, occas forest, mont-alp, in all our mtns; Alas s to e Can, n Cal, RM; Greenland, Iceland, Eurasia.

ANDERSON'S SWORD FERN, *Polystichum andersonii*. Fronds evergreen, usu pinnate, relatively soft, 12″–40″ long, with short, very scaly stipes and one or more scaly buds beneath near tip of rachis; pinnae deeply cleft or occas pinnate, smooth or nearly so above, scaly beneath, with serrated margins. Sori in 1 + rows, with shield-like indusia. Moist woods, Alas s in all our mtns to n Ore, e to Idaho and Mont. Braun's Sword Fern, *P. braunii*, very similar but without frond buds (BC only in our range). California Sword Fern, *P. californicum*, also very similar but lacks frond buds, and stipe naked above base.

SHASTA FERN, *Polystichum mohroides*. Fronds evergreen, 2-divided, relatively soft, 4″–20″ long; pinnae overlapping, with pinnules lobed or toothed but never prickly or spiny; stipe straw colored, somewhat sticky or with fine hairs, scaly only toward base. Sori gen only on mid and upper pinnae, the indusia shieldlike. Rocky slopes, oft on serpentine, mont-subalp, Wenatchee Mtns, Cal Cas, s to S Amer.

ROCK SWORD FERN, *Polystichum scopulinum*. Fronds evergreen, pinnate, 4″–16″ long, with scaly stipe and pale green blade, the stipe brown toward base, straw colored above; pinnae with stiff marginal prickles (*not* spines) and only one free pinnule. Sori in 2 rows near midrib, with shieldlike indusia. Rocky slopes, mid-high el, lower in CRGorge, mostly E Cas, BC to Cal; e to RM and e Can. Kruckeberg's Sword Fern, *P. kruckebergii*, similar but pinnules only 1–2× long as wide and marginal spines more prominent. Rocky places, subalp-alp, s BC to Cal and Utah.

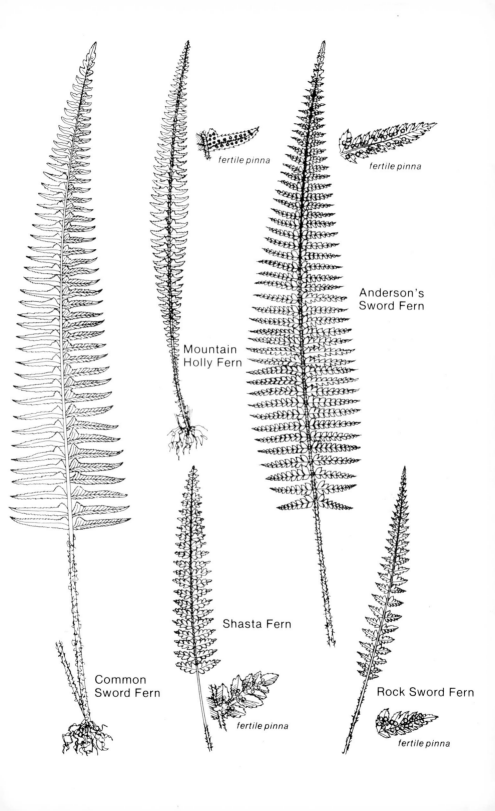

fertile pinna

fertile pinna

Anderson's
Sword Fern

Mountain
Holly Fern

Shasta Fern

Common
Sword Fern

Rock Sword Fern

fertile pinna

fertile pinna

PLATE 5

Common Fern Family (Polypodiaceae)

BRACKEN, *Pteridium aquilinum.* Fronds large, deciduous, gen 20″–80″ long, 3-divided, coarse, stiff, densely hairy beneath, ± smooth above; stipe stout, straw colored. Sori covered by curled margins. Com, open places, low–mid el in all our mtns; widespread throughout the world.

MOUNTAIN FERN, *Thelypteris limbosperma.* Fronds deciduous, pinnate, to 40″ long, the pinnae lobed; stipe short, scaly, straw colored with darker base. Sori marginal, on veins, indusia horseshoe shaped. Open woods, subalp mdws, Vanc I, CMtns, Wn Cas; Alas to n Wn; Eurasia. Sierra Wood Fern, *T. nevadensis,* similar but smaller, more delicate, with narrower blades. Uncom, Cas s of Rainier.

BEECHFERN, *Thelypteris phegopteris.* Fronds deciduous, 8″–18″ long, pinnate, nearly triangular, ± hairy above and beneath, with lobed pinnae and straw-colored stipe much longer than blade. Sori on veins, not marginal, no indusia. Moist, open woods, rocky places in all our mtns, Alas to e Can, e US, s to Ore; Eurasia.

OREGON WOODSIA, *Woodsia oreganá.* Fronds 1- 2-divided, gen 4″–8″ long, bright green, hairless; pinnae lobed; stipe stiff, slender, brown and scaly at base, smooth and straw colored above. Indusia minute, divided into threadlike segm. Dry, rocky places, CMtns, Cas s to Ore; e to RM, mid US, e Can. Rocky Mountain Woodsia, *W. scopulina,* similar but lvs sticky and white haired.

CHAIN FERN, *Woodwardia fimbriata.* Fronds deciduous, gen 20″–80″ long, firm, pinnate; pinnae with long, sharp-tipped, serrated lobes; stipe stout. Sori in 2 chain-like rows near midrib, indusia flaplike. Moist woods, stream banks, mostly near coast, but to mid el in mtns, s BC to Cal and Ariz.

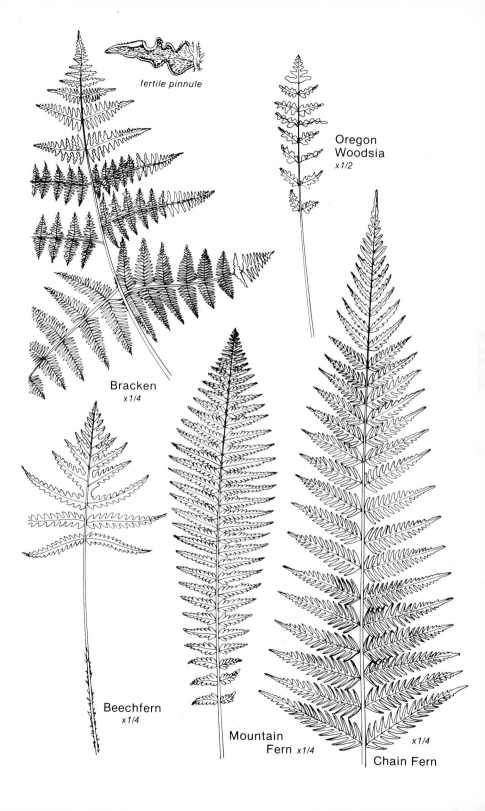

fertile pinnule

Oregon
Woodsia
x1/2

Bracken
x1/4

Beechfern
x1/4

Mountain
Fern *x1/4*

x1/4

Chain Fern

6

FLOWERING PLANTS

The mountains of our region, with their varied topography and climate, support a few thousand species of flowering plants. Species that are at once common, conspicuous, distinctive, and showy, however, make up only a fraction of the total. This guide depicts more than 320 species and provides information for identifying several dozen more. The flowering plants have been separated for convenience into three groups: wildflowers, shrubs, and trees.

The term *wildflower* has no precise botanical meaning and may refer to any flowering plant growing outside of cultivation. In common parlance, however, it usually refers to herbaceous plants, which have nonwoody stems that grow anew each year and die back after seed production. Annuals sprout each year from seed and complete their life cycles in a single growing season. Biennials require two years. Perennial herbs live for several seasons, but during months of dormancy, they persist in the form of mostly underground parts such as bulbs, corms, tubers, rhizomes, or root crowns. Some perennial herbs die back to woody bases, but each year's new growth is herbaceous. Such plants are called subshrubs. In addition to reproducing from seed, some perennials may form new plants through such means as the division of bulbs and corms, the sprouting of tubers, and the formation of new plantlets along rhizomes and runners.

Trees and shrubs are perennial plants with woody stems that persist, with or without leaves, from one year to the next. A tree is often defined as a woody plant at least 15 feet tall, usually with a single trunk at least several inches thick and a well-developed crown of branches. A shrub, therefore, is a woody plant less than 15 feet tall with more than one main stem. Some trees, however, may be decidedly shrubby, especially in harsh environments where conditions inhibit normal growth. Moreover, some shrubs may exceed 15 feet in height or have one short, trunklike stem.

As used here, the term *flowering plant* includes cone-bearing plants (*gymnosperms*) and true flowering plants (*angiosperms*). Gymnosperms bear naked seeds on the undersides of cone scales. Angiosperms bear seeds in protective capsules called ovaries.

Scientific names used in the following species accounts conform to *Flora of the Pacific Northwest* by C. Leo Hitchcock and Arthur Cronquist. Common names are derived from a variety of sources.

The following glossary defines the technical terms used in the species descriptions. Most terms, in addition, are illustrated in figures 7 through 10, which depict types of flowers and leaves as well as plant parts. Wherever possible, common words have been used to replace technical terms.

GLOSSARY

Alternate: *Having one leaf per node (see figure 5).*

Anther: *The pollen-bearing part of the stamen (see figure 3).*

Axil: *The point of the upper angle formed where a leaf or petiole joins a stem (see figure 5).*

Basal: *Referring to leaves that emerge from the base of a flowering stem, either from the stem itself, a woody base, runners, or underground parts (see figure 5).*

Blade: *The expanded part of a leaf or petal (see figure 5).*

Bract: *Any more or less modified or reduced leaf associated with an inflorescence (see figures 3 and 4).*

Calyx: *All the sepals of a flower considered together; the outer set of modified floral leaves (see figure 7).*

Catkin: *An erect or drooping spikelike inflorescence consisting of numerous tiny flowers and their associated bracts (see figure 4).*

Clasping: *Referring to leaves that partially wrap around a stem at the point of attachment (see figure 5).*

Composite Head: *An inflorescence typical of the sunflower family (Compositae) that consists of numerous tubular disk flowers surrounded by a few to many straplike ray flowers, the whole resembling a single regular flower; examples include asters, daisies, and sunflowers (see figures 3 and 4).*

Compound: *Referring to leaves with two or more distinct leaflets (see figure 5).*

Compound-pinnate: *Referring to compound leaves having two or more pinnate leaflets (see figure 5).*

Corolla: *All the petals of a flower considered together; the innermost set of modified floral leaves (see figure 3).*

Corymb: *A round- or flat-topped inflorescence in which the lower (outer) pedicels are progressively longer (see figure 4).*

Deciduous: *Falling off, as leaves in autumn or petals after flowering.*

Disk flower: *The generally small, tubular flowers making up the central disk of a composite head (see figures 3 and 4).*

Dissected: *Cut or divided into lobes or segments; said of leaves.*

Double-toothed: *Referring to leaf margins divided into large teeth that are themselves divided into smaller teeth (see figure 6).*

Elliptic: *Resembling an ellipse (see figure 6).*

Entire: *Referring to undivided leaf margins (see figure 6).*

Evergreen: *Referring to plants that retain leaves throughout the year.*

Fascicled: *Referring to leaves that are attached to a stem in tight bundles, or fascicles (see figure 5).*

Filament: *The stalk of a stamen (see figure 7).*

Glandular: *Having glands that secrete a sticky or greasy substance.*

Inflorescence: *A flower cluster sharing a single main stem (see figure 4).*

Involucre: *A set of bracts beneath an inflorescence (see figure 3).*

Irregular flower: *A flower displaying bilateral, rather than radial, symmetry (see figure 4).*

Leaflet: *The ultimate division of a compound leaf that resembles a single, simple leaf (see figure 5).*

Linear: *Long, narrow, of more or less uniform width; said of leaves (see figure 6).*

Lobe: *A segment of a leaf blade, usually blunt or rounded and not cut all the way from margin to midrib (see figure 6); a projecting segment of a corolla or calyx.*

Node: *Place on a stem where a leaf is or was attached (see figure 5).*

Oblanceolate: *Inversely lancelike (see figure 6).*

Oblong: *Much longer than broad with nearly parallel sides (see figure 6).*

Obovate: *Inversely egg shaped (see figure 6).*

Opposite: *Having a pair of leaves per node (see figure 5).*

Oval: *Broadly elliptic (see figure 6).*

Ovary: *The swollen, seed-bearing portion of the pistil (see figure 3).*

Ovate: *Egg shaped (see figure 6).*

Ovule: *Unfertilized or undeveloped seed; borne in the ovary (see figure 3).*

Palmate: *Resembling the palm of a hand; having leaves or veins radiating from a central point (see figure 6).*

Panicle: *An inflorescence with branched pedicels (see figure 4).*

Pedicel: *The stalk of a single flower in an inflorescence (see figures 3 and 4).*

Peduncle: *The stalk of an inflorescence.*

Perfoliate: *With a leaf completely surrounding the stem (see figure 5).*

Petal: *One of the modified leaves making up the corolla of a flower; usually brightly colored to attract insects (see figure 3).*

Petiole: *Leaf stalk (see figure 5).*

Petioled: *Having a petiole.*

Pinnate: *A compound leaf with the leaflets arranged on each side of a common axis (see figure 5).*

Pistil: *The female reproductive organ of a flower, consisting of a stigma, style, and ovary (see figure 3).*

Raceme: *An inflorescence bearing flowers on pedicels (see figure 4).*

Ray *or* Ray Flower: *The strap-shaped, petallike peripheral flowers of a composite head (see figures 3 and 4).*

Receptacle: *The swollen part of a floral stalk to which the flower parts are attached (see figure 3).*

Regular flower: *A flower displaying radial symmetry (see figure 4).*

Rhizome: *A trailing underground stem producing leafy shoots on the upper side and roots on the underside.*

Rosette: *A leaf cluster, usually basal, in which the leaves are arranged in a concentric configuration like that of the petals of a rose.*

Samara: *Dry, generally one-seeded, winged fruit, as in maples (see plates 41, 53).*

Scalloped: *Having shallow, rounded divisions; said of leaf margins (see figure 6).*

Sepal: *One of the modified leaves making up the calyx of a flower (see figure 3).*

Sessile: *Attached directly to the stem; said of leaves without petioles (see figure 5).*

Sheathing: *Wrapping around the stem like a sheath; said of leaves (see figure 5).*

Simple leaf: *A leaf with a blade undivided into leaflets; opposite of a compound leaf (see figure 5).*

Spadix: *A floral spike with tiny flowers crowded on a fleshy stem (see figure 4).*

Spathe: *A large, usually solitary bract partly surrounding a spadix or other inflorescence (see figure 4).*

Spike: *An inflorescence in which flowers are attached directly to a central stem (see figure 4).*

Spur: *A slender, hollow projection from a petal or sepal.*

Stamen: *The male reproductive organ of a flower, consisting of the anther and filament (see figure 3).*

Stigma: *The pollen receptacle on the tip of a pistil (see figure 3).*

Stipule: *One of a pair of leaflike structures found at the base of leaves on many types of plants (see figure 5).*

Style: *The stalk of a pistil (see figure 3).*

Tepal: *A modified floral leaf performing the function of both sepal and petal when those are lacking.*

Toothed: *Divided into pointed segments, as the margin of a leaf (see figure 6).*

Tufted: *Referring to leaves growing in basal tufts or fascicles.*

Umbel: *Inflorescence in which all the pedicels arise from a central hub (see figure 4).*

Whorled: *Having three or more leaves or flowers radiating from a single node on a stem (see figure 5).*

WILDFLOWERS

More than 200 of the more common or showy species of wildflowers found in our mountains are described and illustrated in the following section of this chapter. They include representatives from each vegetation zone and from most of the important families and genera. The great majority are native to our region, but a few are exotics that have become naturalized.

For easy reference the flowers are grouped by color. A word of caution is in order, however, for color by itself is not always a reliable field mark.

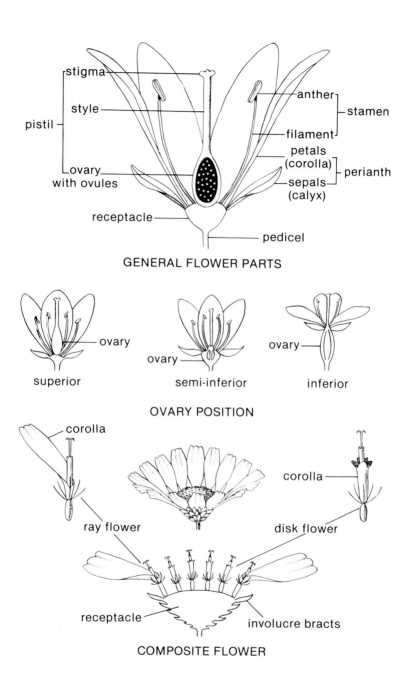

GENERAL FLOWER PARTS

stigma
style
pistil
ovary with ovules
receptacle
anther
stamen
filament
petals (corolla)
sepals (calyx)
perianth
pedicel

OVARY POSITION

ovary
superior

ovary
semi-inferior

ovary
inferior

COMPOSITE FLOWER

corolla
ray flower
corolla
disk flower
receptacle
involucre bracts

Figure 3. Anatomy of a flower

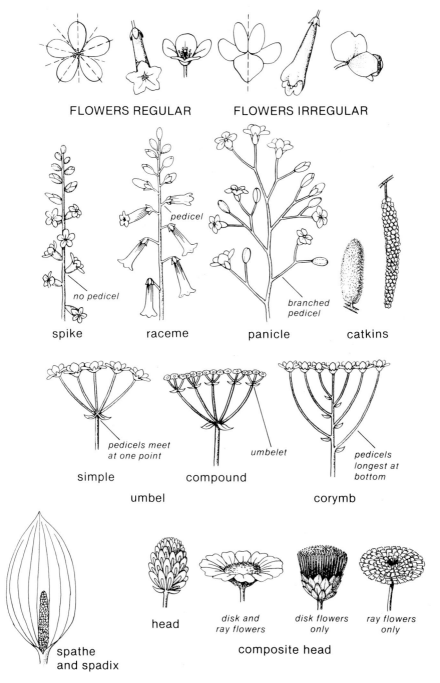

FLOWERS REGULAR   FLOWERS IRREGULAR

spike   raceme   panicle   catkins

no pedicel   pedicel   branched pedicel

simple   compound   corymb

pedicels meet at one point   umbelet   pedicels longest at bottom

umbel

spathe and spadix

head   disk and ray flowers   disk flowers only   ray flowers only

composite head

Figure 4. Types of inflorescence.

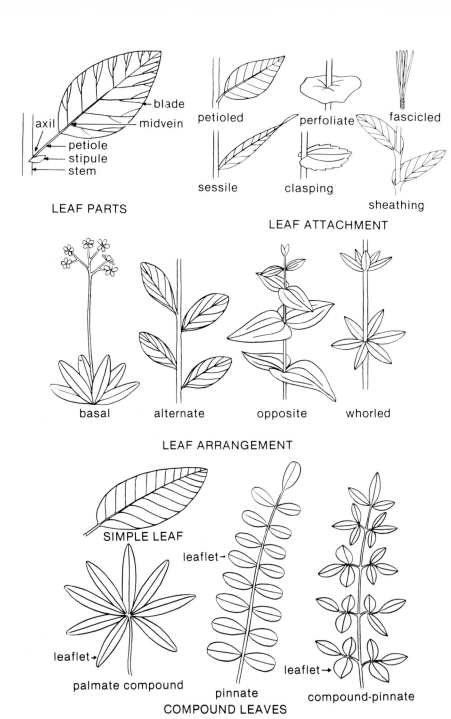

LEAF PARTS

blade
midvein
axil
petiole
stipule
stem

LEAF ATTACHMENT

petioled
perfoliate
fascicled
sessile
clasping
sheathing

LEAF ARRANGEMENT

basal
alternate
opposite
whorled

COMPOUND LEAVES

SIMPLE LEAF
leaflet
palmate compound
pinnate
compound-pinnate
leaflet

Figure 5. Anatomy of leaves.

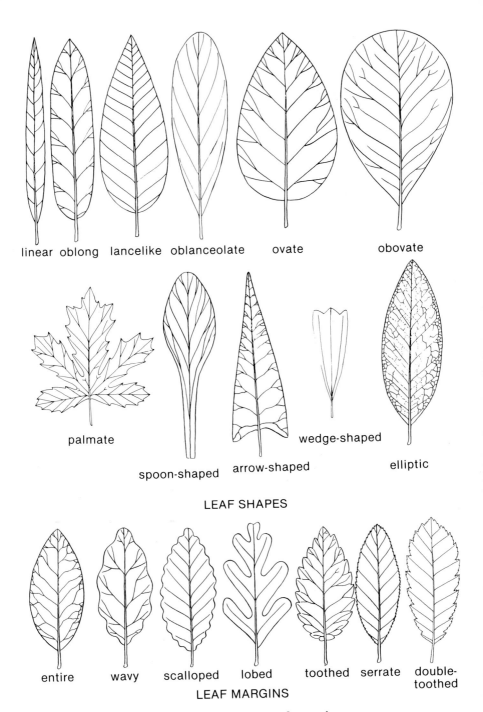

linear oblong lancelike oblanceolate ovate obovate

palmate spoon-shaped arrow-shaped wedge-shaped elliptic

LEAF SHAPES

entire wavy scalloped lobed toothed serrate double-toothed

LEAF MARGINS

Figure 6. Leaf shapes and margins.

First, many species are variable in color. Second, flowers may change color with age. Third, closely related species may have flowers of indentical colors. Fourth, some flowers are more than one color and are therefore difficult to assign to a single color group. Fifth, people differ markedly in their perception of color: what appears creamy white to me may seem pale yellow to you; what I call rosy pink you may consider reddish purple. Therefore, when searching for a wildflower in this guide, turn first to the appropriate color group, but if you do not find your specimen, consult the list of color variations found at the beginning of each color section. This list will direct you to species in other sections that sometimes have flowers the color of your specimen. In addition, don't rely upon color alone. Pay equal attention to flower structure, leaves, stems, general growth habit, habitat, and range. Figures 3 through 6 will help you recognize flowers and leaves.

Species are grouped under each color heading by family. To assist your search, immediately following each family name is a brief statement characterizing the flowers of family members appearing on each plate. If you find a species that does not exactly match your specimen, but is very similar, refer to the brief descriptions of similar species that may be included in the species account. Your specimen may be included there or you may have to settle for identifying it by genus alone. It is also possible, of course, that you have found a species not covered in this book, in which case you should consult Hitchcock and Cronquist's *Flora of the Pacific Northwest* or one of the other exhaustive floras covering our region.

For information on the organization and use of the species accounts and illustrations, as well as for a list of the abbreviations used in the accounts, see the Introduction. The general flowering period for each species is indicated at the end of each account.

I. White Flowers

This section includes not only flowers that are truly white but also those that appear white even though lightly tinged with other colors. The following species from other color sections sometimes have white or whitish flowers.

Sulfur-flowered Buckwheat, *plate 18*
Oval-leaved Buckwheat, *plate 18*
Martindale's Lomatium, *plate 20*
Coiled-beak Lousewort, *plate 21*
Rosy Twisted-stalk, *plate 23*
Western Spring Beauty, *plate 23*
Steer's Head, *plate 24*
Alpine Willow-herb, *plate 25*
Candystick, *plate 25*
Skyrocket, *plate 26*
Spreading Phlox, *plate 26*
Foxglove, *plate 27*
Common Camas, *plate 29*
Monkshood, *plate 29*
Wild Crocus, *plate 29*
Oregon Anemone, *plate 29*
Nuttall's Pea, *plate 30*
Marsh Violet, *plate 30*
Mountain Pennyroyal, *plate 32*
Western Meadowrue, *plate 35*
Fringecup, *plate 35*
Pinedrops, *plate 35*

PLATE 6

Lily Family (Liliaceae): usually 3 petals and 3 sepals, or 6 tepals, but see *Maianthemum*

SUBALPINE MARIPOSA LILY, *Calochortus subalpinus.* Flr creamy white, occas lavender tinged; petals broadly ovate, yellow haired, oft with purple crescent at base. Single grasslike basal lf as long or longer than stem. Ht 2″–12″. Volcanic soils in open woods, mid-high el, Cas, S Wn to cen Ore. Sum.

LYALL'S MARIPOSA LILY, *Calochortus lyallii.* Similar to *C. subalpinus* but petals lancelike, fringed, without yellow hairs. Dry woods and brush, low el, E Cas, BC to cen Wn. Late spr-midsum.

QUEEN'S CUP (BEAD LILY), *Clintonia uniflora.* Flrs bell shaped with spreading tepals, 1 (occas 2) per stem. Lvs 2–3, basal, oblong, 3″–10″ long. Fruit a turquoise berry. Ht ca 4″. Com, forest, open places, low-high el, in all our mtns; Alas to Cal, e to RM, e Ore. Sum.

HOOKER'S FAIRY BELL, *Disporum hookeri.* Flrs to ¾″ long, creamy white, with undivided stigma usu in pairs, nodding. Lvs sessile, nearly clasping, hairy, wavy margined. Ht 12″–24″. Dense woods in all our mtns, BC to Cal, E Cas to coast; n RM. Spr-midsum. Fairy lantern, *D. smithii,* similar but flrs ca 1″ long, with divided stigma and lvs broader, not clasping, hairless above. BC to n Cal, coast to W Cas.

AVALANCHE LILY, *Erythronium montanum.* Flrs white with yellow throat, nodding, ca 2½″ diam, usu 1–3 on lfless stem. Lvs basal, broadly ovate or lance shaped, 4″–8″ long. Ht to 10″. Abun, wet mdws, mid-high el, Vanc I, OMtns, s Wn Cas s to Hood. Early to midsum, just after snow melts.

WASHINGTON LILY, *Lilium washingtonianum.* Flrs white or pale pink, oft with purplish spots, aging purple, fragrant, in loose raceme, 3″–4″ diam, nearly as long. Lvs ± lancelike, 2″–4″ long, alt on lower stem, whorled on upper stem. Ht 24″–80″. Open forest, brush, Cas of Ore and Cal, s in SNev. Sum.

FALSE LILY-OF-THE-VALLEY, *Maianthemum dilatatum.* Flrs tiny, in raceme; only lily with 2 petals, 2 sepals. Lvs heart shaped, glossy green, usu 2 (1–3) per stem, the lower ones 2″–4½″ long, the upper one smaller. Fruit a red berry ¼″ diam. Ht 4″–8″. Moist woods, low-mid el, in all our mtns, Alas to Cal, e to n RM. Late spr-early sum.

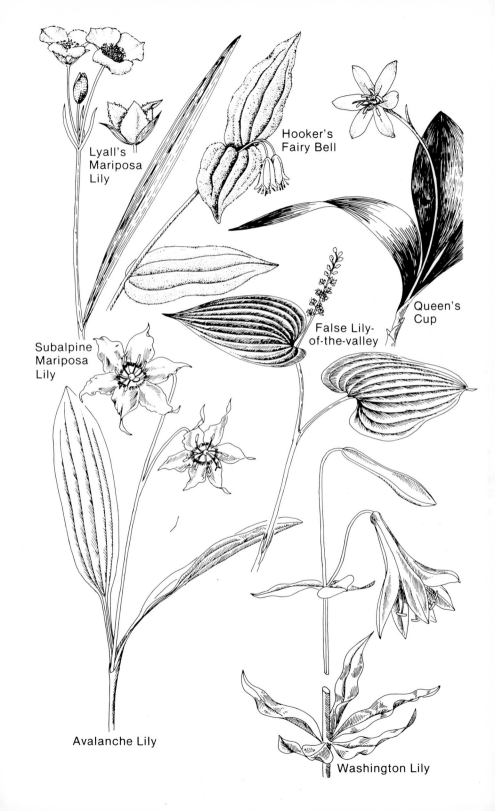

Lyall's
Mariposa
Lily

Hooker's
Fairy Bell

Queen's
Cup

Subalpine
Mariposa
Lily

False Lily-
of-the-valley

Avalanche Lily

Washington Lily

PLATE 7

Lily Family (*Liliaceae*): 3 petals and 3 sepals, or 6 tepals

STARRY SOLOMON'S PLUME (FALSE SOLOMON'S-SEAL), *Smilacina stellata*. Flrs starlike, ca ¼" diam, 5 – 10+ in zigzag raceme. Lvs lancelike to elliptic, clasping stem, gen glossy green above, sometimes downy beneath. Fruit a greenish berry, aging black. Ht 8"–28". Com, usu moist woods to open rocky slopes in all our mtns, Alas to Cal; RM s to Ariz, e to Atl. Late spr-midsum. False Solomon's-Seal (False Spikenard), *S. racemosa*, similar to above but flrs tiny, numerous in panicle, lvs broader, and berries red. Moist woods, stream banks, low-mid el in all our mtns, Alas to Cal, e to Atl. Early spr-midsum.

CLASPING-LEAVED TWISTED-STALK, *Streptopus amplexifolius*. Flrs white, green tinged, usu 1 borne below ea lf. Stems oft kinked or zigzag, freely branching, 12"–36" tall. Lvs ± ovate, clasping. Fruit a translucent red berry. Moist forest, stream banks in all our mtns, Alas to Cal, e in much of US and Can. Late spr. Cf other twisted-stalks, plates 23 and 34.

STICKY TOFIELDIA, *Tofieldia glutinosa*. Flrs greenish white, to ¼" diam, in cluster atop sticky, lfless stem. Lvs grasslike, clasping, basal. Ht 4"–20". Wet mdws, bogs, low-high el in all our mtns, Alas to Cal, e to Atl. Sum.

WESTERN TRILLIUM (WAKE-ROBIN), *Trillium ovatum*. Flrs 1½"–3" diam, gen white, aging pink to dark red, 1 above whorl of 3 (occas 4–5) ovate lvs. Ht 4"–16". Com, moist, oft shaded sites lowl-mid el, in all our mtns, Alas to Cal, e to RM. Late win-early sum.

CORN-LILY (WHITE FALSE-HELLEBORE), *Veratrum californicum*. Flrs white or occas greenish, numerous in dense, upright terminal panicle. Lvs gen ovate to oval 8"–12" long, numerous. Ht 36"–84"+. Wet places, lowl-subalp, W Cas (occas E Cas), Wn s to SNev. Sum. Cf Green False-hellebore, plate 34.

BEARGRASS, *Xerophyllum tenax*. Flrs tiny, creamy, starlike, in dense terminal inflor. Lvs grasslike, stiff, the basal ones gen 6"–24" long, clumped, the stem lvs shorter, numerous. Ht 24"–60". Open woods, clearings, gen mid-high el, in all our mtns, BC to cen Cal, e to RM. Sum.

ELEGANT DEATH-CAMAS. *Zigadenus elegans*. Flrs creamy or green tinged, with green glands at base, in terminal inflor. Lvs mostly basal, grasslike, 6"–12" long, with powdery bloom. Ht 6"–28". Mdws, rocky places, gen mid-high el, Alas and BC s to Wn Cas and OMtns; e to RM, s to Ariz and n Mex. Sum.

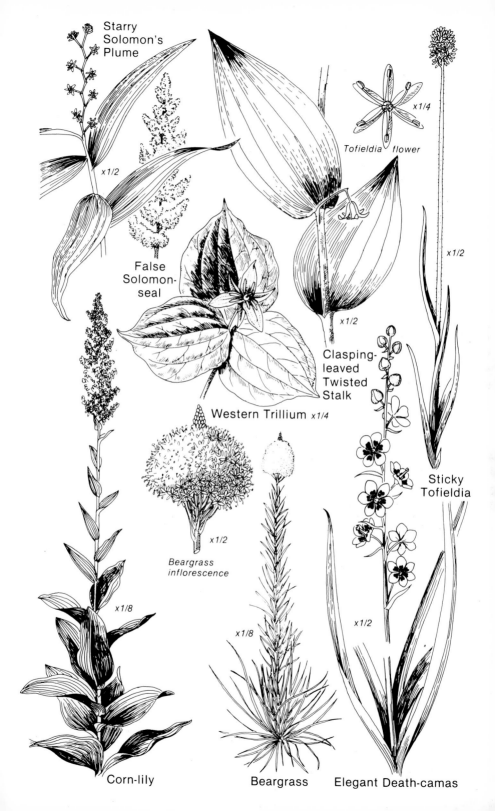

Starry Solomon's Plume

x1/2

Tofieldia flower x1/4

False Solomon-seal

Clasping-leaved Twisted Stalk

x1/2

x1/2

x1/2

Western Trillium x1/4

Sticky Tofieldia

x1/2

Beargrass inflorescence

x1/8

x1/8

x1/2

Corn-lily

Beargrass

Elegant Death-camas

PLATE 8

Orchid Family (*Orchidaceae*) flowers irregular, 3 petals, 3 sepals

MOUNTAIN LADY-SLIPPER (MOCCASIN FLOWER), *Cypripedium montanum*. Flrs usu 2, orchidlike; sepals brownish purple, the 2 lower ones fused; 2 upper petals like sepals but twisted, lower one white, pouchlike, occas purple veined. Lvs oval to ovate, 2"–6" long, sheathing stem. Ht 4"–24"; stem leafy, sticky haired. Mostly E Cas, Alas to Cal, e to RM. Late spr-sum. Cf Clustered Lady-slipper, plate 34.

PHANTOM (SNOW) ORCHID, *Eburophyton austiniae*. Entire plant white, aging brown, with 5–20 fragrant flrs on single stem. Lvs bractlike on lower stem. Ht 8"–20". Moist, shady forest, OMtns, Cas, Wn to s Cal, e to Idaho. Sum.

RATTLESNAKE-PLANTAIN (ORCHID), *Goodyera oblongifolia*. Flrs small, gen in 1-sided raceme on sticky-haired stem. Lvs basal, dk green, mottled or striped with white. Ht gen 10"–16". Shady woods in all our mtns, Alas e to Atl, s in most of w Can and US. Sum-early fall.

ROUNDLEAF BOG ORCHID (REIN ORCHIS), *Habenaria orbiculata*. Flrs creamy white to greenish, 5–25 per stem, with spur to 1" long. Lvs round, rather fleshy, ca 2½"–6" long, 2 (3) at base, lying flat on ground. Ht 8"–24". Moist, mossy forest in our mtns s to Ore; Alas e to Atl and RM. Sum.

WHITE BOG ORCHID, *Habenaria dilatata*. Flrs white, fragrant, spurred. Lvs clasping, lower ones ± lancelike to 4" long, upper ones linear, 2"–12" long. Ht 6"–40". Wet places in all our mtns; Alas s in w Can and US, e to e Can, ne US. Sum-early fall. Short-spurred Bog Orchid, *H. unalascensis*, has basal lvs and yellow green flrs. Elegant Bog Orchid, *H. elegans*, has nearly basal lvs and green flrs with white spur; prefers dry woods. Slender Bog Orchid, *H. saccata*, has green flrs with sack-shaped spur.

LADY'S TRESSES *Spiranthes romanzoffia*. Flrs white or creamy to greenish white, up to 60 in dense, spiraling spike. Lvs linear, 2"–10" long, ± basal, bractlike above. Ht 4"–24". Moist or wet places in all our mtns, Alas s to Cal, Ariz, NMex, e to e Can, ne US. Late sum-early fall.

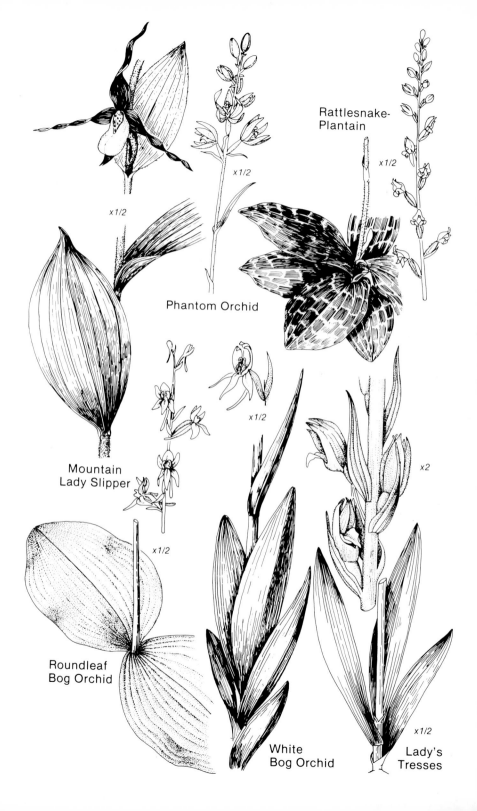

Rattlesnake-
Plantain

x1/2

x1/2

Phantom Orchid

x1/2

Mountain
Lady Slipper

x1/2

x2

Roundleaf
Bog Orchid

White
Bog Orchid

x1/2

Lady's
Tresses

PLATE 9

Buckwheat Family (*Polygonaceae*): no petals, 4–9 petallike sepals

ALPINE (PYROLA-LEAVED) BUCKWHEAT, *Eriogonum pyrolaefolium*. Flrs creamy or greenish white, aging pink, in umbels with 2 linear bracts at base. Lvs numerous, ± oval, basal, petioled. Cushion plant ca 4″. Subalp-alp, Wn Cas to Cal, e to RM. Sum.

COMMON (AMERICAN, MOUNTAIN, WESTERN) BISTORT, *Polygonum bistortoides*. Flrs tiny, in dense clublike inflor. Lvs mostly basal, elliptic to oblong, to 8″ long; stem lvs smaller, bractlike. Ht 12″–24″. Abun, subalp-alp mdws, stream banks, in all our mtns, BC to Cal, e to RM. Sum. The showiest and most common of the more than dozen knotweeds in our range.

Purslane Family (*Portulacaceae*): generally 5 petals, 2 sepals

MINER'S LETTUCE, *Montia perfoliata*. Flrs small, in raceme above round, perfoliate lf (2 lvs fused). Basal lvs usu spoon shaped. Plant edible. Ht 1″–14″. Moist places, low-mid el, Cas, BC s to Baja; e to RM and mid US. Spr-sum.

SIBERIAN MONTIA (WESTERN SPRING BEAUTY, CANDYFLOWER), *Montia sibirica*. Flrs white or pale pink, lined with darker pink, in loose racemes. Basal lvs numerous, broadly spoon shaped, long petioled; stem lvs opp, 1 pair per stem, oval, sessile. Ht 2″–16″. Moist, shaded places, low-mid el, in all our mtns, Alas to Cal, e to RM. Sum. Heartleaf Montia, *M. cordifolia*, has broad, heart-shaped lvs. Littleleaf Montia, *M. parvifolia*, has alt stem lvs and spoon-shaped basal lvs. Cf Western Spring Beauty, plate 23.

PYGMY (DWARF, ALPINE) LEWISIA, *Lewisia pygmaea*. Flrs white to pink or rose, 1 per stem, with 2 sepals, 5-9 petals. Lvs fleshy, basal, linear, 1½″–6″ long. Ht to 4″. Open, rocky places, Cas and OMtns, Wn to Cal, e to RM. Sum.

Pink Family (*Caryophyllaceae*): 5 petals, 5 sepals

MOUNTAIN (BEAUTIFUL, FESCUE) SANDWORT, *Arenaria capillaris*. Flrs to ½″ diam, in open, branched inflor. Lvs grasslike, mostly basal, but with 2–5 opp pairs on stems. Ht 4″–8″, mat forming. Dry, rocky places, in all our mtns, Alas to n Ore; e to Mont, s to Nev. Sum. Other sandworts in our range ± similar.

PARRY'S (WHITE, FESCUE) SILENE (CAMPION, CATCHFLY), *Silene parryi*. Plant hairy, ± sticky. Flrs white, aging pink, with 4–lobed petals ca ⅓″ long; calyx tubular, 5–lobed, with green or purplish veins. Lvs linear-oblanceolate, basal and in 2–3 opp pairs on stem. Ht 4″–24″. Mdws, mont-alp, in all our mtns, BC and Wn e to RM. Sum. Note distinctive petals of other white silenes in our range (see illustrations).

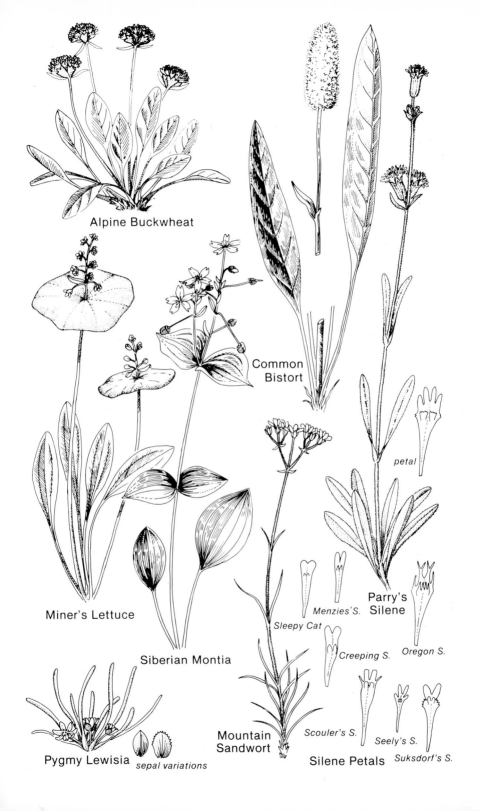

Alpine Buckwheat

Common Bistort

petal

Miner's Lettuce

Siberian Montia

Parry's Silene

Menzies' S.

Sleepy Cat

Creeping S.

Oregon S.

Pygmy Lewisia   sepal variations

Mountain Sandwort

Scouler's S.

Seely's S.

Suksdorf's S.

Silene Petals

PLATE 10

Buttercup Family (*Ranunculaceae*): 5–12 petallike sepals

WESTERN RED BANEBERRY, *Actaea rubra.* Flrs tiny, tinged purple, in dense racemes. Lvs compound pinnate, long petioled, the ultimate segm toothed and lobed. Fruit, clusters of poisonous red berries. Ht 16″–40″. Moist places, in all our mtns, Alas to Cal; e to RM, e Can, ne US. Late spring-midsum.

COLUMBIA WINDFLOWER (ANEMONE), *Anemone deltoidea.* Flrs solitary, tinged blue, 1½″ diam, with 5 petallike sepals. Basal lf usu solitary with 3 ovate, toothed lflets; 3 simple, toothed stem lvs in whorl. Ht 4″–12″. Forest, W Cas, Wn to n Cal. Spr. Lyall's Anemone, *A. lyalli,* similar but stem lvs ea have 3 lflets. Northern Anemone, *A. parvifolia,* has numerous basal lvs and simple, 3–lobed stem lvs and is usu less than 6″ tall. Cf Oregon Anemone, plate 29.

DRUMMOND'S ANEMONE, *Anemone drummondii.* Flrs gen 1 per stem, ca 1″ diam, the 5 petallike sepals white tinged with blue. Lvs finely divided, silky haired, several on long petioles from base; smaller but similar lvs in whorl on upper stem. Ht 4″–12″. Alp-subalp in all our mtns, Alas to Cal, e to RM. Sum. Cliff Anemone, *A. multifida,* similar but flrs oft 2–3 per stem, usu yellowish, tinged with red, blue, or purple.

WESTERN PASQUEFLOWER, *Anemone occidentalis.* Entire plant hairy. Flrs 1″–2″ diam, occas blue tinged, with 5–7 petallike sepals. Lvs basal, downy, finely divided, the ultimate segm linear. Stems ca 4″ tall at flowering, to 24″ at maturity. Fruit a mop of feathery seeds. Wet mdws, mont-alp, in all our mtns, BC to Cal, e to RM. Early sum.

TWINFLOWER MARSH-MARIGOLD, *Caltha biflora.* Flrs white with yellow center, ca 1½″ diam, 5–12 petallike sepals, usu 2 flrs per stem. Lvs basal, nearly round to ovate, to 4″ long, nearly as wide or wider. Wet places, subalp-alp, in all our mtns, Alas to Cal, e to RM. Sum. Elkslip Marsh-marigold, *C. leptosepala,* similar, also com, but lvs much longer than wide and flrs usu 1 per stem.

FALSE BUGBANE, *Trautvetteria caroliniensis.* Flrs with 3–7 tiny greenish sepals and numerous white stamens, in loose corymbs. Lvs mostly basal, 4″–12″ broad, palmately lobed and toothed. Ht 6″–40″. Moist places in all our mtns; N Amer, Japan. Late spr-sum.

GLOBEFLOWER, *Troillus laxus.* Flr solitary, creamy or greenish white, ca 1½″ diam. Lvs palmately 5–lobed or divided, basal and alt on stem. Ht 4″–20″. Wet places, mid-high el, mtns of BC, OMtns, Wn Cas; e to RM and in US to Atl. Late spr-early sum.

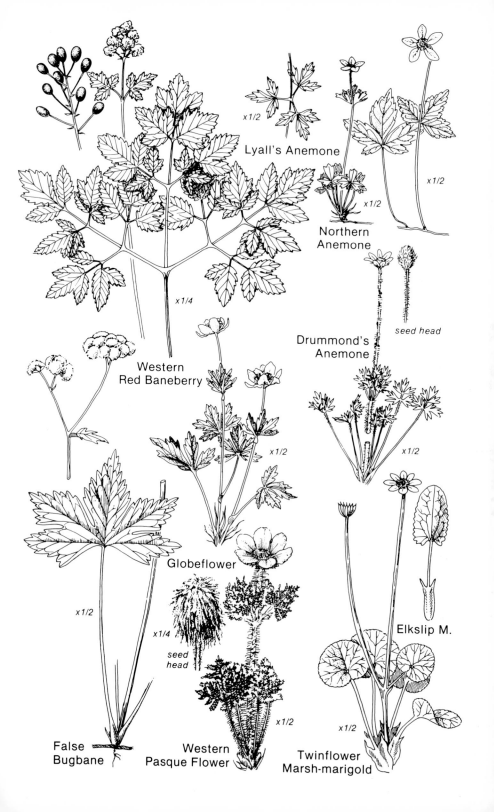

Lyall's Anemone

x1/2

Northern
Anemone

x1/2

Drummond's
Anemone

seed head

Western
Red Baneberry

x1/2

x1/2

x1/4

Globeflower

Elkslip M.

False
Bugbane

x1/2

Western
Pasque Flower

seed
head

x1/4

x1/2

Twinflower
Marsh-marigold

x1/2

PLATE 11

Barberry Family (*Berberidaceae*): flowers 3—parted

VANILLA LEAF, *Achlys triphylla*. Flrs inconspicuous, numerous in dense spike 1″–2″ long. Lvs basal, long petioled, compound, the 3 lflets fan shaped with wavy, toothed margins. Ht 8″–16″. Moist forest, stream banks, low-mid el, in all our mtns, BC to Cal. Spr-sum.

Mustard Family (*Cruciferae*): 4 petals in a cross

ALPINE SMELOWSKIA, *Smelowskia calycina*. Flrs white, creamy, or purple tinged, in racemes. Lvs mostly basal, pinnately lobed, gray haired, with long, stiff hairs on petioles. Cushion plant 2″–8″ tall. Subalp-alp, BC s to Wn Cas, OMtns; widespread in N Amer e to RM; Asia. Sum. Shortleaf Smelowskia, *S. ovalis*, very similar but without long, stiff hairs on petioles; Cas, Wn to Cal.

Sundew Family (*Droseraceae*): usually 5 petals, 5 sepals

ROUNDLEAF SUNDEW, *Drosera rotundifolia*. Flrs white or pinkish, small, on slender, bent stalk. Lvs basal, spreading, long petioled, covered with sticky red hairs. Ht to 10″. Insectivorous. Bogs, in all our mtns, Alas s to Cal and Nev, e in Can and n US to Atl. Sum-early fall. Great Sundew, *D. anglica*, very similar but lvs ± oblong and gen upright, not spreading.

Saxifrage Family (*Saxifragaceae*): 5 petals, 5 sepals

ELMERA (ALUMROOT), *Elmera racemosa*. Flrs 10–35 in raceme, with tiny, white and greenish yellow calyx. Lvs basal and on flr stem, kidney shaped, sticky haired, the margins lobed. Ht 4″–10″. Rock crevices, mont-subalp, OMtns, Wn Cas, se Ore. Sum-early fall.

SMALL FLOWERED ALUMROOT, *Heuchera micrantha*. Similar to *Elmera* but flrs in panicle and lvs gen basal, with white or red hairs on petioles and base of flr stem. Ht to 36″. Stream banks, moist rock crevices, lowl-subalp, in all our mtns, BC to Cal, e to ne Ore, Idaho. Late spring-sum. Smooth Alumroot, *H. glabra*, very similar but petioles hairless. Other spp similar, but flrs yellow or greenish.

FRINGED GRASS-OF-PARNASSUS, *Parnassia fibriata*. Flrs solitary on stem, ca 1″ diam, with 5 fringed petals and feathery structure at base of stamens. Lvs basal, long petioled, heart-kidney shaped. Ht 6″–20″. Wet places, mont-alp, in all our mtns, Alas to Cal, e to RM. Midsum-early fall.

FOAMFLOWER (FALSE MITREWORT, COOLWORT), *Tiarella trifoliata*. Flrs tiny, nodding, in branched inflor. Lvs gen basal, hairy, toothed, either compound with 3 lflets or simple and palmately lobed. Plants with simple lvs oft considered a separate sp, *T. unifoliata*. Ht to 16″. Damp forest in all our mtns, Alas to Cal, e to RM. Late spr-fall.

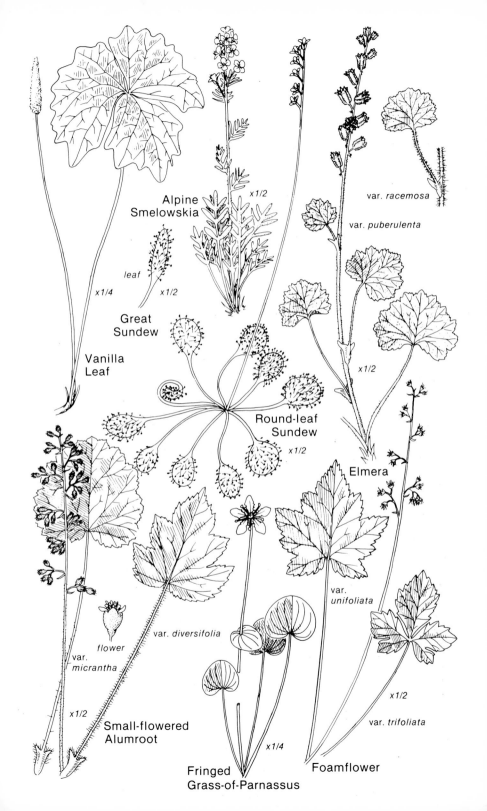

Alpine
Smelowskia

x1/2

var. *racemosa*

var. *puberulenta*

leaf   *x1/2*

Great
Sundew

Vanilla
Leaf

x1/4

Round-leaf
Sundew

x1/2

x1/2

Elmera

var.
unifoliata

var. *diversifolia*

flower

var.
micrantha

x1/2

Small-flowered
Alumroot

x1/2

var. *trifoliata*

Foamflower

x1/4

Fringed
Grass-of-Parnassus

PLATE 12

Saxifrage Family (*Saxifragaceae*): 5 petals, 5 sepals

BROOK SAXIFRAGE, *Saxifraga arguta.* Flrs in sticky, red-haired panicles, the petals round and oval. Lvs kidney shaped, toothed, basal, on long petioles. Ht 8"–24". Wet places, mont-alp, in all our mtns, Alas to Cal, e to RM. Sum. Dotted Saxifrage, *S. punctata,* similar but petals oblong and inflor white haired, not sticky.

SPOTTED (MATTED, COMMON) SAXIFRAGE, *Saxifraga bronchialis.* Flrs with many yellow, orange, red, and/or maroon spots. Lvs tiny, leathery, fringed, in basal tufts. Ht 2"–6", mat forming. Rocky places, lowl-alp, in all our mtns, Alas to n Ore, Ida, e Colo; Greenland, Eurasia. Sum.

TUFTED SAXIFRAGE, *Saxifraga caespitosa.* Flrs plain white. Lvs tiny, wedge shaped, sticky, 3–lobed at tip, in basal tufts, Stems sticky, 2"–6" tall; mat-forming plant. Rocky places, in all our mtns; widespread in n hemis. Sum.

RUSTY SAXIFRAGE, *Saxifraga ferruginea.* Flrs irreg, the 2 lower petals spoon shaped, white; the 3 upper, lancelike, slender stalked, white with 2 yellow spots. Lvs basal, spoon shaped, toothed. Plant hairy. Ht 4"–24". Flrs oft replaced by leafy bulb-lets. Moist cliffs, stream banks, in all our mtns, Alas to Cal, e to RM. Sum.

LYALL'S SAXIFRAGE, *Saxifraga lyallii.* Flrs white, aging pink, with 2 yellow spots on ea petal. Lvs basal, fan shaped, nearly as broad as long, petioled, toothed. Plant matlike, sparsely downy. Ht to 12". Moist places, mont-alp, in all our mtns, Alas to NCas, e to RM. Sum.

MERTEN'S SAXIFRAGE, *Saxifraga mertensiana.* Flrs tiny, white with pink an-thers, oft replaced by pinkish bulblets. Lvs round, sparsely hairy, succulent, doubly toothed, 1"–4" diam, on long-haired petioles with membranous sheathing stipules. Flr stem branched, hairy. 4"–16" tall. Stream banks, low-mid el, in all our mtns, Alas to Cal, e to RM. Spr-sum.

WESTERN SAXIFRAGE, *Saxifraga occidentalis.* Flrs white (purple in OMtns), with or without yellow spots; inflor variable. Lvs ovate, petioled, strongly toothed, gen with red hairs beneath. Highly variable sp. Ht 2"–12". Mdws, cliffs, stream banks, in all our mtns, BC to n Ore, e to RM. Spr-sum.

TOLMIE'S (ALPINE) SAXIFRAGE, *Saxifraga tolmiei.* Flrs white with smooth bowl-shaped calyx. Lvs fleshy, thick, to ½" long, basal. Ht ca 1"–3", mat forming. Mdws, stream banks, wet rocks, gen alp, Alas to Cal, e to RM. Sum.

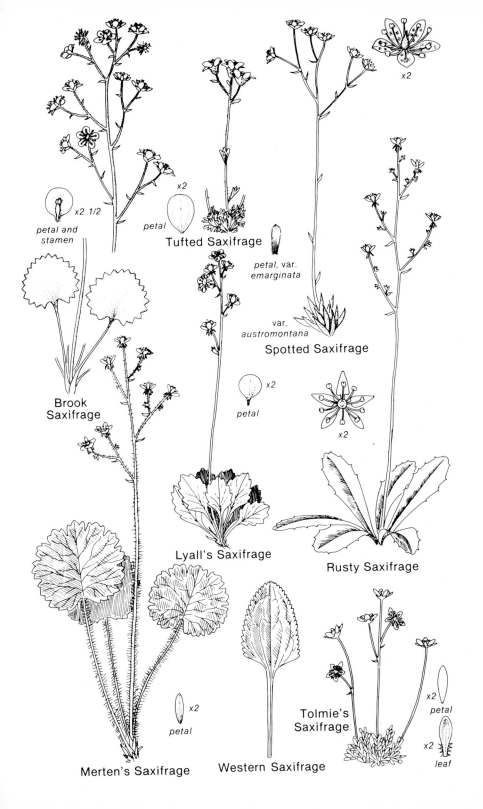

x2

x2 1/2

*petal and
stamen*

petal

x2

Tufted Saxifrage

*petal, var.
emarginata*

var.
austromontana

Spotted Saxifrage

**Brook
Saxifrage**

x2

petal

x2

x2

Lyall's Saxifrage

Rusty Saxifrage

x2

petal

x2

petal

**Tolmie's
Saxifrage**

x2

leaf

Merten's Saxifrage

Western Saxifrage

PLATE 13

Rose Family (*Rosaceae*): 5 petals, 5 sepals

GOATSBEARD, *Aruncus sylvester*. Flrs tiny, in plumelike panicles. Lvs compound, large, long petioled, with ovate, toothed, slender-tipped lflets to 6″ long. Ht 36″–84″. Moist places, in all our mtns, Alas to n Cal, e in BC to RM; Eurasia. Spr-sum.

WOODS STRAWBERRY, *Fragaria vesca*. Flrs, lvs, fruit like domestic strawberries. Mdws, stream banks, open woods, in all our mtns; widespread in N Amer and Eurasia. Sum.

STRAWBERRY BRAMBLE, *Rubus pedatus*. Flrs similar to above. Lvs compound, with 5 (or 3) toothed lflets. Stems trailing, to 84″ long. Forest, lowl-subalp, in all our mtns, Alas to s Ore, e to Mont, Idaho. Late spring. Dwarf Bramble, *R. lasiococcus*, very similar but lvs gen 3- 5-lobed, not compound.

PARTRIDGEFOOT, *Luetkea pectinata*. Flrs tiny, creamy white, in headlike racemes. Lvs finely divided, tiny, numerous at base, fewer on stems. Ht 2″–6″, mat forming. Moist or shaded places, subalp-alp, Vanc I, OMtns, W CMtns-Cas, Alas to n Cal, e to RM. Sum.

Oxalis Family (*Oxalidaceae*): 5 sepals, 5 petals

OREGON OXALIS (WOOD SORREL, REDWOOD SORREL), *Oxalis oregana*. Flrs single on long stalks, white to pink with yellow in center, ½″–¾″ diam. Lvs 3-divided, cloverlike, the lflets heart shaped. Ht 2″–6″. Moist, dense forest, OPen s to Cal, e to Cas, CRGorge. Spr-fall.

Violet Family (*Violaceae*): flowers irregular, 5 sepals, 5 petals

SMALL WHITE VIOLET, *Viola mackloskeyi*. Flrs to ½″ wide, lower 3 petals purple veined. Lvs heart shaped, not tapering to slender tip. Ht ca 1½″–2½″. Mtn bogs, in all our mtns; widespread in N Amer. Late spring-sum. Canada Violet, *V. canadensis*, 4″–15″ tall, the flrs with yellow centers and without purple veins.

Parsley Family (*Umbelliferae*): flowers in umbels, 5 petals

COW PARSNIP, *Heracleum lanatum*. Flrs in compound, flat-topped umbel to 12″ diam. Lvs 3-divided, the lflets 6″–16″ long, nearly as wide, deeply 3-lobed, coarsely toothed. Stem single, smooth to woolly. Ht 36″–120″. Widespread in N Amer; Siberia. Sum.

GRAY'S LOVAGE, *Ligusticum grayi*. Flrs tiny, in compound umbel. Lvs compound-pinnate, finely divided, the ultimate segm lancelike, 4″–12″ long, all but 1 or 2 gen basal. Stem smooth, solitary, 8″–24″ tall. Open woods, dry mdws, gen mid el, Cas, BC to SNev, also n RM. Sum-fall.

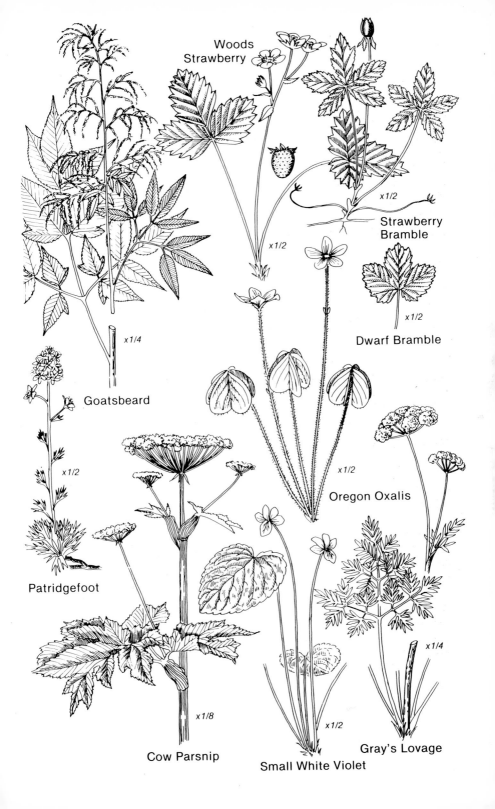

Woods
Strawberry

x1/2

Strawberry
Bramble

x1/2

Dwarf Bramble

x1/4

Goatsbeard

x1/2

Patridgefoot

Oregon Oxalis

x1/2

x1/2

Cow Parsnip

x1/8

Small White Violet

x1/2

Gray's Lovage

x1/4

PLATE 14

Heath Family (*Ericaceae*): 5 petals, 5 sepals

INDIAN PIPE, *Monotropa uniflora*. Entire plant white. Flrs nodding. Lvs scalelike. Stems clustered, thick, succulent. Ht 2″-6″. Shady forest in all our mtns, Alas to Cal, e to Atl. Sum.

PINESAP, *Hypopitys monotropa*. Flrs white, yellowish, or pinkish, with hairy petals, in nodding racemes. Lvs scalelike. Stem pinkish or pale yellow, drying black, fleshy, stout, unbranched. Ht 2″-10″. OMtns, W Cas, s Wn to n Cal, e to Atl; Europe. Sum. Fringed Pinesap, *Pleuricospora fimbriolata*, very similar but flrs in erect spikelike raceme, the petals not hairy.

WHITE-VEINED WINTERGREEN, *Pyrola picta*. Flrs greenish white, creamy or pink. Lvs sometimes absent; if present, oval or ovate, leathery, dk green mottled with white along veins, mostly basal, long petioled. Stems reddish brown. Ht 4″-10″. Forest, in all our mtns, BC to s Cal, e to RM. Sum.

ONE-SIDED WINTERGREEN, *Pyrola secunda*. Flrs greenish white, 6–20 in 1-sided raceme. Lvs ovate, clear green, toothed or scalloped. Ht 2″-6″. Moist forest in all our mtns, Alas s to s Cal, e to RM and Atl. Sum.

WOOD NYMPH (ONE-FLOWERED WINTERGREEN), *Pyrola uniflora*. Flr white or pink, solitary. Lvs oval or ovate, on lower part of stem, long petioled, fine toothed. Ht 1½″-6″. Moist forest, rotting wood, in all our mtns, Alas to Cal, e to RM, e Can, e US. Sum.

Primrose Family (*Primulaceae*): flowers generally 5-lobed

FAIRY CANDELABRA, *Androsace septentrionalis*. Flrs tiny, tubular, with spreading lobes, in open umbels. Lvs straplike, toothed toward tip, in basal rosette. Ht 1″-10″. Dry rocky places in all our mtns; widespread in mtns of N Amer and Eurasia. Spr-sum.

WHITE SHOOTING STAR, *Dodecatheon dentatum*. Flrs with short tubes, and longer, reflexed lobes; white with yellow center and purplish stamens, in umbel. Lvs basal, ovate, toothed or scalloped, petioled. Ht 6″-16″. Wet places, E Cas, BC to n Ore, e to Idaho. Spr-sum.

Gentian Family (*Gentianaceae*): flowers generally 4– 5-lobed

NEWBERRY'S (ALPINE) GENTIAN, *Gentiana newberryi*. Flrs tubular, 5-lobed, white with green spots within, bluish on outside. Basal lvs spoon shaped; stem lvs much smaller, narrower. Ht 1″-2″. Mdws, subalp slopes, Cas to SNev, cen Ore to Cal. Sum.

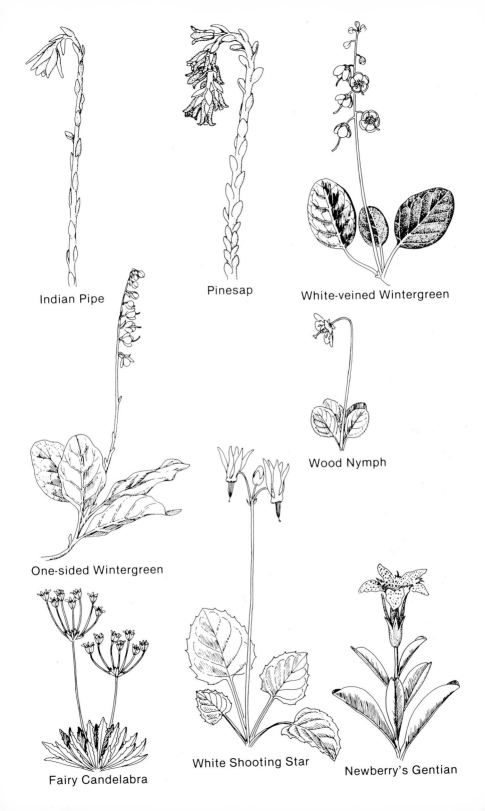

Indian Pipe

Pinesap

White-veined Wintergreen

One-sided Wintergreen

Wood Nymph

Fairy Candelabra

White Shooting Star

Newberry's Gentian

PLATE 15

Phlox Family (Polemoniaceae): 5-lobed flowers

ALPINE COLLOMIA, *Collomia debilis.* Flrs white to pale blue or pink, tubular, ½"–1½" long, to ¾" diam. Lvs ½"–1¼" long, variable (lancelike to finely divided). Ht ca 2", mat forming. Talus, subalp-alp, OMtns, Cas, Wn to Cal. Sum.

Waterleaf Family (Hydrophyllaceae): 5-lobed flowers

FENDLER'S WATERLEAF, *Hydrophyllum fendleri.* Flrs to ⅜" long, bell shaped, white to lavender, in terminal inflor. Lvs pinnate, to 10" long and 6" wide, hairy, with 7–15 sharp-toothed lflets. Stems hairy. Ht 8"–32". Moist open places, thickets, lowl-subalp, OMtns, Cas s to Cal; e to Idaho, Utah, NMex. Spr-sum.

VARILEAF PHACELIA, *Phacelia heterophylla* var *pseudohispida.* Flrs white, occas purple, in bristly-hairy inflor. Lvs gray green, entire on upper stem, pinnate or pinnately lobed on lower stem, with 1 terminal lflet or lobe and 1–2 pairs of basal lflets or lobes. Plant hairy, sticky, oft bristly. Ht usu to 20". Dry, open places, low-mid el, E Cas. Spr-sum.

Mint Family (Labiatae): flowers irregular, 2-lipped

YERBA BUENA, *Satureja douglasii.* Flrs small, white or pale purple, 1 in ea upper lf axil. Lvs opp, ± round, ½"–1" long. Creeping plant with erect flr stems to 12" tall, trailing stems to 36" long. Shaded woods, low el, W Cas to coast, BC to Baja, n Idaho. Spr-fall.

Figwort Family (Scrophulariaceae): flowers irregular

SMALL-FLOWERED PAINTBRUSH, *Castilleja parviflora* var *albida.* Corolla white or pink, tiny, tubular, 2-lipped; flrs in terminal spike, with numerous white, 3-5-lobed bracts. Lvs 3– 5-lobed, numerous on stem. Ht to 12". Subalp-alp mdws, NCas s to Cascade Pass. Sum. Cf Magenta Paintbrush, plate 27.

RAMSHORN (SICKLETOP) LOUSEWORT, *Pedicularis racemosa.* Flrs ca ½" long, white or pink, 2-lipped, the upper one beaklike, twisted on one side, the lower 3-lobed. Lvs lancelike, 2"–4" long, toothed. Ht 6"–20". Open forest in all our mtns, BC to Cal, e to RM. Sum.

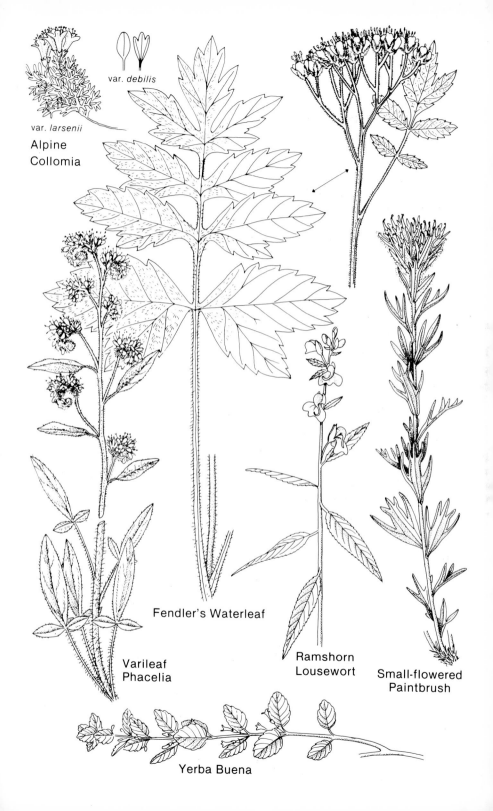

var. *debilis*

var. *larsenii*

Alpine
Collomia

Fendler's Waterleaf

Varileaf
Phacelia

Ramshorn
Lousewort

Small-flowered
Paintbrush

Yerba Buena

PLATE 16

Madder Family (Rubiaceae): 3- 4-lobed flowers

SWEET-SCENTED BEDSTRAW, *Galium triflorum*. Flrs tiny, greenish white, in 3s from upper lf axils and stem tip, fragrant. Lvs vanilla scented, narrow to oval or oblanceolate, pointed, usu 5–6 in whorls. Stems gen trailing, to 32″ long. Moist woods, oft near seeps or streams, low-mid el, in all our mtns; widespread in N Amer. Sum.

Valerian Family (Valerianaceae): 5-lobed flowers

SITKA VALERIAN, *Valeriana sitchensis*. Flrs small, slightly irreg, fragrant, in round heads. Lvs mostly in 2–5 pairs on stem, pinnate, long petioled, the lflets toothed and the terminal one longest. Ht 12″–48″. Moist open or wooded places, esp in wet subalp mdws, mid-high el, CMtns, Cas, BC to n Cal. Sum.

Aster or Sunflower Family (Compositae): flowers in composite heads

TRAIL PLANT, *Adenocaulon bicolor*. Flr heads tiny, with disk flrs only, at ends of short, thin stems. Lvs mostly near base, broadly arrow shaped, with wavy margins, smooth above, white-woolly beneath, long petioled. Ht to ca 36″. Moist forest, low-mid el, in all our mtns, BC to Cal, e to mid US. Sum.

PEARLY EVERLASTING, *Anaphalis margaritacea*. Flr heads small, with numerous minute yellow disk flrs and white, papery bracts. Lvs ca 2″–4″ long, linear or lancelike, numerous, white-woolly. Stems 8″–36″ tall, white-woolly. Dry open places, lowl-subalp, in all our mtns, Alas s to s Cal, e to ne US; Eurasia. Sum.

WOOLLY PUSSYTOES (EVERLASTING), *Antennaria lanata*. Flrs very like those of above sp, but plant only 4″–8″ tall and densely woolly throughout. Lvs mostly basal, oblanceolate, to 4″ long, stem lvs narrower. Not mat forming. Subalp-alp, s BC to Ore, e to n RM. Sum.

ALPINE PUSSYTOES (EVERLASTING), *Antennaria alpina*. Flrs white to yellowish, similar to those of above 2 spp. Stem lvs linear; basal lvs ± spoon shaped, to 1″ long, mostly on runners. Entire plant woolly, mat forming. Ht to 4″. Moist gravelly sites, subalp-alp, in all our mtns, BC to Cal, e to RM. Sum.

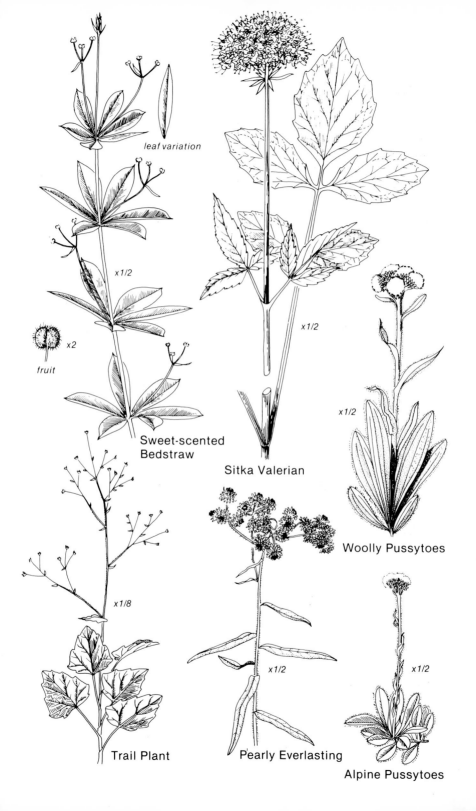

leaf variation

x1/2

x2

fruit

Sweet-scented
Bedstraw

Sitka Valerian

Woolly Pussytoes

x1/8

Trail Plant

Pearly Everlasting

Alpine Pussytoes

PLATE 17

Aster or Sunflower Family (Compositae): flowers in composite heads

YARROW, *Achillea millefolium*. Disk flrs yellow, ray flrs white or pink; heads small, in terminal inflor. Lvs finely divided, fernlike, aromatic. Stems mostly un-branched and solitary, covered with cottony hairs. Ht 4″–30″+. Lowl-alp in all our mtns; widespread in n hemis. Spr-fall.

OLYMPIC ASTER, *Aster paucicapitatus*. Flr heads ca 1″ diam, with tiny yellow disk flrs and gen 13 white, straplike ray flrs, 1 or few heads per stem. Lvs elliptic, sessile, 1″–2″ long, alt on stem. Plant downy or sticky. Ht 8″–20″. Open subalp slopes, OMtns, Vanc I. Sum. Engelmann's Aster, *A. engelmannii,* also white flrd but lvs 2″–4″ long and plant gen 24″–60″ tall; Wn Cas.

OXEYE DAISY, *Chrysanthemum leucanthemum*. Flr heads 1″–3″ diam, with yellow disk flrs, gen 15–30 ray flrs. Lvs cleft and scalloped, lower ones wedge or spoon shaped, 1½″–6″ long, long petioled; upper ones smaller, narrower, sessile. Ht 8″–32″. Com. disturbed places, esp roadsides, in all our mtns; widespread in N Amer; introduced from Europe. Spr-fall.

DWARF MOUNTAIN (CUTLEAF) DAISY (FLEABANE), *Erigeron compositus*. Flr heads ca 1″ diam, with yellow disk and white (pink or blue), slender ray flrs, solitary. Mostly basal lvs, finely cleft, fernlike. Plant sticky-hairy to nearly smooth. Flr stems 1½″–10″ tall. Gen rocky places, low-high el, in all our mtns; widespread in N Amer. Sum. Several other spp very similar.

WHITE-FLOWERED HAWKWEED, *Hieracium albiflorum*. Flr heads with rays only. Lvs oblong, the basal ones hairy, 2″–6″ long, ± entire, petioled; the stem lvs smaller, without petioles, less hairy. Stems long haired below, ± hairless above. Ht 12″–48″. Moist slopes, open woods in all our mtns but E CMtns-Cas, Alas to Cal and Colo. Sum.

COLTSFOOT, *Petastites frigidus*. Flr heads white or pinkish, usu with disk flrs only, in dense terminal inflor. Lvs basal, palmate, ± hairy, deeply lobed and toothed, up to 12″ diam. Stems coarse, thick, succulent, with large, sheathing, parallel-veined bracts. Ht 6″–24″. Moist places, lowl-subalp. Circumboreal. Late win-midsum.

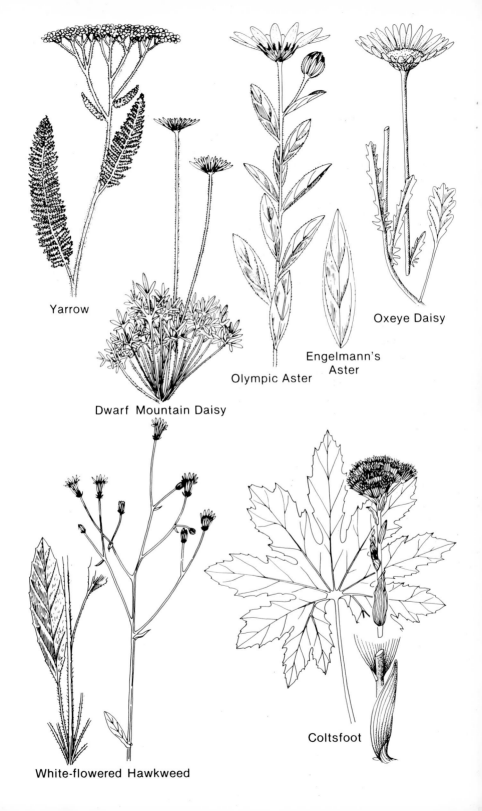

Yarrow

Dwarf Mountain Daisy

Olympic Aster

Engelmann's Aster

Oxeye Daisy

White-flowered Hawkweed

Coltsfoot

II. Yellow and Orange Flowers

This section includes only flowers that are distinctly yellow or truly orange. Cream-colored flowers are covered in section 1, red orange flowers in section 3. Compositae (members of the sunflower family) with yellow disks but ray flowers of other colors are grouped according to the color of the rays. The following species from other color sections sometimes have yellowish or orangish flowers.

Cliff Anemone, cf Drummond's Anemone, *plate 10*
Indian Pipe, *plate 14*
Alpine Pussytoes, *plate 16*
Yarrow, *plate 17*
Coltsfoot, *plate 17*
Rosy Twisted-stalk, *plate 23*
Western Spring Beauty, *plate 23*
Tweedy's Lewisia, *plate 23*
Applegate Paintbrush, *plate 27*
Common Paintbrush, *plate 27*
Explorer's Gentian, *plate 31*
Brewer's Mitrewort, *plate 35*
Pinedrops, *plate 35*

PLATE 18

Arum Family (Araceae): flowers in spike (spadix) partly enclosed by showy bract (spathe)

SKUNK CABBAGE, *Lysichitum americanum.* Flrs tiny, on a fleshy spadix 1½"–4" long, ½"–1" diam, the spathe up to 8" long. Lvs oval, basal, 12"–36" long, half as wide. Wet places, in all our mtns, Alas to Cal, e to Mont, Idaho. Spr-early sum.

Lily Family (Liliaceae): 3 petals and 3 sepals, or 6 tepals

GLACIER LILY (YELLOW FAWN-LILY), *Erythronium grandiflorum.* Flrs 1–2 per stem, with 6 reflexed tepals ca ½" long. Lvs basal, elliptic, 4"–8" long. Ht 6"–12". Damp, recently snow-free sites, mont-subalp, in all our mtns, s BC to n Ore, e to RM. Sum.

TIGER (COLUMBIA) LILY, *Lilium columbianum.* Flrs 2"–3" diam, with strongly reflexed tepals. Lvs lancelike, usu in whorls, but may be scattered on stem. Ht 12"–48". Open areas, dry woods, BC to n Cal, e to Idaho, Nev. Sum.

Buckwheat Family (Polygonaceae): no petals, 4-9 petallike sepals

SULFUR-FLOWERED BUCKWHEAT, *Eriogonum umbellatum.* Flrs tiny, occas cream colored, hairy, in compound umbels. Lvs spoon shaped, mostly in basal tufts, ½"–1½" long, smooth or hairy on 1 or both sides; whorl of smaller lvs at base of umbel, but not at mid-stem. Dwarf plants under 4" tall; others to 12". Dry, rocky places, lowl-alp, mostly E Cas, s BC to Cal, e to RM. Sum.

OVAL-LEAVED BUCKWHEAT, *Eriogonum ovalifolium.* Similar to above sp, but inflor not branched, lvs rounder, and no whorl of lvs at base of umbel. Flrs occas pinkish; lvs silvery to pale green. Various habitats, lowl-alp, BC s in OMtns, Cas and RM to Cal and NMex. Late spr-sum. This and above sp are 2 of many, very similar yellow-flowered buckwheats in our region.

Water-lily Family (Nymphaeaceae): tiny petals, 9 sepals

YELLOW POND-LILY (WATER-LILY), *Nuphar polysepalum.* Flrs with tiny, inconspicuous petals, small outer green sepals, large yellow inner sepals, to 2" diam. Lvs heart shaped, 6"–8" long, nearly as wide, floating on pond surfaces. Aquatic plant in ponds, other standing water, low-mid el, in all our mtns, Alas to s Cal, e to Colo. Sum-fall.

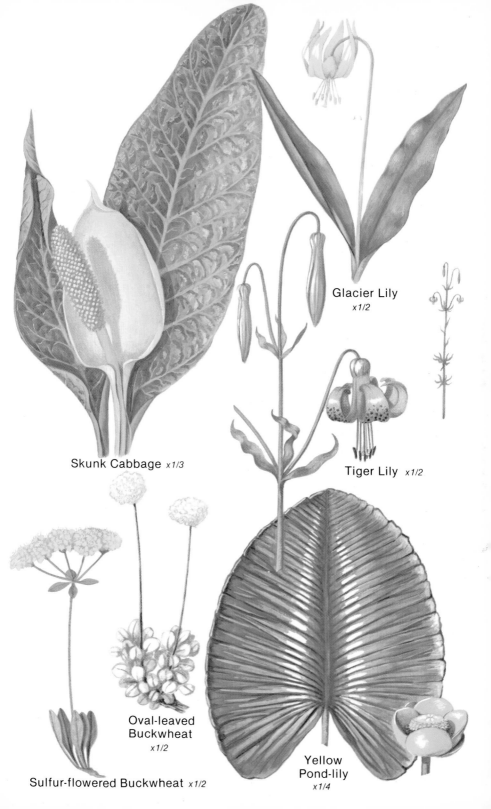

Glacier Lily
x1/2

Skunk Cabbage x1/3

Tiger Lily x1/2

Oval-leaved
Buckwheat
x1/2

Sulfur-flowered Buckwheat x1/2

Yellow
Pond-lily
x1/4

PLATE 19

Buttercup Family (Ranunculaceae): 5 petals, 5 sepals

YELLOW COLUMBINE, *Aquilegia flavescens*. Flrs nodding, with spurred petals and spreading petallike sepals. Lvs mainly basal, compound, long petioled, ea lflet 3-lobed and toothed, waxy blue green. Ht 18″–24″. Moist mdws, subalp-alp, Cas, BC to s Wn, e to RM. Sum.

SUBALPINE (MOUNTAIN) BUTTERCUP, *Ranunculus eschscholtzii*. Flrs glossy yellow, ca ½″ diam. Basal lvs long petioled, the blade 3-lobed, to 1⅛″ long, the lobes toothed or the mid one sometimes entire. Ht to 8″. Moist, oft rocky places, subalp-alp, in all our mtns; Alas to Cal, e to RM. Sum. Several other similar spp found at all elevations.

Mustard Family (Cruciferae): 4 petals in a cross

PAYSON'S WHITLOW-GRASS, *Draba paysonii*. Flrs in small racemes. Lvs slender, to ½″ long, basal, fringed with forked and unforked hairs, old lvs persisting. Cushion plant to 2″ tall. Rocky places, subalp-alp, BC to Cal, e to RM. Sum. One of several very similar spp in our range.

MOUNTAIN WALLFLOWER, *Erysimum arenicola*. Flrs in short racemes. Lvs toothed, ± linear to narrowly oblanceolate, numerous at or near base, several to many on stem. Ht gen 4″–10″. Dry, rocky places, mont-alp, OMtns, Cas, Wn to s Ore. Sum. Rough Wallflower, *E. asperum*, of the E Cas s to CRGorge, is very similar.

Stonecrop Family (Crassulaceae)

SPREADING STONECROP, *Sedum divergens*. Flrs starlike, with petals distinct. Lvs opp, ± oval, thick, fleshy, sessile. Flr stems branching from prostrate, rooting stems. Ht to 6″. Rocky places at high el, OMtns, CMtns-Cas, s BC to n Ore. Sum. Oregon Stonecrop, *S. oreganum*, has petals united near base, alt lvs, and flr stems sprouting from rhizomes. Creamy Stonecrop, *S. oregonense*, has white to creamy flrs and spoon-shaped lvs. Lanceleaf Stonecrop, *S. lanceolatum*, has alt linear to lancelike lvs with many basal rosettes. Rough Stonecrop, *S. stenopetalum*, has slender, pointed lvs and bulblets in upper lf axils oft replacing flrs.

Rose Family (Rosaceae)

FANLEAF CINQUEFOIL, *Potentilla flabellifolia*. Flrs ca 1″ diam, not waxy, the petals notched. Lvs compound, with 3 toothed lflets. Ht 4″–14″. Moist mdws, talus, high el in all our mtns s to Cal, e to RM. Sum. Varileaf Cinquefoil, *P. diversifolia*, has 5–7 lflets, white haired beneath. Hairy Cinquefoil, *P. villosa*, is a cushion plant with small hairy lvs. Drummond's Cinquefoil, *P. drummondii*, has 5–7 lflets, the 3 upper fused at base. Cf Shrubby Cinquefoil, plate 39.

SIBBALDIA, *Sibbaldia procumbens*. Flrs ca ⅓″ diam, with greenish sepals far exceeding petals. Lvs compound, with 3 toothed, wedge-shaped lflets and membranous stipules. Stems prostrate, mat forming. Alp zone, N Amer, Eurasia. Ht to 3″. Sum.

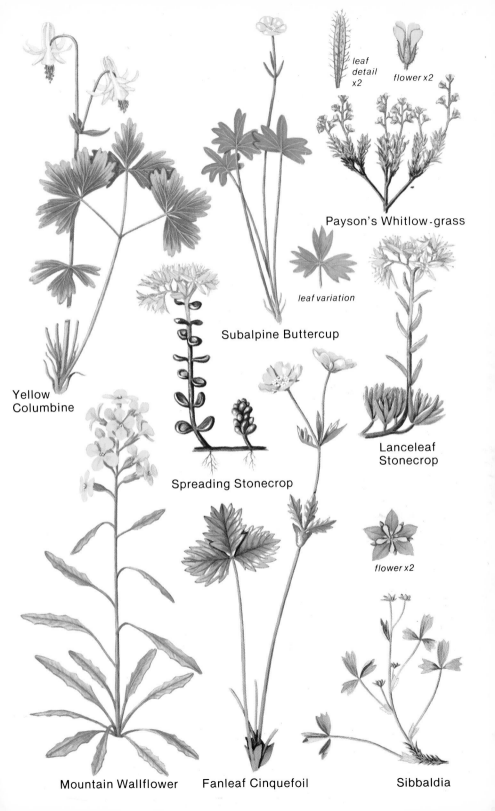

leaf detail x2

flower x2

Payson's Whitlow-grass

leaf variation

Subalpine Buttercup

Yellow Columbine

Spreading Stonecrop

Lanceleaf Stonecrop

flower x2

Mountain Wallflower

Fanleaf Cinquefoil

Sibbaldia

PLATE 20

Pea Family (Leguminosae): flowers irregular

GOLDEN-PEA, *Thermopsis montana.* Flrs sweetpealike, ¾"–1" long, in racemes. Lvs compound, with 3 broadly lancelike lflets ea 2"–4" long and large leaflike stipules. Fruit, erect; hairy pods 1½"–3" long. Ht 12"–48". Mdws, forest openings, BC to n Cal, e to RM. Spr-sum.

Violet Family (Violaceae): flowers irregular, 5 petals, 5 sepals

WOOD (PIONEER) VIOLET, *Viola glabella.* Flrs pansylike, with maroon lines on lower petals, ¾"–1" wide. Lvs to 2" long, heart shaped, toothed, with slender tip. Ht to 12". Moist places, in all our mtns, Alas to Cal, e to Mont. Spr-sum. Our most com yellow violet. Evergreen Violet, *V. sempervirens,* has thick, glossy green, round-tipped, heart-shaped lvs and creeping stems. Round-leaved Violet, *V. orbiculata,* has thin, round or heart-shaped lvs and erect stems. Purplish Violet, *V. purpuraea,* has petals purple tinged on the back.

Evening-primrose Family (Onagraceae): 4 petals, 4 sepals

YELLOW WILLOW-HERB, *Epilobium luteum.* Flrs 1"–1½" diam, petals notched. Lvs lancelike, toothed, ¾"–3" long, opp. Ht 8"–28". Moist sites, mont-alp, in all our mtns, Alas to Ore. Midsum-early fall.

Parsley Family (Umbelliferae): flowers in umbels, 5 petals

MARTINDALE'S LOMATIUM, *Lomatium martindalei.* Flrs yellow or white, small, in flat-topped umbels. Lvs finely dissected, parsleylike. Ht 2"–8". Late spring-sum. Barestem Lomatium, *L. nudicale,* has oval lflets. Other spp similar to Martindale's Lomatium.

Figwort Family (Scrophulariaceae): flowers tubular, 2-lipped

ALPINE YELLOW (MOUNTAIN) MONKEYFLOWER, *Mimulus tilingii.* Flrs ca 1" diam, 2-lipped, the lower red spotted, with calyx teeth of uneven length. Lvs opp, smooth, toothed, on prostrate stems. Plant mat forming, ht only 2"–4". Wet mdws, bogs, subalp-alp, BC to s Cal, e to RM. Sum. Common Monkeyflower, *M. guttatus,* very similar but not mat forming, ht 2"–24", commoner at lower el. Coast Monkeyflower, *M. dentatus,* only 4"–12" tall, but not mat forming, and calyx teeth of equal length (OMtns only). Primrose Monkeyflower, *M. primuloides,* has solitary flr on erect stem rising above basal rosette. Musk-flowered Monkeyflower, *M. moschatus,* has musky scent and slimy, sticky-haired lvs. Chickweed Monkeyflower, *M. alsinoides,* is a tiny lowland sp with long-petioled lvs and a single reddish spot on base of lower corolla lip.

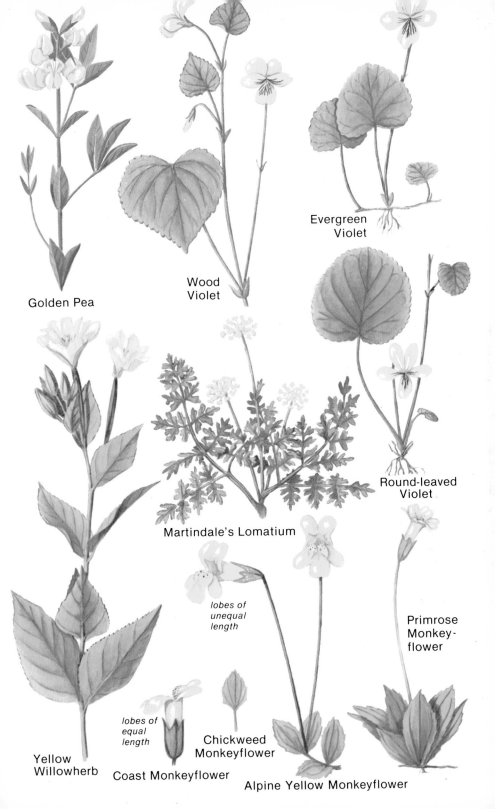

Golden Pea

Wood
Violet

Evergreen
Violet

Round-leaved
Violet

Martindale's Lomatium

Yellow
Willowherb

*lobes of
unequal
length*

*lobes of
equal
length*

Coast Monkeyflower

Chickweed
Monkeyflower

Alpine Yellow Monkeyflower

Primrose
Monkey-
flower

PLATE 21

Figwort Family (Scrophulariaceae): flowers 2-lipped or 5-lobed

BRACTED LOUSEWORT (WOOD BETONY), *Pedicularis bracteosa.* Flrs yellow, red, or purple, 2-lipped, the upper hoodlike, ± beakless. Lvs pinnate, 3"–10" long, the lflets ± double toothed; stem lvs as large as those, if any, at base. Ht 12"–36". Moist mdws, forest openings, mont-alp, BC to n Cal, e to RM. Sum. Mt. Rainier Lousewort, *P. rainierensis,* very similar but only 6"–16" tall, with many basal lvs and fewer, smaller stem lvs; Mt. Rainier only.

COILED-BEAK LOUSEWORT, *Pedicularis contorta.* Flrs yellow or creamy, 2-lipped, the upper beaklike, slender, strongly curved or coiled downward. Lvs pinnate, long petioled, the lflets toothed. Ht 8"–20". Mdws, open places, mont-alp, mostly Cas, Wn to n Cal. Sum.

WOOLLY MULLEIN, *Verbascum thapsus.* Flrs nearly reg, 5-lobed, in dense bracteose spike. Lvs of 1st year basal, oblong to oblanceolate, 4"–16" long; lvs of 2nd year on flr stem, elliptic to lancelike, sheathing, oft droopy, 2"–12" long. Plant woolly throughout. Ht 12"–78". Disturbed places, esp roadsides; widespread in N Amer; introduced from Europe. Sum.

Aster or Sunflower Family (Compositae): flowers in composite heads

ORANGE MOUNTAIN-DANDELION, *Agoseris auriantiaca.* Flr heads dandelion-like, ca 1" diam, distinctly burnt orange, unique. Lvs basal, variable, broadest above middle, oft slightly toothed. Ht 4"–24". Grassy places, mdws, in all our mtns; widespread in mtns of w N Amer. Sum.

PALE MOUNTAIN-DANDELION, *Agoseris glauca.* Flr heads like those of common dandelion, ½"–1¼" diam. Lvs basal, variable, 2"–14" long, lancelike to oblanceolate, nearly smooth or finely haired, entire or slightly toothed. Ht 4"–30". Mdws, rocky places, lowl-alp, in all our mtns, w Can s to Cal and NMex, e to Minn. Late spring-sum. Other yellow mountain-dandelions very similar, but this sp is the most com in our range.

MOUNTAIN (BROADLEAF) ARNICA, *Arnica latifolia.* Flr heads 1 to few per stem, with both disk and ray flrs. Lvs opp, ovate, sessile above, petioled below, sharply toothed, in 2–4 pairs on stem. Ht 8"–18". Gen moist, open places, in all our mtns, Alas to Cal and Colo. Sum. The most com of several, similar spp in our range.

ARROWLEAF BALSAMROOT, *Balsamorrhiza sagitatta.* Flr heads very large (4"–5" diam), with 8–25 rays, ea 1"–1½" long. Lvs basal, arrow shaped, long petioled, the blades to 12" long. Open places, pine-fir forests, E Cas, BC to SNev, e to RM. Sum. Com and conspicuous.

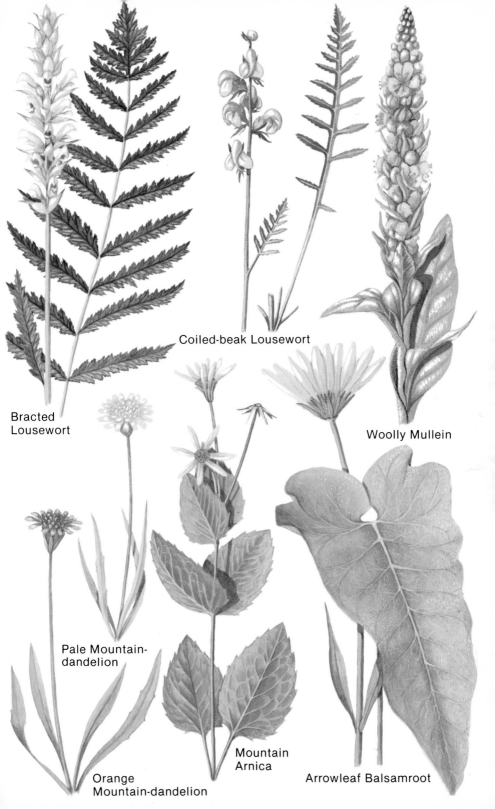

Coiled-beak Lousewort

Woolly Mullein

Bracted
Lousewort

Pale Mountain-
dandelion

Mountain
Arnica

Orange
Mountain-dandelion

Arrowleaf Balsamroot

PLATE 22

Aster or Sunflower Family (Compositae): flowers in composite heads

GOLDEN FLEABANE (DAISY), *Erigeron aureus*. Flr heads solitary, ½"–1" diam. Lvs mostly basal, petioled, spoon shaped. Plant woolly. Ht 2"–6". Rocky places, sub-alp-alp, Wn Cas, n to s BC and Albta. Sum.

WOOLLY SUNFLOWER, *Eriophyllum lanatum*. Flr heads 1"–1½" diam, with 9–11 ray flrs. Lvs entire to deeply pinnately cut, very woolly. Ht 4"–12". Dry, open places, lowl-mont (subalp in OMtns), BC to Cal, e to RM. Late spr-sum.

LYALL'S GOLDENWEED, *Haplopappus lyallii*. Flr heads solitary, ca 1" diam. Lvs ± oblanceolate, sessile, sticky haired, ½"–3" long. Stems sticky haired, 2"–6" tall. Rocky places, gen alp, BC and Wn e to Albta, ne Ore, ne Nev, Col. Mid-sum-early fall.

SILVERBACK LUINA, *Luina hypoleuca*. Flr heads rayless, in branched, terminal inflor on ea stem. Lvs sessile, oval or ovate, densely white haired below. Stems numerous, clustered. Ht 6"–16". Rocky places w of Cas, BC to Cal. Sum.

ARROWHEAD GROUNDSEL, *Senecio triangularis*. Flr heads 1"–1½" diam, with 5–10 rays, in branched inflor. Lvs like arrowheads, 2"–6" long, sharply toothed. Ht 12"–36". Moist places, lowl-high el, in all our mtns, Alas to Cal, Ariz, NMex. Late sum.

TALL WESTERN GROUNDSEL, *Senecio integerrimus*. Flr heads usu yellow, occas white or rayless in Wn Cas, with black-tipped involucre bracts. Basal lvs 2½"–10" long, gen oblanceolate or elliptic, long petioled; stem lvs alt, smaller upward, becoming sessile, lancelike. Ht 12"–36". Open places below timberline in all our mtns; widespread in N Amer. Late spr-mid-sum.

CREEK (MEADOW, CANADA) GOLDENROD, *Solidago canadensis*. Flr heads small, numerous, in dense spraylike panicles. Lvs lancelike, toothed, numerous, 2"–5" long. Ht 12"–36". Moist places, lowl-mont, in all our mtns; widespread in N Amer. Late sum-fall. Other tall spp similar.

NORTHERN (ALPINE) GOLDENROD, *Solidago multiradiata*. Flr heads small, gen with 13 rays, in panicles. Stem lvs spoon shaped or lancelike, gen pointed, sessile, ± entire. Basal lvs spoon shaped, ± toothed, with bristly hairs along petiole margins. Ht gen to 12". Subalp-alp; mtns of w N Amer, but missing from Ore Cas. Sum.

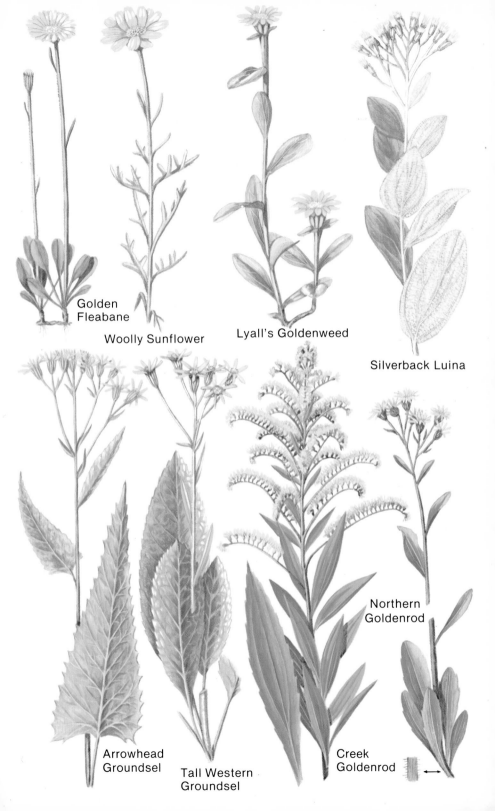

Golden
Fleabane

Woolly Sunflower

Lyall's Goldenweed

Silverback Luina

Arrowhead
Groundsel

Tall Western
Groundsel

Northern
Goldenrod

Creek
Goldenrod

III. Pink to Red Flowers

Flowers in this section range in color from pale pink to red orange or reddish purple. Compounded of red and blue, purple comes in shades that are difficult to assign to one color or the other. When attempting to identify plants with reddish purple flowers, also consult section 4. Truly orange flowers are covered in section 2. White flowers tinged with pink are found in section 1. The following species sometimes have pink or reddish flowers.

Washington Lily, *plate 6*
Western Trillium, *plate 7*
Alpine Buckwheat, *plate 9*
Miner's Lettuce, *plate 9*
Siberian Montia, *plate 9*
Pygmy Lewisia, *plate 9*
Roundleaf Sundew, *plate 11*
Lyall's Saxifrage, *plate 12*
Oregon Oxalis, *plate 13*
Indian Pipe, *plate 14*
Wood Nymph, *plate 14*
Alpine Collomia, *plate 15*
Small-flowered Paintbrush, *plate 15*
Ramshorn Lousewort, *plate 15*
Yarrow, *plate 17*
Dwarf Mountain Daisy, *plate 17*
Tiger Lily, *plate 18*
Oval-leaved Buckwheat, *plate 18*
Bracted Lousewort, *plate 21*
Oregon Anemone, *plate 29*
Nuttall's Pea, *plate 30*
Flett's Violet, *plate 30*
Davidson's Penstemon, *plate 32*
Cascade Aster, *plate 33*
Wandering Daisy, *plate 33*
Giant Helleborine, *plate 34*
Mountain-sorrel, *plate 35*
Fringecup, *plate 35*
Pinedrops, *plate 35*

PLATE 23

Lily Family (Liliaceae): 6 tepals

OLYMPIC ONION, *Allium crenulatum*. Flrs pink or white with pink lines on lance-like tepals, in upright umbel. Lvs 2, fleshy, narrow, basal, oft coiled at tip, present with flrs. Stem ± flattened and "winged." Ht 3"–8" tall. Dry, gravelly places, subalp-alp, Vanc I, OMtns, Cas, cen Wn s to sw Ore. Sum. Nodding Onion, *A. cernuum*, has nodding head and ± oval tepals. Tapertip Onion, *A. acuminatum*, is dk rose and lvs wither before flowering.

ROSY TWISTED-STALK, *Streptopus roseus*. Flrs rosy to white or greenish with magenta spots, 1–2 below ea leaf. Lvs ovate, sessile, minutely toothed. Stems zig-zag, gen unbranched. Ht 12"–24". Damp forest, mid-high el in all our mtns, Alas to Ore. Sum. Cf plates 7 and 34.

Orchid Family (Orchidaceae): 3 petals, 3 sepals, flowers irregular

FAIRY (VENUS) SLIPPER, *Calypso bulbosa*. Flr solitary on single unbranched stalk. One (occas 2) basal lf, oval to ovate, 1¼"–2½" long; 2–3 bracts on stem. Ht 2"–8". Moist forest, lowl-mont, in all our mtns, Alas to Cal; Ariz, Colo, e across Can to Atl. Spring-early sum.

SPOTTED CORALROOT, *Corallorhiza maculata*. Flrs ca ¾" diam, with 3 sepals, 2 sepallike petals, and a 3rd, lower, drooping 3-lobed lip. Lvs scalelike. Ht 8"–32". Forest in all our mtns; widespread in N Amer. Late spr-sum. Striped Coralroot, *C. striata*, similar but petals red striped and lip unlobed. Western Coralroot, *C. mertensiana*, has ± uniformly reddish brown flrs.

Purslane Family (Portulacaceae): 5+ petals, 2+ sepals

WESTERN SPRING BEAUTY, *Claytonia lanceolata*. Flrs pink or white (occas yellow), red lined, with 2 sepals and 5 petals, in 1-sided racemes. Lvs 2 per stem, opp, lancelike, ½"–3" long, just below inflor; occas 1–2 basal lvs. Ht 2¾"–6". Open places, lowl-alp, in all our mtns, BC to Cal, e to RM. Spr-sum.

COLUMBIA LEWISIA, *Lewisia columbiana*. Flrs with 2 sepals, 6–11 petals, ¾"–1" diam, several per stem. Lvs basal, fleshy, straplike. Ht 4"–8". Open, rocky places, s BC to Cal, e to ne Ore, Idaho. Late spr-sum. Threeleaf Lewisia, *L. triphylla*, lacks basal lvs when in flower. Tweedy's Lewisia, *L. tweedyi*, has pale pink to peach or apricot flrs 1½"–3" diam; endemic to Wenatchee Mtns.

PUSSYPAWS, *Spraguea umbellata*. Flrs in fuzzy, round headlike umbels. Lvs basal, spoon shaped, leathery. Mat-forming plants to 6" tall, either perennial with branched woody base (var *caudicifera*) or annual without woody base (var *umbellifera*). Dry open places, E Cas, BC to Cal, e to RM. Spr-sum.

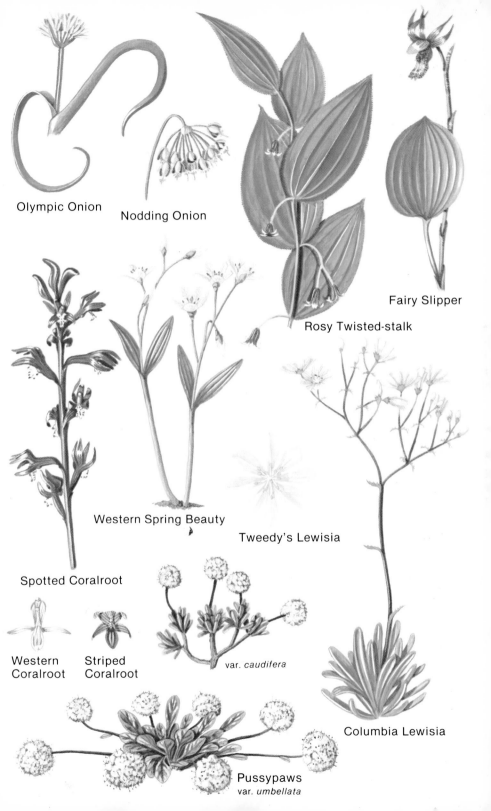

Olympic Onion

Nodding Onion

Fairy Slipper

Rosy Twisted-stalk

Western Spring Beauty

Tweedy's Lewisia

Spotted Coralroot

Western Coralroot

Striped Coralroot

var. *caudifera*

Columbia Lewisia

Pussypaws
var. *umbellata*

PLATE 24

Pink Family (Caryophyllaceae): 5 petals, 5 sepals

MOSS CAMPION, *Silene acaulis*. Flrs pink to lavender, numerous, ca ½" diam, with tubular calyx. Lvs needlelike, ca ½" long, mostly basal. Ht 2"–4¾", mat or cushion forming. Rocky places, subalp-alp in all our mtns; Alas s in mtns of N Amer; arctic tundra. Sum.

Buttercup Family (Ranunculaceae): 5 petals, 5 sepals

RED COLUMBINE, *Aquilegia formosa*. Flrs with flaring petallike sepals and scoop-like and spurred petals. Lvs gen basal, long petioled, compound, the lflets lobed. Ht 12"–36". Woods, moist mdws, lowl-mont, in all our mtns, Alas to Cal, e to RM. Spr-sum.

Fumitory Family (Fumariaceae): 4 petals, 2 sepals

SCOULER'S (WESTERN) CORYDALIS, *Corydalis scouleri*. Flrs irreg, spurred. Lvs usu 3, gen compound-pinnate. Ht 12"–48". Moist, shaded places, Cas to coast, BC to Ore. Spr-sum.

WESTERN BLEEDING HEART, *Dicentra formosa*. Flrs nodding, heart shaped. Lvs compound-pinnate, the lflets lobed and toothed, long petioled. Ht gen 6"–26". Moist woods, low-mid el, BC to Cal, e to Cas. Spr-sum.

STEER'S HEAD, *Dicentra uniflora*. Flrs pink to white, resembling cow's skull, with 2 outer petals forming horns, 2 inner petals the skull. Lvs basal, 1"–4" long, 3-compound, the lflets lobed. Ht 1½"–4". Open places, lowl-subalp, Wn Cas s to Cal; e to Idaho, Wyo, Utah. Spr-sum.

Mustard Family (Cruciferae): 4 petals in a cross

LYALL'S ROCKCRESS, *Arabis lyalli*. Flrs to ½" long, in racemes. Lvs both basal and on stem, rather flashy, entire, linear to lancelike, or spoon shaped, ± smooth. Ht 4"–10". Subalp-alp, BC to Cal, e to RM. Sum. One of several very similar spp in our range.

SLENDER TOOTHWORT (LARGE-FLOWERED BITTERCRESS), *Cardamine pulcherrima*. Flrs pink to reddish or purplish, in racemes. Lvs basal, long petioled, either compound with lobed lflets or simple, round, lobed. Ht gen 4"–8". Moist woods, BC to Cal, W Cas to coast. Spr.

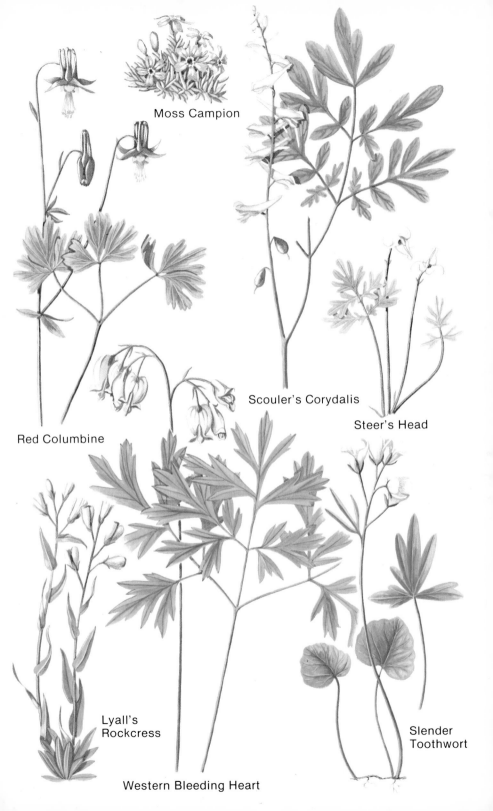

Moss Campion

Red Columbine

Scouler's Corydalis

Steer's Head

Lyall's
Rockcress

Western Bleeding Heart

Slender
Toothwort

PLATE 25

Stonecrop Family (Crassulaceae): 5 petals, 5 sepals

ROSEROOT (ROSY SEDUM OR STONECROP), *Sedum roseum.* Flrs fleshy, tiny, crowded in flat inflor. Lvs fleshy, lancelike, alt, crowded on stem. Ht to 6". Moist, rocky places, subalp-alp, BC to Cal, e to RM; Greenland, Eurasia. Sum.

Saxifrage Family (Saxifragaceae): 5 petals, 5 sepals

PURPLE SAXIFRAGE, *Saxifraga oppositifolia.* Flrs starlike, pink to reddish purple, the petals much smaller than sepals and "stemmed" at base. Lvs ovate, gen opp, in 4 overlapping rows on stems. Cushion plant to 2" tall. Rocky alp slopes, tundra, N Amer s to Wn, ne Ore and Wyo RM. Sum.

Rose Family (Rosaceae): 5 petals, 5 sepals

MARSH CINQUEFOIL, *Potentilla palustris.* Flrs starlike, deep wine red to purple. Lvs pinnate, with 5-7 sharply toothed lflets. Stems oft trailing or floating. Wet places, lowl-subalp, Alas to Cal; e to mid US, e Can. Sum.

Evening-primrose Family (Onagraceae): 4 petals, 4 sepals

ALPINE WILLOW-HERB, *Epilobium alpinum.* Flrs occas white, to ½" diam, petals notched. Lvs ovate to elliptic, to 2" long, opp, occas alt near tip of stem. Ht 2"-12". Moist places, subalp-alp, Alas to Cal, e to RM and Atl; Eurasia. Sum.

FIREWEED, *Epilobium angustifolium.* Flrs in spirelike raceme, opening from bottom to top of inflor. Lvs alt, willowlike, 3"-6" long. Ht 36"-120". Abun on burns and clearcuts, other disturbed places, Alas to Cal, e to Atl; Eurasia. Late spr-sum.

RED WILLOW-HERB, *Epilobium latifolium.* Flrs to 1½" diam; raceme not spirelike. Lvs opp, lancelike, 1"-2" long. Ht to 16". Moist rocky or gravelly places, subalp-alp, Alas to Cal, e to e Ore and RM. Sum.

Heath Family (Ericaceae): 5 petals, 5 sepals

CANDYSTICK, *Allotropa virgata.* Flrs urn shaped, in spikelike raceme. Lvs scalelike, brownish. Stem fleshy, striped like candycane. Ht 4"-16". Moist, shady forest, E Cas to coast, BC to Cal. Sum.

PRINCE'S PINE (PIPSISSEWA), *Chimaphila umbellata.* Flrs gen 5-15 in oft ± nodding inflor. Lvs evergreen, leathery, oblanceolate, toothed, 1"-3" long, in 1-2 whorls. Stems slightly woody. Ht 4"-12". Gen conifer forest, Alas to s Cal, e to RM and e US; Eurasia. Sum. Little Prince's Pine, *C. menziesii,* similar but lvs elliptic and gen 1-3 flrs.

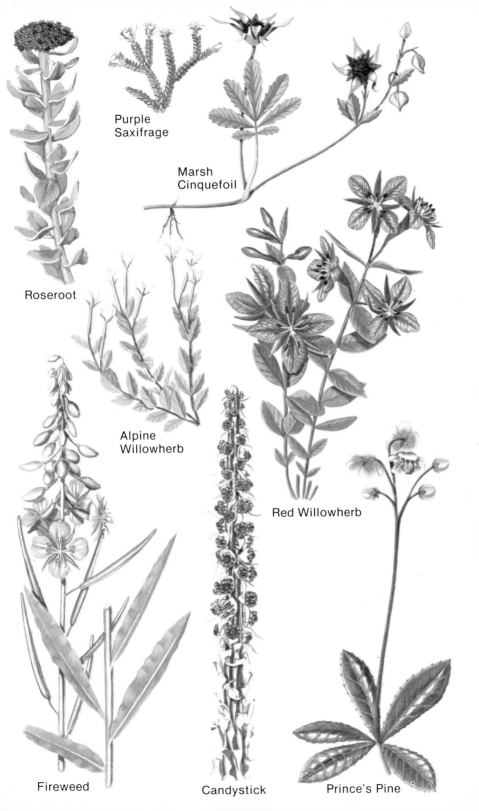

Purple
Saxifrage

Marsh
Cinquefoil

Roseroot

Alpine
Willowherb

Red Willowherb

Fireweed

Candystick

Prince's Pine

PLATE 26

Heath Family (Ericaceae): 5 petals, 5 sepals

PINK WINTERGREEN, *Pyrola asarifolia.* Flrs 10–25 in raceme. Lvs basal, heart shaped to ± oval, minutely toothed to nearly entire, petiole and blade ea to ca 3″ long; lvs occas absent. Ht to 16″. Moist woods, Alas s in most of w N Amer, e across Can and n US. Sum-early fall.

Primrose Family (Primulaceae): 4–9 petals, 4–9 sepals

JEFFREY'S SHOOTING STAR, *Dodecatheon jeffreyi.* Flrs gen with 5 (occas 4) reflexed petals and enlarged stigma tip, in sticky-haired umbel. Lvs spoon shaped, smooth or sticky haired, broad petioled, basal, 2″–16″ long, entire or scalloped or slightly toothed. Ht to 24″. Moist places, Alas to Cal, e to n RM. Sum. One of several very similar spp in our range. Cf White Shooting Star, plate 14.

SMOOTH DOUGLASIA, *Douglasia laevigata.* Flrs ca ⅜″ diam, tubular with flaring lobes. Lvs to ¾″ long, smooth or hairy margined, lancelike, in rosettes at stem ends. Stems creeping, to 12″ long, with flr stalks to 2½″ high; mat forming. Open rocky places, W Cas to coast, Wn and Ore, very rare in w BC. Spr-sum.

WESTERN STARFLOWER, *Trientalis latifolia.* Flrs white to rose, ca ½″ diam. Lvs elliptic, 1¼″–4″ long, 4–8 in whorl right below flrs. Ht 4″–6″. Woods, mdws, s BC to Cal, e to n RM. Spr-sum. Northern Starflower, *T. arctica,* a bog plant, has white flrs and lvs along entire stem.

Dogbane Family (Apocynaceae): 5-lobed flowers

SPREADING DOGBANE, *Apocynum androsaemifolium.* Flrs tubular or bell shaped, to ½″ diam, gen in terminal inflor, occas in lf axils. Lvs ovate to elliptic, opp, 1″–2½″ long. Ht 8″–20″. Dry places, lowl-subalp, in all our mtns; widespread in N Amer. Sum-early fall.

Phlox Family (Polemoniaceae): 5-lobed flowers

SKYROCKET, *Gilia aggregata.* Flrs ¾″–1¼″ long, occas white. Lvs 1″–2″ long, most numerous near base of stem, divided into linear segm. Ht 8″–40″. Dry, open places, E Cas, BC to Cal, e to RM and s to n Mex. Sum.

SPREADING PHLOX, *Phlox diffusa.* Flrs usu pink, occas pale blue or white, ¾″ diam, oft hiding lvs. Lvs opp, needlelike, ¼″–¾″ long. Stems woody at base, prostrate, mat forming. Ht 4″–12″. Dry, rocky places, gen subalp-alp, in all our mtns; widespread in w N Amer. Early sum.

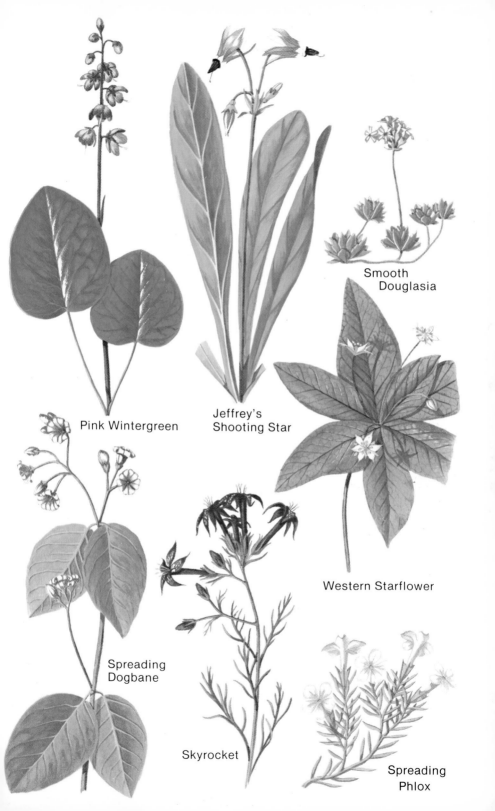

Pink Wintergreen

Jeffrey's
Shooting Star

Smooth
Douglasia

Western Starflower

Spreading
Dogbane

Skyrocket

Spreading
Phlox

PLATE 27

Figwort Family (Scrophulariaceae): flowers irregular, 5-lobed

APPLEGATE PAINTBRUSH, *Castilleja applegatei.* Flrs slender, tubular, spout-like, gen inconspicuous among scarlet (occas orange or yellow) 3- to 5-lobed bracts. Lvs either 3-lobed on upper stem and entire below, or all entire; margins wavy. Stems sticky haired below inflor. Ht 4″–24″. Open woods, rocky places, Cas, Ore to Cal, e to e Ore, Idaho, Nev. Sum.

COMMON (SCARLET) PAINTBRUSH, *Castilleja miniata* var. *miniata.* Flrs similar to those of *C. applegatei;* floral bracts scarlet to crimson (occas orange or yellow), 3-lobed. Lvs entire, lancelike, margins not wavy. Ht 12″–36″. Moist places, lowl-mont, s Alas, w Can, s in w US to Cal, e to NMex. Late spring-early fall. Elmer's Paintbrush, *C. elmeri,* also has entire lvs, but inflor gen crimson to purplish, and strongly sticky haired. Subalp-alp, cen Wn Cas n to s BC.

MAGENTA PAINTBRUSH, *Castilleja parviflora* vars. *oreopola* and *olympica.* Flrs similar to those of *C. applegatei,* but corolla obscured by calyx. Floral bracts 3- 5-lobed, gen magenta or rose. Ht to 12″. Subalp mdws, OMtns, Cas, Rainier to cen Ore. Sum. Cf Small-flowered Paintbrush, plate 15.

CLIFF PAINTBRUSH, *Castilleja rupicola.* Flrs similar to those of *C. applegatei,* but corolla beak extends far beyond calyx; floral bracts entirely red, 3– 7-lobed. Plant densely hairy. Ht to 8″. Rocky places, subalp-alp, Cas, BC to s Ore. Sum. Harsh Paintbrush, *C. hispida,* also densely hairy but gen taller, with flr bracts green at base.

SUKSDORF PAINTBRUSH, *Castilleja suksdorfii.* Flrs similar to those of *C. applegatei,* with beak extending well beyond calyx; floral bracts gen 5-lobed, yellow at base, red toward tips. Lvs ± smooth, entire or lobed. Ht to 20″. Moist subalp mdws, Cas, cen Wn to s Ore. Sum-early fall.

FOXGLOVE, *Digitalis purpuraea.* Flrs pink to lavender, purple, and white, 1″–2″ long, in dense 1-sided raceme. Lvs ovate, toothed or scalloped, to 12″ long at base, smaller upward on stem. Ht to 72″. Moist sites, roadsides and waste places, lowl-mont throughout our region; introduced from Europe. Late spr-sum.

BREWER'S MONKEYFLOWER, *Mimulus breweri.* Flrs very nearly reg, ca ¼″ diam. Lvs entire, lancelike. Plant sticky haired. Ht to 6″. Dry places, E Cas, low-mid el, BC s to Cal. Sum.

LEWIS' MONKEYFLOWER, *Mimulus lewisii.* Flrs 1¼″–2¼″ long. Lvs opp, ovate, toothed, clasping stem. Ht 12″–24″. Moist-wet subalp-alp mdws in all our mtns, w Can s to Cal, e to n RM. Sum.

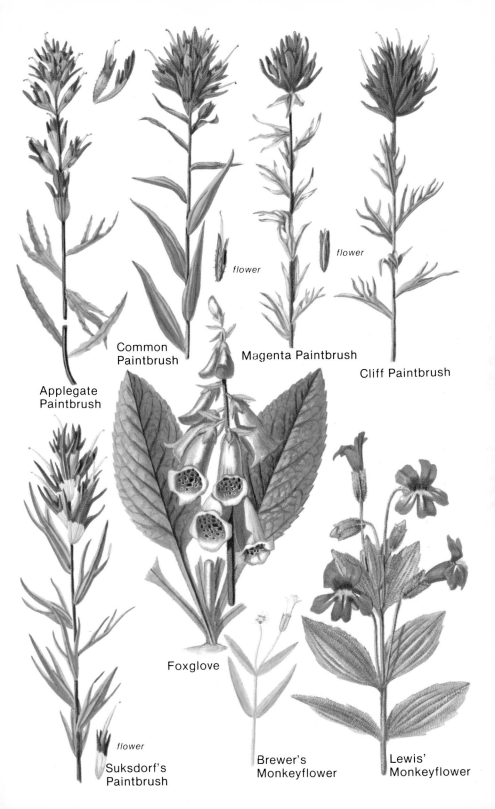

Applegate
Paintbrush

Common
Paintbrush

Magenta Paintbrush

Cliff Paintbrush

flower

flower

Foxglove

Suksdorf's
Paintbrush

flower

Brewer's
Monkeyflower

Lewis'
Monkeyflower

120

PLATE 28

Figwort Family (Scrophulariaceae): flowers irregular, 2-lipped

ELEPHANT'S HEAD, *Pedicularis groenlandica.* Flrs rose to purple like tiny elephant heads, upper lip forming trunk, lateral lobes forming ears. Lvs pinnate, to 6″ long, basal and reduced upward on stem. Plant hairless. Ht to ca 24″. Wet mdws in all our mtns; widespread in w N Amer. Sum.

LITTLE ELEPHANT'S HEAD, *Pedicularis attolens.* Similar to above sp but plant hairy and the "trunk" no longer than lower lip. Ht to only 16″. Wet mdws, Ore Cas s to SNev. Sum.

BIRDSBEAK LOUSEWORT, *Pedicularis ornithoryncha.* Flrs dark rose to purple, with short, straight beak. Lvs pinnate, basal, and up to 3 small ones on stem. Ht to 6″. Subalp-alp mdws, s Alas in CMtns and Vanc I. to Wn Cas. Sum.

WOODLAND BEARDTONGUE, *Nothochelone nemorosa.* Flr to 1″ long, 2–5 in terminal panicle. Lvs ovate, opp, toothed, 2″–3″ long. Ht to 24″. Moist places, W Cas to coast, BC to n Cal. Sum.

CLIFF (ROCK) PENSTEMON, *Penstemon rupicola.* Flrs rose to lavender or red, 1″–1½″ long. Lvs opp, ovate, thick, toothed, to ¾″ long. Stems creeping, woody at base. Ht 3″–6″. Cliffs, rocky places, Cas, Wn to Cal. Sum. Cf Penstemons, plate 32.

Sunflower or Aster Family (Compositae): flowers in composite heads

ROSY PUSSYTOES, *Antennaria microphylla.* Flr heads with tiny yellow disk flrs bordered by pink or rosy bracts, in tight inflor. Basal lvs spoon shaped, pointed; stem lvs linear, all white-woolly. Ht to 18″, mat forming. Open places, mtns of w N Amer. Late spring-sum. Cf Woolly Pussytoes, plate 16.

EDIBLE THISTLE, *Cirsium edule.* Flr heads with disk flrs only, 2″–3″ diam, surrounded by spiny bracts. Lvs pinnately lobed and spiny margined, mostly basal to 16″ long, fewer and smaller on stem. Ht 24″–28″. Entire plant webby haired. Moist mdws, open woods, lowl-alp, cen BC to n Ore, e to W Cas. Sum-early fall.

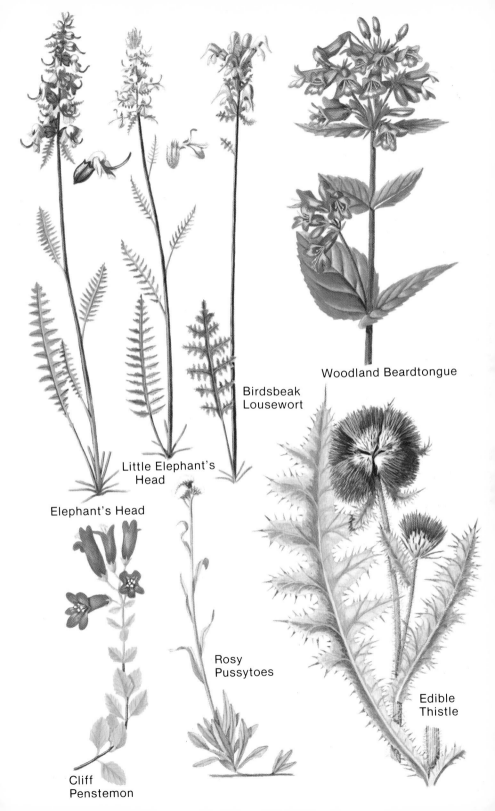

Woodland Beardtongue

Birdsbeak
Lousewort

Little Elephant's
Head

Elephant's Head

Rosy
Pussytoes

Edible
Thistle

Cliff
Penstemon

IV. Blue to Purple Flowers

This section includes flowers that are distinctly blue, violet, or bluish purple. Compounded of equal parts red and blue, purple comes in shades that are difficult to assign to one color or the other. When attempting to identify plants with purplish flowers, also consult section 3. White flowers tinged with blue or lavender are covered in section 1. Brownish flowers tending toward maroon or purple are covered in section 5. The following species from other sections may have bluish or purplish flowers.

Subalpine Mariposa Lily, *plate 6*
Lyall's Mariposa Lily, *plate 6*
Mountain Lady Slipper, *plate 8*
Western Red Baneberry, *plate 10*
Drummond's Anemone, *plate 10*
Western Pasqueflower, *plate 10*
Alpine Smelowskia, *plate 11*
Alpine Collomia, *plate 15*
Varileaf Phacelia, *plate 15*
Yerba Buena, *plate 15*
Dwarf Mountain Daisy, *plate 17*
Bracted Lousewort, *plate 21*
Purple Saxifrage, *plate 25*
Spreading Phlox, *plate 26*
Magenta Paintbrush, *plate 27*
Foxglove, *plate 27*
Lewis' Monkeyflower, *plate 27*
Elephant's Head, *plate 28*
Birdsbeak Lousewort, *plate 28*
Edible Thistle, *plate 28*
Western Bronze Bells, *plate 34*
Small-flowered Twisted-stalk, *plate 34*
Clustered Lady Slipper, *plate 34*
Giant Helleborine, *plate 34*
Wild-ginger, *plate 35*
Brown's Peony, *plate 35*
Youth-on-age, *plate 35*

PLATE 29

Lily Family (Liliaceae): 6 tepals

COMMON CAMAS, *Camassia quamash.* Flrs 1½"–2" diam, pale blue to deep violet, occas white, gen slightly irreg, in long-bracted raceme. Lvs grasslike. Ht 12"–24". Grassy places, mdws, lowl-subalp s BC to Cal, e to RM. Spring-early sum. Leichtlin's Camas, *C. leichtlinii,* similar but flrs more oft reg and/or white, and inflor bracts short.

Iris Family (Iridae): 6 tepals

BLUE-EYED GRASS, *Sisyrinchium angustifolium.* Flrs ½"–1½" diam, tepals abruptly slender pointed. Lvs grasslike, 2 forming spathe below inflor. Ht 4"–20". Moist places, lowl-mont, s Alas to Baja; e to n RM, e Can. Spr-midsum.

Buttercup Family (Ranunculaceae): 5–7 petallike sepals

MONKSHOOD, *Aconitum columbianum.* Flrs occas white or greenish, upper sepal hoodlike, 2 tiny petals inside hood. Lvs palmately lobed, toothed, 2"–8" wide. Ht 18"–60". Moist places, lowl-subalp, Alas to Cal, e to RM, cen US. Sum.

WILD CROCUS (PASQUEFLOWER), *Anemone nuttalliana.* Flrs blue to purple, rarely white, ca 1½"–3" diam, hairy on the outside. Lvs white haired, finely dissected, mostly basal (these appearing after earliest flrs), but 2–3 in whorl below flr. Ht to ca 12". Mont-subalp slopes, E CMtns to Cas; Alas to Wn; e to RM, cen and s US. Sum. Cf Western Pasqueflower, plate 10.

OREGON (BLUE) ANEMONE, *Anemone oregana.* Flrs gen blue, also pink or white, gen with 35–100 stamens, to 1½" diam, hairless. Lvs compound, 1 basal, 3 in whorl below flr. Ht 4"–12". Moist woods and brush, E Cas, n Wn to CRGorge; also sw Wn, e Ore. Spr-early summer. Lyall's Anemone, *A. lyallii,* very similar but flr gen white and less than 35 stamens. Cf Columbia Windflower, plate 10.

ROCKSLIDE (LARGE-FLOWERED) LARKSPUR, *Delphinium glareosum.* Flrs irreg, with 5 sepals, the upper spurred, and 4 smaller, deeply notched blue petals; raceme hairy, ca ½ length of stem. Lvs fleshy, deeply 5–7-lobed, the petioles progressively smaller upward on stem so that blades tend to be clumped near mid-stem. Ht to 12". Talus, rocky ridges, alp-subalp, OMtns, E Cas, cen Wn, Ore Cas. Sum. One of 9 very similar spp in our mtns. Pale Larkspur, *D. glaucum,* is 40"–80" tall and has basal lvs 6"–8" wide (smaller on stem) and hairless stems with powdery bloom. Menzies' Larkspur, *D. menziesii,* has deep blue sepals, pale blue or white petals, and most of its lvs on stem. Upland Larkspur, *D. nuttallianum,* has a few 2–4-lobed, mostly basal lvs.

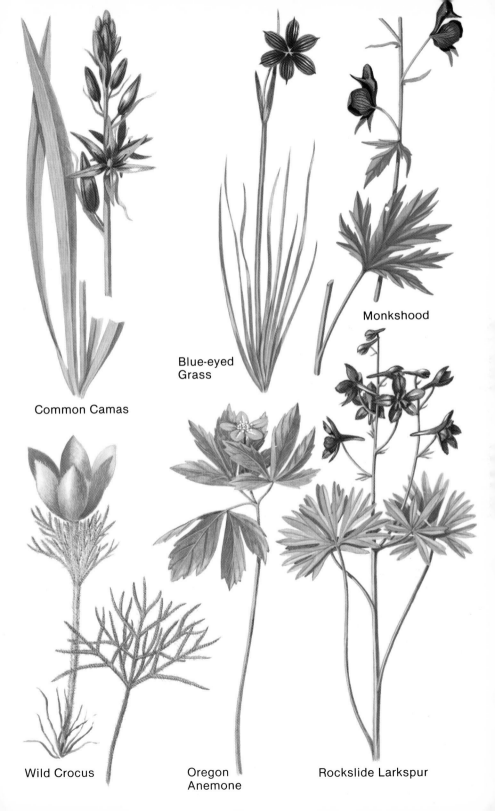

Common Camas

Blue-eyed
Grass

Monkshood

Wild Crocus

Oregon
Anemone

Rockslide Larkspur

PLATE 30

Pea Family (Leguminosae): flowers irregular, 5 petals

NUTTALL'S PEA, *Lathyrus nevadensis* sbsp *lanceolatus*. Flrs blue, white, pink, or purple, to ca ¾ " long, gen 17 or less per inflor. Lvs pinnate, with 8–14 lflets, ending in forked tendril. Ht to 32". Open woods, grassland, s BC to Cal, e to Idaho. Spr-sum.

BROADLEAF LUPINE, *Lupinus latifolius*. Flrs irreg, in long dense racemes. Lvs palmately compound, the lflets gen 7–9, usu 1¼"–2⅜" long. Plant usu hairy, the stems branched. Ht to 40". Com, open places, lowl-subalp in all our mtns, Alas to Cal, e to Cas. Sum. Bigleaf Lupine, *L. polyphyllus,* best recognized through much of our range by unbranched stem and lvs usu with 9–13 lflets up to 4" long.

ALPINE LUPINE, *Lupinus lepidus* var *lobbii*. Flrs irreg, in short, dense racemes. Lvs palmately compound, the 6–8 lflets silky haired, ⅝" long. Ht 3"–4", mat forming. Rocky alp slopes, BC to s Cal; e to Idaho, Nev. Sum. Other varieties of this sp occur from lowl to subalp in our region.

AMERICAN VETCH, *Vicia americana*. Flrs irreg, sweetpealike, 4–8 per stalk from lf axil. Lvs pinnately compound, gen with 8–12 lflets, usu ending in branched tendril. Plant trailing or climbing, roadsides, open places, in all our mtns; widespread in N Amer. Late spr-sum.

Violet Family (Violaceae): flowers irregular, 5 petals, 5 sepals

EARLY BLUE (HOOK) VIOLET, *Viola adunca*. Flrs lilac or white with purple lines, to ¾ " wide, with prominent spur, white-haired side petals. Lvs ovate or heart shaped, scalloped, long petioled, stipules oft slenderly toothed. Ht to 4". Moist mdws, woods, open places, lowl-subalp, in all our mtns, but esp E Cas; widespread in N Amer. Spr-sum.

MARSH VIOLET, *Viola palustris*. Flrs lilac, or white with blue lines, 1 per short stalk. Lvs rounded or heart shaped, to 1⅜" wide. Lvs and flrs both rise directly from rhizome. Ht 3"–6". Bogs, marshes, wet mdws, BC to Cal, e to RM, Atl; Europe. Spr-sum.

FLETT'S VIOLET, *Viola flettii*. Flrs purple and yellow. Lvs kidney shaped, fleshy, finely scalloped or toothed, ca ½"–1½" wide. Ht 1"–6". Rocky places, high el, OMtns. Sum.

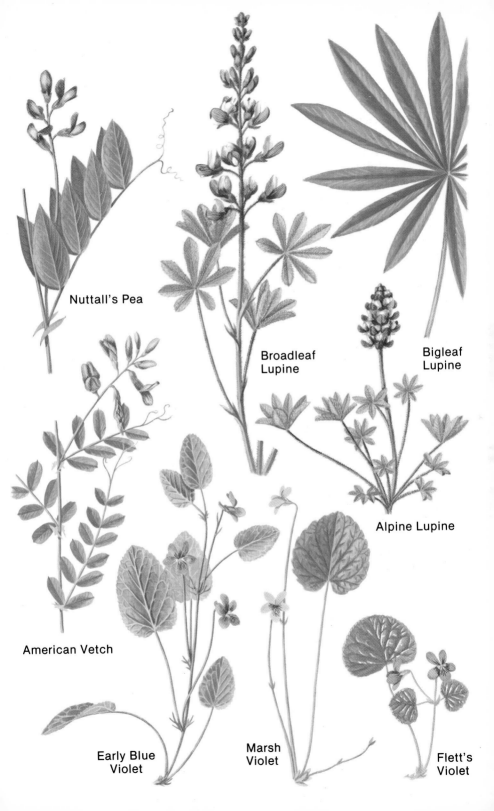

Nuttall's Pea

Broadleaf
Lupine

Bigleaf
Lupine

Alpine Lupine

American Vetch

Early Blue
Violet

Marsh
Violet

Flett's
Violet

PLATE 31

Gentian Family (Gentianaceae): 4– 5-lobed flowers

EXPLORER'S (MOUNTAIN, BOG, PLEATED) GENTIAN, *Gentiana calycosa.* Flrs 1″–1⅝″ long, vaselike, 5-lobed, rarely yellowish, with 2– 4-toothed pleats between corolla lobes, gen 1 per stem, occas 3 in inflor. Lvs to 1″ long, ovate, opp, 7–9 pairs on stem. Ht 2″–12″. Gen subalp-alp mdws, streamsides, BC to Cal, e to RM. Late sum-fall. Northern Gentian, *G. amarella,* has several flrs in crowded inflor, ea flr 4– 5-lobed and without pleats.

HIKER'S GENTIAN, *Gentiana simplex.* Flr solitary, with 4 corolla lobes oft spreading to form cross. Lvs opp, lancelike, 3–6 pairs on single stem. Ht 2″–8″. Mtn bogs, mdws, Ore Cas to SNev. Sum.

Phlox Family (Polemoniaceae): 5-lobed flowers

ELEGANT SKY PILOT, *Polemonium elegans.* Flrs funnel shaped with flaring corolla lobes, in terminal head. Lvs pinnate, gen basal, the lflets tiny, rounded. Entire plant sticky and strongly ill-smelling. Ht 2″–4″. Rocky alp slopes, Cas, BC to Wn, OMtns. Sum.

SHOWY JACOB'S LADDER, *Polemonium pulcherrimum* var *calycinum.* Flrs bell shaped, in headlike inflor, ill-smelling. Lvs pinnate, basal and on stem, the 11–25 lflets elliptic, to 1½″ long. Inflor sticky but herbage otherwise hairless or nearly so. Ht gen 12″–20″. Gen rocky places, mid el, Cas, Wn to Cal, e to Mont, Nev. Late spring-sum. *P.p.* var *pulcherrium,* is a compact version found at high el in all our mtns.

Waterleaf Family (Hydrophyllaceae): 5 petals, 5 sepals

SILKY (ALPINE) PHACELIA, *Phacelia sericea.* Flrs ca ¼″ diam, stamens longer than petals, in spikelike inflor. Lvs pinnately lobed, fernlike, 1″–4″ long, silky haired (except in Ore). Ht 4″–24″. Various habitats, mid-high el, s BC to Cal, e to RM. Sum. Cf Varileaf Phacelia, plate 15.

Borage Family (Boraginaceae): 5 sepals, 5-lobed

JESSICA'S STICKSEED, *Hackelia micrantha.* Flrs ca ¼″ diam, in open, branched inflor. Lvs lancelike, long petioled below, sessile above. Stems hairy. Ht 12″–40″. Open places, Cas to SNev, e to RM. Sum.

PANICLED BLUEBELLS (LUNGWORT), *Mertensia paniculata.* Flrs tubular, nodding, in loose clusters. Lvs ovate, stems lvs 2″–3″ long, short petioled, with slender, pointed tip; basal lvs, when present, heart shaped, long petioled. Ht to 60″. Moist places, Alas, Can, s to RM, Cas, OMtns, s Ore. Sum. Oregon Lungwort, *M. bella,* has bell-shaped flrs; Cas, cen Ore-Cal. Fringed Lungwort, *M. ciliata,* has hairy sepals and sessile upper-stem lvs; cen Ore-Cal.

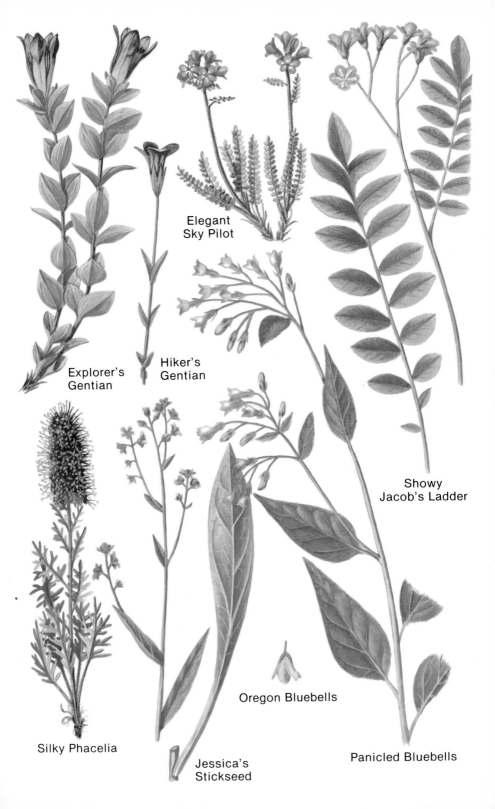

Explorer's Gentian

Hiker's Gentian

Elegant Sky Pilot

Showy Jacob's Ladder

Silky Phacelia

Jessica's Stickseed

Oregon Bluebells

Panicled Bluebells

PLATE 32

Mint Family (Labiatae): flowers irregular

MOUNTAIN PENNYROYAL (COYOTE MINT), *Monardella odoratissima.* Flrs occas white, ca ½" long, in dense head, cupped by membranous bracts. Lvs opp, lancelike, to 1¼" long. Ht 6"–20". Dry woods, rocky places, E Cas, Wn to SNev; also e Wn and n Idaho s to Ariz and NMex. Sum.

SELFHEAL, *Prunella vulgaris.* Flrs to ¾" long, 2-lipped, the upper lip hoodlike, the lower 3-lobed, in short, dense spikes. Lvs opp, lancelike to ovate, toothed, petioled. Ht 4"–20". Moist places, lowl-mont; widespread in N Amer; Europe. Sum.

COOLEY'S HEDGENETTLE, *Stachys cooleyae.* Flrs ½"–1" long, 2-lipped, the upper lip hoodlike, the lower longer, 3-lobed, droopy, in whorls on upper stem. Lvs opp, narrowly ovate or triangular, toothed, petioled, hairy on both sides, 2½"–6" long. Stems 4-sided, bristly. Ht 24"–60". Damp places, BC to s Ore, Cas to coast. Sum.

Figwort Family (Scrophulariaceae): flowers irregular

LARGE-FLOWERED BLUE-EYED MARY, *Collinsia grandiflora.* Flrs ca ¾" long, corolla attached at right angle to calyx, in whorls on upper stem. Lvs opp, ovate to spoon shaped and toothed on lower stem, narrower and entire above. Stem simple or branched. Ht 4"–16". Moist places, lowl-mont, BC to n Cal, W Cas to coast. Sum.

SMALL-FLOWERED BLUE-EYED MARY, *Collinsia parviflora.* Flrs like those of above sp, but only ca ¼" long. Lvs opp, oblong to nearly round on lower stem, 2"–4" long, short petioled; upper lvs lancelike, sessile. Stem simple or branched. Ht 2"–16". Moist places, BC s to Cal, Ariz; e to Colo, e Can, n US. Spring.

DAVIDSON'S PENSTEMON, *Penstemon davidsonii.* Flrs to 1½" long, 2-lipped, hairy at base of lower lip, 1 per stalk. Lvs to ¾" long, oval, oft toothed, petioled. Stems woody at base. Ht 2"–6", mat forming. Rocky places, mont-alp, BC to Cal. Sum.

SMALL-FLOWERED PENSTEMON, *Penstemon procerus.* Flrs ca ½" long, 2-lipped, whorled. Lvs entire; the lower ones ovate, petioled, to 4" long; the upper ones lancelike, mostly sessile, to 3" long. Plant singly stemmed. Ht 6"–12", mat forming. Moist places, mid-high el, in all our mtns, s to Cal and Nev. Sum. Cascade Penstemon, *P. serrulatus,* similar but flrs ⅜"–1" long, and plant taller with several stems, and larger, toothed lvs.

CUSICK'S SPEEDWELL, *Veronica cusickii.* Flrs 4-petaled, ± irreg, ca ½" diam. Lvs oval, opp, shiny, to 1" long. Ht 2"–8". Com, moist mdws, talus, stream banks, subalp, Wn Cas, OMtns, s to SNev, e to RM. Sum. Alpine Speedwell, *V. wormskjoldii,* very similar but lvs gen oblong, not crowded on stem.

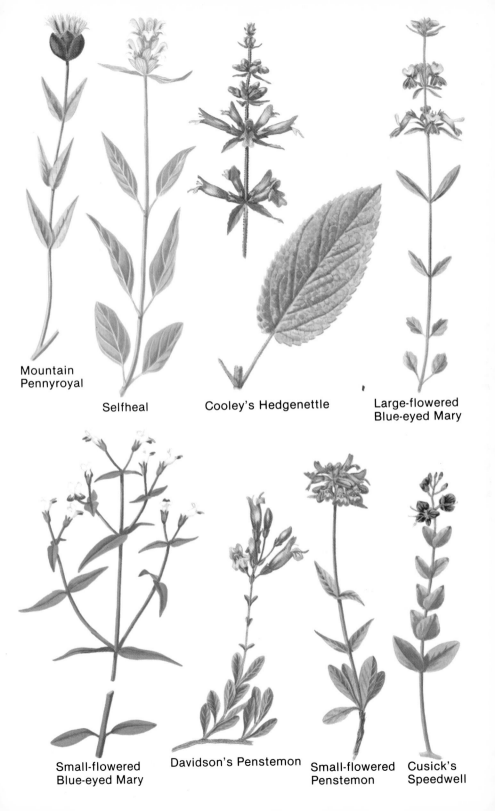

Mountain
Pennyroyal

Selfheal

Cooley's Hedgenettle

Large-flowered
Blue-eyed Mary

Small-flowered
Blue-eyed Mary

Davidson's Penstemon

Small-flowered
Penstemon

Cusick's
Speedwell

PLATE 33

Bladderwort Family (Lentibulariaceae): flowers irregular, 5-lobed

COMMON BUTTERWORT, *Pinguicula vulgaris*. Flrs 2-lipped, spurred, to 1" long, 1 per stem. Lvs basal, ± spoon-shaped, short petioled, succulent, slimy above, 1"–2" long. Ht 2"–6". Bogs, wet places in mtns, Alas to n Cal, e to e Can, ne US; Eurasia. Spr-sum.

Bellflower Family (Campanulaceae): 5-lobed flowers

BLUEBELLS OF SCOTLAND (ROUNDLEAF BELLFLOWER, HAREBELL, BLUEBELL), *Campanula rotundifolia*. Flrs bell shaped ca ¾" long, lobes barely spreading. Lvs both basal and alt; basal ones round or heart shaped, long-petioled, toothed; alt lvs linear, entire. Ht 4"–32". Many places, lowl-subalp, in all our mtns; widespread in n hemis. Sum. Parry's Bellflower, *C. parryi*, similar but basal lvs spoon shaped, short-petioled. Rough Harebell, *C. scabrella*, covered with downy hairs.

PIPER'S HAREBELL, *Campanula piperi*. Flrs dish shaped, ca 1" diam. Lvs all ± spoon shaped, sharply toothed. Stems unbranched. Ht to 4". Rocky places, subalp-alp, OMtns only. Sum.

SCOULER'S HAREBELL, *C. scouleri*. Flrs tubular with flaring lobes longer than tube and style exceeding upper corolla rim. Lvs toothed, ± round and long petioled at base, ± oval and shorter petioled on stem. Ht 4"–16". Woods, rocky places below 4000', W CMtns-Cas to coast, Alas to n Cal. Sum.

ALASKA BELLFLOWER, *Campanula lasiocarpa*. Flrs funnel shaped, the calyx woolly, with toothed, lancelike segm. Lvs mostly basal, spoon shaped, sharply toothed. Ht 2"–6". Alp in all our mtns; Alas s to Wn; Asia. Sum.

Aster or Sunflower Family (Compositae): flowers in composite heads

ALPINE ASTER, *Aster alpigenus*. Flr head daisylike, 1 per stem, the rays lavender to violet. Lvs entire, mostly basal, linear to spoon shaped; stem lvs few, smaller. Ht 2"–6". Subalp-alp, OMtns, Cas, Wn to Cal, e to n RM. Sum.

CASCADE ASTER, *Aster ledophyllus*. Flr heads daisylike, gen several per stem, with 6–21 blue or pink rays. Lvs lancelike to elliptic, sessile, ± gray-cottony beneath, scalelike on lower stem. Ht gen 12"–24". Open woods, mdws, mont-subalp, Cas, BC to Cal. Midsum-fall. Leafy Aster, *A. foliaceus*, has purple or blue rays and long-petioled, spoonlike lvs on lower stem.

WANDERING DAISY (FLEABANE), *Erigeron peregrinus*. Flr heads with 30–80 blue, lavender, or pink rays, gen 1 or few per stem. Lower lvs spoonlike, long petioled; upper ones smaller, sessile, linear to ovate. Ht 12"–30"; alp plants oft less than 8" tall. Com, mdws, moist places, mont-alp, in all our mtns; widespread in mtns of w N Amer. Sum. One of numerous very similar spp. in our range.

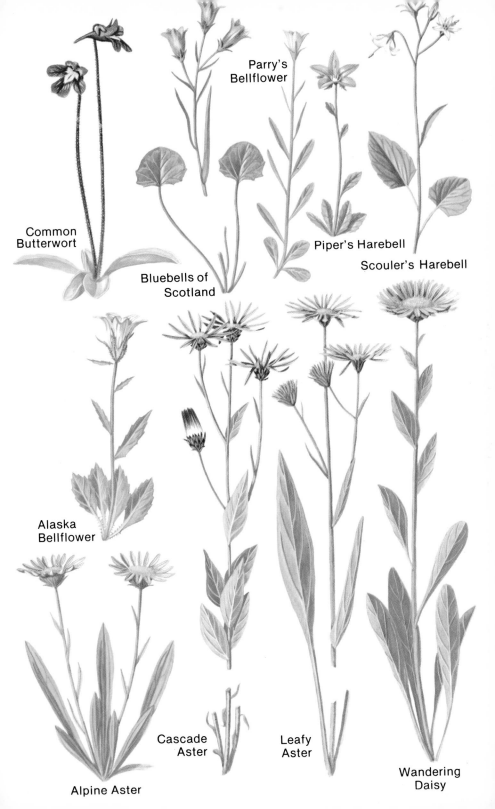

Parry's
Bellflower

Common
Butterwort

Bluebells of
Scotland

Piper's Harebell

Scouler's Harebell

Alaska
Bellflower

Cascade
Aster

Leafy
Aster

Wandering
Daisy

Alpine Aster

V. Green or Brown Flowers

This section includes flowers that are conspicuously green or brown, at least in part. The green may tend toward yellow or white, the brown toward maroon or purple. The following species may also have greenish or brownish flowers.

Clasping-leaved Twisted-stalk, *plate 7*
Sticky Tofieldia, *plate 7*
Corn-lily, *plate 7*
Elegant Death-camas, *plate 7*
Mountain Lady Slipper, *plate 8*
Roundleaf Bog Orchid, *plate 8*
Lady's Tresses, *plate 8*
False Bugbane, *plate 10*
Globeflower, *plate 10*
White-veined Wintergreen, *plate 14*
One-sided Wintergreen, *plate 14*
Sweet-scented Bedstraw, *plate 16*
Sibbaldia, *plate 19*
Rosy Twisted-stalk, *plate 23*
Spotted Coralroot, *plate 23*
Monkshood, *plate 29*

PLATE 34

Lily Family (Liliaceae): 6 tepals

CHECKER (CHOCOLATE) LILY, *Fritillaria lanceolata*. Flrs nodding, ¾"-1½" long, mottled green (or yellow) and brown (or purple). Lvs both scattered on upper stem and in 1-2 whorls. Ht 6"-40". Forest, grassy places, lowl-mont, BC to Cal, e to Idaho. Spr-sum.

WESTERN BRONZE BELLS, *Stenanthium occidentale*. Flrs greenish bronze or purplish green, nodding, in loose raceme. Lvs basal, grasslike, 4"-12" long. Ht 4"-20". Moist places, gen subalp-alp, in all our mtns s to Cal, e to RM. Sum.

SMALL-FLOWERED TWISTED-STALK, *Streptopus streptopoides*. Flrs greenish, oft purple tinged, the tepals spreading. Lvs ovate, sessile, to 2¼" long. Ht 4"-8". Mid-mtn forest, Alas to OMtns and Wn Cas, e to Idaho. Sum. Cf twisted-stalks, plates 7 and 23.

GREEN FALSE-HELLEBORE, *Veratrum viride*. Flrs greenish, in drooping, tasseled panicle. Lvs clasping, 6"-14" long, 3"-6" wide. Ht 36"-84". Wet places, lowl-subalp, Alas to n Ore; e to RM and e Can. Sum. Cf Corn-lily, plate 7.

Orchid Family (Orchidaceae): flowers irregular

CLUSTERED LADY-SLIPPER, *Cypripedium fasciculatum*. Flrs ca ½" wide, sepals and 2 petals brownish purple, lip pouchlike, pale green mottled with purple. Lvs 2, opp, ovate, 2"-6" long. Stem hairy, 2"-8" tall. Open forest, s BC to Cal, E Cas to n RM. Sum. Cf Mountain Lady-slipper, plate 8.

GIANT HELLEBORINE (STREAM ORCHID), *Epipactis gigantea*. Flrs to 1½" wide; 3 green, lancelike sepals; 2 pink or purplish lancelike petals; a 3rd petal tonguelike, pinkish, purple-streaked at base. Lvs broadly lancelike, 2"-8" long. Ht 12"-36". Moist-wet places, gen lowl-mont, s BC to Mex, e to RM. Spr-sum.

HEARTLEAF TWAYBLADE, *Listera cordata*. Flrs greenish or brownish, small, orchidlike, with forked lower lip, gen 5-16 in raceme. Lvs 2, opp, heart shaped. Ht to 10". Gen damp-wet places, Alas s to Cal and NMex; e to e Can, se US; Greenland. Sum. Western Twayblade, *L. convallarioides*, similar but flr lip merely notched, not deeply forked, and lvs ovate. Broad-lipped Twayblade, *L. caurina*, also similar but lower lip wedge shaped and neither notched nor forked.

Nettle Family (Urticaceae): no petals, 4 sepals

STINGING NETTLE, *Urtica dioica*. Flrs small, greenish, in stringy inflor from lf axils. Lvs lancelike to ovate, opp, petioled, toothed. Stems 36"-84" tall, smooth or hairy. Lvs and sometimes stems covered with stinging hairs; avoid contact! Moist places, N Amer, Eurasia. Spr-sum.

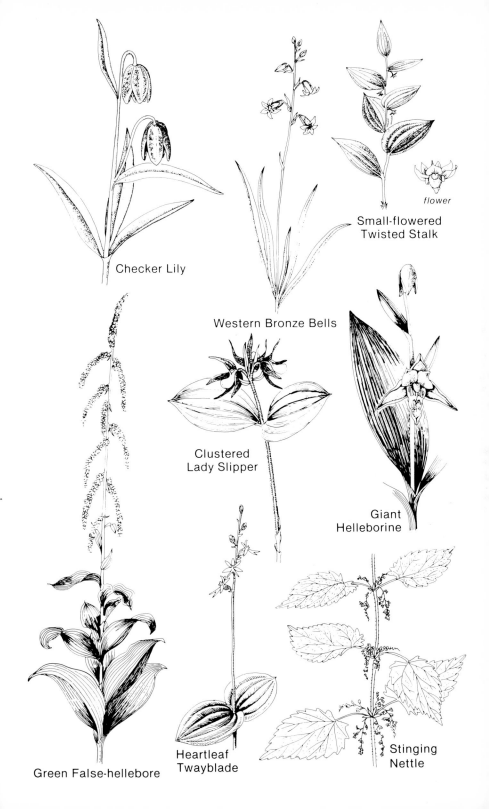

Checker Lily

Small-flowered
Twisted Stalk

flower

Western Bronze Bells

Clustered
Lady Slipper

Giant
Helleborine

Green False-hellebore

Heartleaf
Twayblade

Stinging
Nettle

PLATE 35

Birthwort Family (Aristolochiaceae): 3-lobed flowers, no petals

WILD-GINGER, *Asarum caudatum*. Flrs brownish or occas greenish, the calyx bowl shaped, with very long, slender sepals. Lvs heart or kidney shaped, in pairs. Stems trailing, mat forming. Moist shady woods, lowl-mont, BC to Cal, e to Idaho, Mont. Spr-sum.

Buckwheat Family (Polygonaceae): no petals, 4 sepals

MOUNTAIN (ALPINE)-SORREL, *Oxyria digyna*. Flrs greenish to reddish, small, in slender panicles. Lvs green or reddish, heart or kidney shaped, long petioled, gen basal. Ht gen 4"–16". Moist rocky places, subalp-alp, mtns of n hemis. Sum.

Peony Family (Paeoniaceae): 5 petals, 5 sepals

BROWN'S (WESTERN) PEONY, *Paeonia brownii*. Flrs green and brown to maroon, 1"–1½" diam. Lvs 3-divided 2×, the ultimate segm lobed, the blades to 2½" long, smooth, fleshy-leathery, waxy blue green. Ht 8"–24". Pine forest, E Cas, Wn to Cal, e to Idaho, Wyo, Utah. Late spr-early sum.

Buttercup Family (Ranunculaceae): no petals, 4–5 sepals

WESTERN MEADOWRUE, *Thalictrum occidentale*. Flrs small, in panicles, greenish white (M flrs) or purplish (F flrs). Lvs compound, divided in 3s, the ultimate segm round. Young plants dk purplish. Ht to 40". Moist woods, BC s to n Cal, e to RM states. Late spr-midsum.

Saxifrage Family (Saxifragaceae): 4–5 petals

BREWER'S MITREWORT, *Mitella breweri*. Flrs greenish yellow, feathery, 20–60 in raceme. Lvs basal, 1½"–3½" diam, heart or kidney shaped, shiny green, 7–11-lobed and toothed. Flr stems lfless, 4"–16" tall. Moist places, gen in mtns, BC s in Cas and OMtns to Cal, e to n RM. Spr-sum. Naked Mitrewort, *M. nuda,* similar but lvs small, hairy, Three-toothed Mitrewort, *M. caulescens,* has lvs on stems. Oval-leaved Mitrewort, *M. ovalis,* has narrower, white-haired lvs.

FRINGECUP, *Tellima grandiflora*. Flrs with fringelike greenish to reddish petals, gen 10–35 in 1-sided racemes. Lvs mostly basal, also 1–3 on stem, coarse haired, 5–7-lobed, scalloped or toothed. Ht to 32". Moist places, lowl-low mtn, s Alas to cen Cal, gen W Cas to coast in Ore and Wn. Spr-sum.

YOUTH-ON-AGE, *Tolmiea menziesii*. Flrs tiny, bristly, green and brown, with tubular calyx and 4 threadlike petals, in raceme 4"–12" long. Lvs hairy, toothed, and lobed, reduced upward on stem. Ht to 32". Moist places, Alas to Cal, W CMtns and Cas to coast. Spr-sum.

Heath Family (Ericaceae): 5-lobed corolla

PINEDROPS, *Pterospora andromedea*. Flrs urn shaped, nodding, gen pale yellowish brown, also pink or white, 40–60 in spirelike raceme. Lvs bractlike. Stems rose to reddish or yellowish brown, 12"–40" tall, sticky, persisting as dry stalks. Forest, Alas to Cal, s in RM to NMex, e to Atl. Sum.

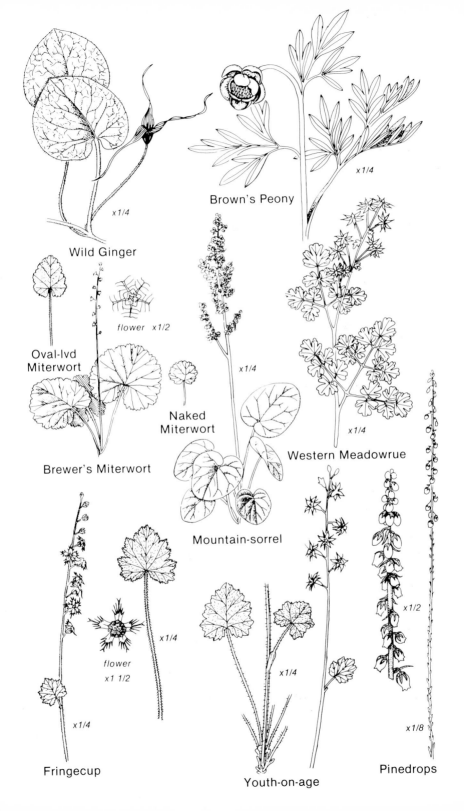

Brown's Peony

x1/4

x1/4

Wild Ginger

Oval-lvd
Miterwort

flower x1/2

Naked
Miterwort

x1/4

Brewer's Miterwort

Western Meadowrue

x1/4

Mountain-sorrel

flower
x1 1/2

x1/4

x1/4

x1/2

Fringecup

x1/4

Youth-on-age

x1/8

Pinedrops

Shrubs

Well over 100 species of shrubs occur within our range. These include: erect shrubs, some large and treelike; prostrate or mat-forming plants; woody vines; and a few species, such as twinflower and bunchberry dogwood, which are herblike in general appearance but have more or less woody stems. Subshrubs are included with wildflowers in the preceding section. Plants that are typically treelike and only occasionally shrubby in our region are included among the trees in the following section.

While herbaceous plants are usually conspicuous only when in flower, shrubs catch our attention the year around. Some species have showy flowers or fruits, but these aids to identification may not always be present. Many other species have inconspicuous fruits and flowers that may be of little help to an untrained observer even when they are present. It is important, then, when attempting to identify shrubs, to pay particular attention to the stems and leaves.

The great majority of shrubs occurring in our region are illustrated in the following pages. The chief exceptions include members of the larger genera, such as *Ribes* (currants and gooseberries) and *Salix* (willows), which are represented only by about a half-dozen species each. In both cases, species often may be distinguished largely or solely on the basis of rather obscure, technical differences. One should be content to identify such plants by genus alone.

Among the trees, the following species are sometimes shrubby.

Elfinwood (prostrate timberline trees): lodgepole pine, whitebark pine, subalpine fir, Engelmann spruce, mountain hemlock, Alaska yellow-cedar.

Broadleaf trees: Pacific willow, water birch (cf paper birch), golden chinquapin, Oregon oak, western crabapple, cascara buckthorn.

For information on the organization and use of the species accounts and illustrations, as well as for a list of the abbreviations used in the accounts, see the Introduction.

PLATE 36

Cypress Family (Cupressaceae)

COMMON (DWARF) JUNIPER, *Juniperus communis*. Prostrate, evergreen shrub, mat forming. Lvs awl shaped, with shallow white channels, in whorls of 3, numerous on stems. Fruit a dk blue berrylike cone with whitish bloom. Bark scaly, gray brown. Rocky places, subalp-alp, Alas to Cal, e to Atl; Eurasia. Cf Junipers, plate 50.

Willow Family (Salicaceae)

WILLOWS, *Salix* spp. Prostrate shrubs to trees. Lvs simple, alt, deciduous, short petioled, linear to oval or obovate, toothed or entire, smooth, hairy, or covered with powdery bloom on 1 or both sides. Flrs tiny, in erect M and F catkins on different plants. Nearly 24 spp in our mtns from BC to n Cal, most easily recognized as willows but notoriously difficult to separate by species. Following spp com and ± representative. Snow Willow, *S. nivalis*, one of 3 similar, prostrate, mat-forming, timberline shrubs in our mtns. Undergreen Willow, *S. commutata*, a com shrub, 3'–9' tall, of wet places below timberline. Scouler's Willow, *S. scouleriana*, a com shrub or small tree, 3'–35'+, along streams at low-mid el throughout the region. Also cf Pacific Willow, plate 51.

Birch Family (Betulaceae)

SITKA (SLIDE) ALDER, *Alnus sinuata*. Deciduous shrub gen 10'–15' tall. Lvs ovate, with sharply pointed but *not* spiny tip, to 4" long, double toothed. Catkins borne after lvs in sum. Fruit, clusters of 3–6 woody cones ca ½" long. Very com, moist places, avalanche tracks, in all our mtns, Alas to n Cal, e to Idaho. Mountain Alder, *A. incana*, similar but lvs have rounded, ± blunt, or only slightly pointed tip and catkins appear in spring before lvs; E CMtns-Cas. Cf Red Alder, plate 51.

BOG (SWAMP) BIRCH, *Betula glandulosa*. Deciduous shrub gen to 10' tall. Lvs oval, ca ¾" long, scalloped or toothed, thick and leathery. Bark reddish brown with white spots, smooth on trunk, sticky and warty on branches. Wet places, lowl-mont, Alas to Cal, e to RM, ne US, e Can. Cf Paper Birch, plate 51.

CALIFORNIA HAZELNUT, *Corylus cornuta* var *californica*. Deciduous shrub gen 3'–12' tall. Lvs ovate to heart shaped, coarsely toothed, ± hairy on both surfaces and pale beneath. Catkins yellow, borne before lvs. Fruit a hard-shelled edible nut in leafy cover. Com, lowl-low mont, BC to Cal, e to Idaho.

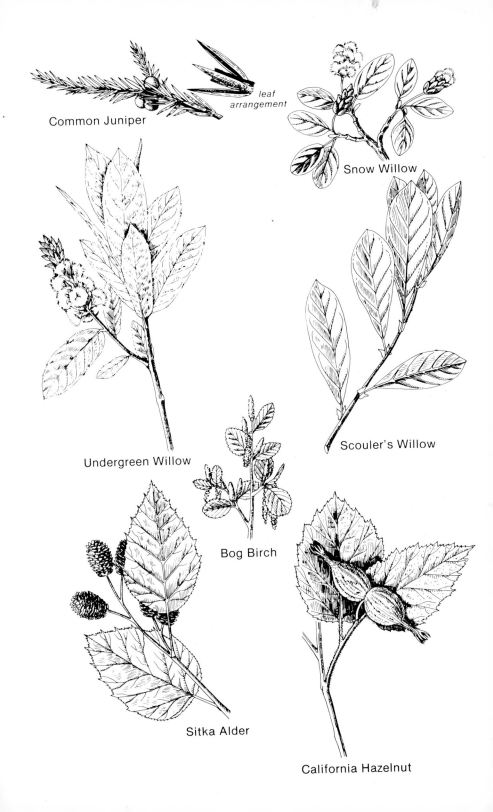

Common Juniper

leaf arrangement

Snow Willow

Undergreen Willow

Scouler's Willow

Bog Birch

Sitka Alder

California Hazelnut

PLATE 37

Barberry Family (Berberidaceae)

CASCADE OREGON-GRAPE, *Berberis nervosa.* Low, spreading shrub gen 4″–12″ tall, with persistent bud scales on stems. Lvs pinnately compound, oft 12″–20″ long, with 9–19 dull green, palmately veined, spiny toothed, leathery lflets. Flrs in erect racemes. Fruit a sour blue berry with powdery bloom, in grapelike clusters. Gen open woods, Vanc I e to Cas, s to Cal. Tall Oregon-grape, *B. aquifolium,* very similar but taller (3′–6′), with only 5–9 pinnately veined lflets. Creeping Oregon-grape, *B. repens,* is also a low, spreading shrub, but with 5–7 pinnately veined lflets; E Cas only.

Currant or Gooseberry Family (Grossulariaceae)

GOOSEBERRIES and CURRANTS, *Ribes* spp. Deciduous shrubs. Gooseberries have prickly fruits and stems; currants are without prickles; otherwise the two are similar. More than 24 spp in our range. The following spp are com and representative.

STINK CURRANT, *Ribes bracteosum.* Erect, oft straggly shrubs to 10′ tall. Lvs deeply 5– 7-lobed, ill-smelling, 2″–8″ wide, ½ as long, with yellow resin glands beneath. Flrs saucer shaped, greenish, in erect racemes with leafy bracts. Fruit a rough black berry, in erect clusters 4″–8″ long. Alas to n Cal, gen in and w of Cas.

SWAMP GOOSEBERY, *Ribes lacustre.* Shrub to 3′ tall, prickly with thorns. Twigs gray-hairy. Lvs 3– 5-lobed, toothed, 1″–2″ wide and long, sparsely downy to hairless. Flrs ca ¼″ diam, saucer shaped, usu 4+ in drooping racemes, the sepals reddish, longer than petals. Fruit a black, sticky, bristly berry. Moist places, mont-subalp, Alas to Cal, e to e Can, ne US.

GUMMY GOOSEBERRY, *Ribes lobbii.* Shrub 3′–6½′ tall, with 3-spined nodes on downy, not bristly, stems. Lvs 3– 5-lobed, toothed, less than 1¼″ wide, sticky haired beneath. Flrs ca 1″ long, with sharply reflexed red sepals ca 2× long as petals. Fruit a bristly, sticky, ± palatable purple berry. Moist places, lowl-mont, BC to Cal, mostly E Cas.

RED-FLOWERING CURRANT, *Ribes sanguineum.* Erect shrub 3′–10′ tall. Lvs 3–5-lobed, double toothed, densely hairy beneath, 1¼″–3¼″ wide. Flrs tubular, in showy racemes. Fruit an unpalatable black berry with whitish bloom. Various habitats, lowl-low mont, BC to Cal, coast to E Cas in Wn and Ore.

STICKY CURRANT, *Ribes viscosissimum.* Erect or spreading, oft straggly shrub to ca 6′ tall. Lvs 3– 5-lobed, 1″–3″ wide, glandular, gen hairless except occas on veins. Flrs tubular, greenish white tinged with pink, gen 6–12 in ± erect raceme with large bracts, sticky haired throughout. Fruit a black sticky-haired berry. Various habitats, lowl-subalp, mostly E Cas, BC to Cal; e to RM.

Hydrangea Family (Hydrangeaceae)

LEWIS' SYRINGA (MOCK-ORANGE), *Philadelphus lewisii.* Deciduous shrub ca 5′–15′ tall. Lvs ovate to oval, entire or minutely toothed, smooth or hairy, ca 1″–4″ long, with 3 main veins. Flrs fragrant, white, ca 1″ diam. Streamsides, talus, cliffs, rocky places, gen low-mid el, BC to n Cal, e to Idaho, Mont.

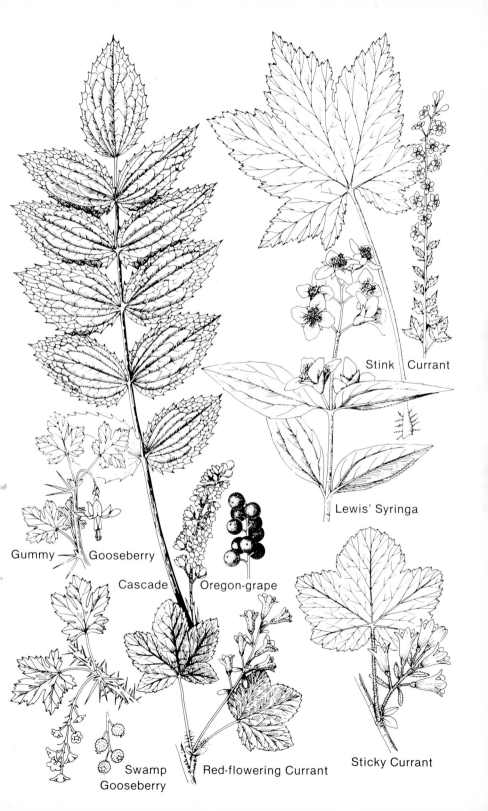

Stink Currant

Lewis' Syringa

Gummy Gooseberry

Cascade Oregon-grape

Swamp Gooseberry

Red-flowering Currant

Sticky Currant

146

PLATE 38

Rose Family (Rosaceae)

WESTERN SERVICEBERRY, *Amelanchier alnifolia*. Spreading or erect shrub, small tree, gen 3'–16' tall. Lvs alt, deciduous, petioled, oval to oblong or wedge shaped, usu toothed toward tip, ¾"–2" long, ± silky to hairless beneath. Flrs fragrant, white, ca 1" diam, 3–20 in short, erect racemes. Fruit an unpalatable reddish or black berry. Open woods, rocky places, lowl-subalp, Alas s to Cal and NMex, e to mid US.

BLACK HAWTHORN, *Crataegus douglasii*. Deciduous shrub, small tree, gen 3'–13' tall. Branches armed with sharp thorns usu ca ¾" long. Lvs oval to wedge shaped, petioled, the blades to 3" long, with sharp teeth or toothed and lobed at tip. Flrs white, ca ½" diam. Fruit small, dk purple "apples." Bark brown or gray, rough. In mtns, gen near water at low el, Alas to Cal, e to mid US and e Can.

MOUNTAIN-AVENS, *Dryas octopetala*. Prostrate, mat-forming shrub. Lvs ca 1" long, narrowly lancelike to oblong, deep green and wrinkled above, hairy and glandular beneath, the margins scalloped and rolled under. Flrs cream or white, 1" diam, with 7 – 8 petals. Fruit a showy head of plumed seeds. Gravel bars, talus, alp ridges, mdws, mont-alp, Alas to Wn Cas; e to e Can, ne US, s in RM to Colo, also ne Ore.

CREAMBUSH (OCEAN SPRAY), *Holodiscus discolor*. Deciduous shrub 1½'–10' tall. Lvs 1½"–3" long, shallowly lobed or toothed, hairy beneath. Flrs white, tiny, numerous in loose panicles 4"–7" long. Rocky places, open forest, lowl-low mont, BC to Cal, e to w Mont, Idaho, ne Ore.

OSOBERRY (INDIAN PLUM), *Oemleria (Osmaronia) cerasmiformis*. Deciduous shrub, 5'–16' tall. Lf blades 2"–5" long, entire, oblanceolate to elliptic, hairless above, paler and oft hairy beneath. Flrs small, greenish white, 5–10 per raceme from lf axils, fragrant. Fruit a bitter blue-black berry. Bark purplish brown. Stream banks, woods, BC to Cal, W Cas to coast.

OLYMPIC ROCKMAT, *Petrophytum hendersonii*. Matted shrublet. Lvs ± spoon shaped, entire, tufted, ± hairy. Flrs tiny, in dense spikelike racemes above lvs. Cliffs, talus, mid-high el, OMtns.

PACIFIC NINEBARK, *Physocarpus capitatus*. Spreading to erect deciduous shrub gen 6½'–13' tall. Lf blades 3– 5-lobed, 1"–4" long, doubly toothed, gen hairy beneath. Flrs ca ¾" diam, in corymbs terminating leafy twigs. Flrs replaced by reddish seed husks in sum. Bark peeling. Damp places, lowl-low mont, Alas to Cal, Cas to coast; n Idaho.

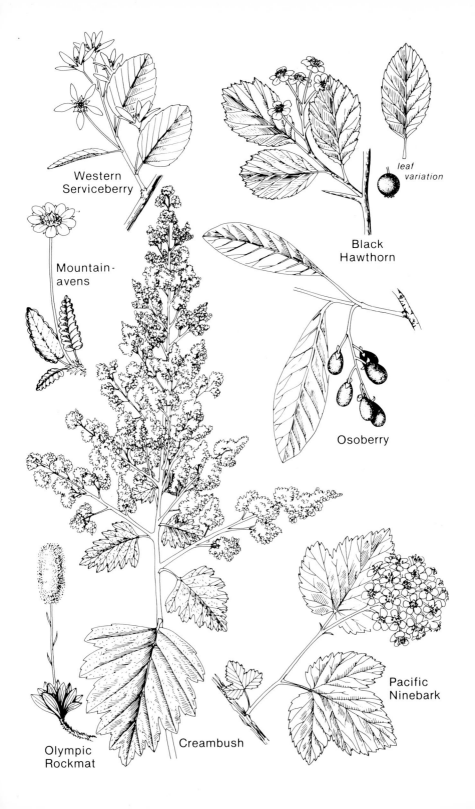

Western
Serviceberry

Mountain-
avens

Black
Hawthorn

leaf
variation

Osoberry

Pacific
Ninebark

Olympic
Rockmat

Creambush

PLATE 39

Rose Family (Rosaceae)

SHRUBBY CINQUEFOIL, *Potentilla fruticosa.* Spreading to erect shrub gen 4"–40" tall. Lvs pinnate, usu with 5 lflets ea to ¾" long, entire, silky haired. Flrs to 1" diam, yellow, showy, single in lf axils or in branched inflor. Bark reddish brown, shreddy. Rocky places, in our range mostly subalp, Alas to Cal, e to RM, e Can, ne US; Eurasia.

BITTER CHERRY, *Prunus emarginata* var *emarginata.* Multistemmed shrub gen 3'–13' tall. Lf blades ± elliptic or oblong, 1¼"–3" long, the margins finely toothed or scalloped, smooth to rather hairy. Flrs ca ¼" diam, white, 5–10 in loose inflor. Fruit a bitter, red to almost black cherry. Bark dk brown to reddish purple. Moist woods, streamsides, mainly in Cas, BC to Cal, e to RM. *P. e.* var *mollis,* gen a tree to 50' tall, occurs mainly w of the Cas from s BC to s Ore.

COMMON CHOKECHERRY, *Prunus virginiana.* Deciduous shrub, small tree, to 20' tall. Lf blades ± elliptic or oblong, 2"–4" long, fine-toothed, paler and downy or hairless beneath, with 2 knobby glands on petiole. Flrs in spikelike racemes gen 3"–5" long. Fruit a puckery red to black cherry, numerous in grapelike clusters. Low-mid el in our mtns; widespread in US and s Can.

ANTELOPE (BITTER) BRUSH, *Purshia tridentata.* Deciduous shrub gen 3'–6' tall. Lvs gen in fascicles, wedge shaped, 3-toothed at tip, to ¾" long, greenish above, densely gray haired beneath, the margins ± curled under. Flrs solitary, yellow, the calyx sticky haired. Fruit a downy "nutlet." Sagebrush steppe and ponderosa pine forest, E Cas, BC to Cal; widespread e to RM, s to NMex.

NOOTKA ROSE, *Rosa nootkana.* Shrub to gen 3'–6" tall, with thorns below ea lf. Lvs pinnate, usu with 5–9 oval or ovate toothed lflets, sticky haired beneath, the lf axis sticky, oft prickly. Flrs to 3½" diam, gen solitary, with persistent sepals. Fruit a rosehip crowned with sepals. Moist, gen wooded places, usu mont, Alas to Cal, e to RM. Baldhip Rose, *R. gymnocarpa,* ± similar but plant and flr (to 1" diam) both smaller, stems prickly, and rosehip without sepals.

RED RASPBERRY, *Rubus idaeus.* Shrub gen to 6½' tall. Branches bristly and spiny, the spines stout, straight. Lvs compound, the 3–5 lflets doubly toothed, gray-woolly beneath. Flrs white, less than ¾" diam, with petals shorter than sepals, in short, sticky, bristly racemes. Fruit a red raspberry. Widespread in N Amer and Eurasia. Blackcap Raspberry, *R. leucodermis,* has hooked spines and ± black berries.

THIMBLEBERRY, *Rubus parviflorus.* Erect, unarmed shrub to 10' tall. Lvs 4"–8" wide, palmate, gen 5-lobed, doubly toothed, velvety above and beneath. Flrs white, to 2" diam. Fruit a bland, rather dry red raspberry. Very com, open places and woods, lowl-subalp, Alas to s Cal, e to RM.

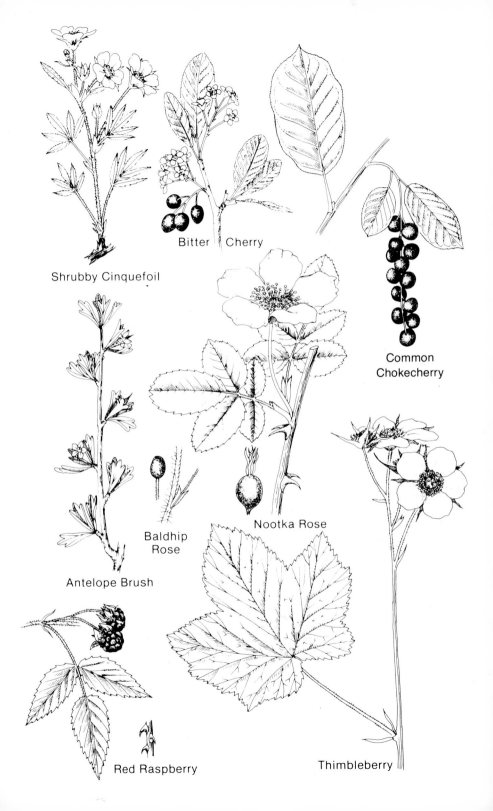

Shrubby Cinquefoil

Bitter Cherry

Common
Chokecherry

Baldhip
Rose

Nootka Rose

Antelope Brush

Red Raspberry

Thimbleberry

PLATE 40

Rose Family (Rosaceae)

SALMONBERRY, *Rubus spectabilis.* Shrub to 16' tall. Stems erect, weakly armed when young, unarmed with age. Lvs 3-compound, toothed. Flrs ca 1" diam, rosy pink, showy, usu solitary. Fruit salmon orange to red, sweet, bland. Moist places, lowl-mid-mtn, Alas to nw Cal, Cas to coast.

PACIFIC BLACKBERRY, *Rubus ursinus.* Trailing shrub. Branches spined. Lvs 3-compound or simple and 3-lobed, the lflets ± oval, toothed, downy. Flrs white or pale pink. Fruit a choice blackberry. Lowl-mont, BC to n Cal, e to Idaho.

SITKA MOUNTAIN-ASH, *Sorbus sitchensis.* Shrub to 13' tall in our region. Lvs pinnate with 7–11 elliptic to oblong lflets with blunt or rounded tips, oft red haired midvein and marginal teeth gen confined to upper ½-¾ of lflet. Flrs small, creamy, numerous in flat-topped inflor. Fruit a red berry with bluish cast from waxy bloom. Open, gen moist places, mont-subalp, Alas to n Cal, e to n RM. Cascade Mountain-ash, *S. scopulina,* very similar but lflets narrower, pointed at tip, oft white haired along midvein, finely toothed entire length, and the berries without waxy bloom.

SUBALPINE SPIRAEA, *Spiraea densiflora.* Deciduous shrub 8"–40" tall. Lvs ±oval, to 1½" long, the tips blunt or rounded and toothed. Flrs small, pink to red, numerous in dense, flat-topped inflor. Moist open places, rocky slopes, low-high mtns, BC to Cal; e to n RM. Douglas' Spiraea, *S. douglasii,* similar but inflor pyramidal.

Pea Family (Leguminosae)

SCOTCH BROOM, *Cytisus scoparius.* Deciduous shrub to 10' tall. Branches numerous, green, broomlike, strongly angled. Lvs compound near base of branches, simple above. Flrs irreg, sweetpealike, yellow, ca ¾" long, ± covering plant. Fruit a flattened pod. Com, roadsides, waste places, BC to Cal; introduced from Europe.

Crowberry Family (Empetraceae)

CROWBERRY, *Empetrum nigrum.* Spreading shrub to 6" tall. Branches ± woolly. Lvs needlelike, alt and whorled in 4s, ca ¼" long, sticky haired, grooved beneath. Flrs obscure, pinkish or purplish, 3-sepaled, no petals. Fruit a ± bitter black berry. Peat bogs, rocky places, Alas to n Cal, Cas to coast.

Sumac Family (Anacardiaceae)

POISON-OAK, *Rhus diversiloba.* Erect deciduous shrub to 6' tall or twining vine on tree trunks. Lvs compound, the 3 lflets gen toothed, lobed. Flrs greenish white, in axillary panicles. Fruit a white or brownish berry. Dry woods, open places, entirely w of Cas crest at low el, sw Wn to Baja. Poison-ivy, *R. radicans,* similar, found sparingly at low el, E Cas of Wn and Ore. Both cause contact dermatitis in most people.

Staff-tree Family (Celastraceae)

MOUNTAIN LOVER, *Pachystima myrsinites.* Evergreen shrub gen 8"–24" tall. Lvs opp, leathery, ± oblong or lancelike, toothed, hairless, ca 1" long.Flrs maroon, flat, 4-petaled. Gen open places at mid el in mtns, BC to Cal, e to RM.

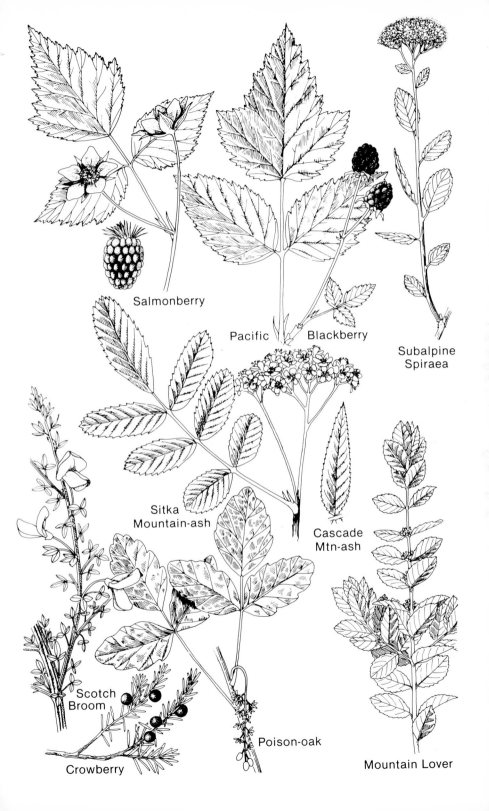

Salmonberry

Pacific   Blackberry

Subalpine
Spiraea

Sitka
Mountain-ash

Cascade
Mtn-ash

Scotch
Broom

Crowberry

Poison-oak

Mountain Lover

PLATE 41

Maple Family (Aceraceae)

VINE MAPLE, *Acer circinatum*. Deciduous shrub or small tree 3'–26' tall. Lvs 2"–6" wide, palmately 7– 9-lobed, doubly toothed, red or yellow in fall. Flrs white, red sepaled, in loose inflor. Fruit a double samara. Com, lowl-subalp, Alas to n Cal, E Cas to coast.

DOUGLAS' MAPLE, *Acer glabrum* var *douglasii*. Deciduous shrub or small tree to 25' tall. Lvs 1"–3" wide, palmate, 3– 5-lobed, red in fall. Flrs yellow, in panicle. Fruit a double samara. Moist places, lowl-mont, BC to Cal, e to Idaho and Mont.

Buckthorn Family (Rhamnaceae)

SNOW BUSH, *Ceanothus cordulatus*. Spreading shrub 3'–6½' tall. Stiff spiny twigs. Lvs ovate or elliptic, ± entire, to ¾" long, 3-veined, hairless or downy, green with bloom above, gray green beneath. Flrs small, white, fragrant, in dense inflor. Bark smooth, whitish. Dry forest openings, mid-high el, Cas, s Ore and Cal, throughout Cal.

DEER BRUSH, *Ceanothus integerrimus*. Shrub 3'–13' tall. Branches green or yellow; twigs smooth or hairy, flexible. Lf blades thin, oblong to ovate, entire, 3-veined, to 2¾" long, pale green and downy to smooth above, paler and usu downy beneath. Flrs white (pink or blue), fragrant, sticky, in dense inflor. Dry mont places, E Cas, Wn to Cal; s to Baja, e to NMex.

SQUAW CARPET (MAHALA MAT), *Ceanothus prostratus*. Prostrate shrub, mat forming. Lvs thick and fleshy, sharp toothed, to 1" long, pale glossy green above, finely haired beneath. Flrs tiny, blue, in umbellike inflor. Dry forest floor, E Cas, Wn to Cal.

REDSTEM CEANOTHUS (OREGON TEA-TREE), *Ceanothus sanguineus*. Erect deciduous shrub 5'–10' tall. Twigs flexible, smooth, reddish. Lf blades ± oval, to 4" long, nearly hairless, rarely shiny or sticky above, with small glandular teeth and deciduous stipules. Flrs white, fragrant, in compound inflor 4"–8" long. Dry open places in mtns, Cas, BC to Cal, e to Idaho and Mont. Tobacco Brush (Mountain Balm, Greasewood, Sticky Laurel), *C. velutinus,* similar but lvs evergreen, varnished and sticky above, and stipules tiny and persistent.

ALDERLEAF BUCKTHORN, *Rhamnus alnifolia*. Erect deciduous shrub to 5' tall. Lf blades ± oval, toothed, thin, bright green, ca 2½" long, with 5-7 pairs of parallel veins. Flrs without petals, greenish, 2–5 in stalkless umbels. Wet, brushy places, E Cas s to Cal, e to Atl.

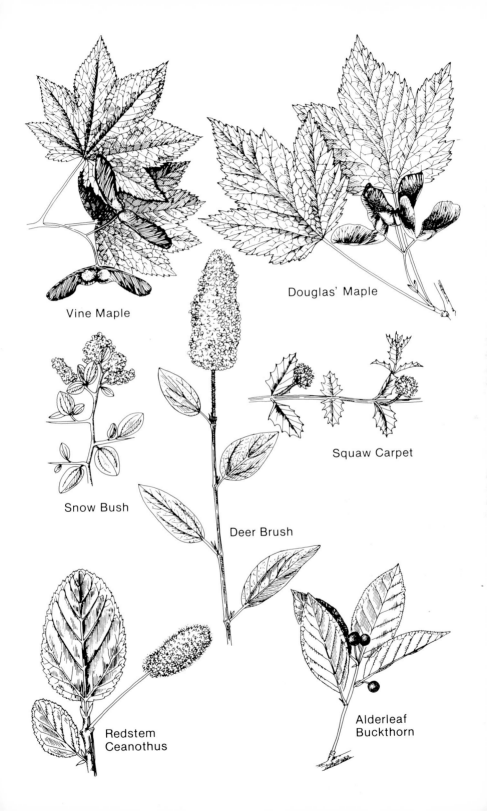

Vine Maple

Douglas' Maple

Snow Bush

Deer Brush

Squaw Carpet

Redstem
Ceanothus

Alderleaf
Buckthorn

PLATE 42

Ginseng Family (Araliaceae)

DEVIL'S CLUB, *Oplopanax horridum*. Deciduous shrub 3'–10' tall, with stems, petioles and lf veins densely armed with yellowish spines to ⅜" long. Lf blades palmately 7– 9-lobed, 4"–14" wide, toothed, long petioled. Flrs small, greenish white, in headlike umbels borne in inflor to 10" long. Fruit a bright red berry. Moist woods, streamsides, Alas s along coast and in mtns to s Ore, e to e Can, Michigan.

Dogwood Family (Cornaceae)

BUNCHBERRY DOGWOOD, *Cornus canadensis*. Low, trailing shrublet 2"–8" tall. Lvs ovate or elliptic, to 3" long, 4–7 in whorl below inflor. Flrs tiny, greenish, in head surrounded by 4 showy, gen white, petallike bracts. Fruit, red berries in tight clusters. Com, moist woods, Alas to Cal and NMex; e to e Can, ne US; Greenland, Asia.

RED-OSIER DOGWOOD, *Cornus stolonifera*. Shrub 6½'–20' tall, with some rooting lower stem. Lf blades ± oval, entire, to 4¾" long, ± hairy above, hairy or with powdery bloom beneath. Flrs tiny, white or bluish, in dense inflor. Bark reddish. Moist thickets, widespread in N Amer.

Silktassel Family (Garryaceae)

FREMONT'S SILKTASSEL, *Garrya fremontii*. Erect shrub 4'–10' tall. Lvs opp, elliptic to ovate or oblong, to 3½" long, entire, shiny yellow green above, paler beneath, oft hairy when young. Flrs in tassellike catkins. Woodland and brush, W Cas, Ore to Cal.

Figwort Family (Scrophulariaceae)

SHRUBBY PENSTEMON, *Penstemon fruticosus*. Shrub 6"–16" tall. Branches ascending from woody base. Lvs variable, ± elliptic or oval, entire or toothed, opp. Flrs lavender, bluish, purplish, occas white, 2-lipped, 1"–2" long, very showy. Fruit a capsule. Lowl-subalp, mostly E Cas, BC to Ore, e to Mont, Wyo.

Aster or Sunflower Family (Compositae)

BIG SAGEBRUSH, *Artemisia tridentata*. Erect evergreen shrub gen 16"–80" tall. Lvs wedge shaped, 3-toothed at tip, gray green with matted hairs above and beneath, alt, oft in fascicles. Flr heads with disk flrs only, numerous in large, loose inflor. E CMtns-Cas, BC to Cal; widespread in w US, BC to Mex.

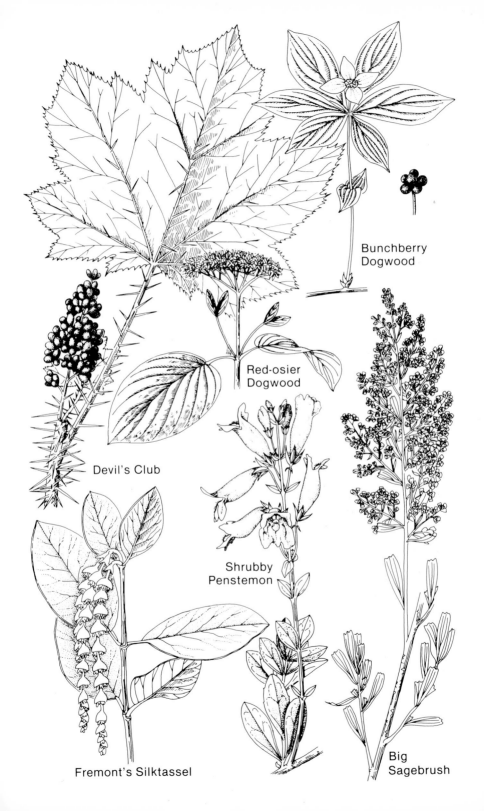

Bunchberry
Dogwood

Red-osier
Dogwood

Devil's Club

Shrubby
Penstemon

Big
Sagebrush

Fremont's Silktassel

PLATE 43

Heath Family (Ericaceae)

PINEMAT MANZANITA, *Arctostaphylos nevadensis.* Evergreen prostrate shrub to 8″ tall. Lvs oblong to spoon shaped, sharply tipped, to 1½″ long, thick and leathery. Flrs white, occas pink, ca ¼″ long, in short racemes. Fruit a smooth, dk brown berry. Bark reddish brown, peeling in strips. Dry woods, openings, Wn Cas to Cal, also ne Ore.

KINNICKINNICK, *Arctostaphylos uva-ursi.* Evergreen prostrate shrub to 6″ tall. Lvs spoon shaped or ovate, to 1″ long, rounded or blunt at tip, thick and leathery. Flrs white or pinkish, ca ¼″ long, in short racemes. Fruit a red berry. Bark reddish brown, shredding. Dry woods, openings, Alas to Cal, e to RM and e US.

GREENLEAF MANZANITA, *Arctostaphylos patula.* Erect shrub 3′–7′ tall. Lvs ovate to ± round, to 1¾″ long, hairless, entire. Flrs pinkish, ca ¼″ long, in dense panicles. Fruit a smooth, dk brown berry. Bark reddish brown, peeling. Gen dry forest, E Cas, s Wn to Cal, W Cas Ore and Cal; Cal mtns, e to RM.

WHITE MOUNTAIN-HEATHER, *Cassiope mertensiana.* Mat-forming shrub to 12″ tall. Lvs broadly lancelike, tiny, in 4 rows flattened to stems, rounded on back. Flrs white, 1 per stalk. Com, open areas, subalp-alp; Alas to Cal, e to RM. Four-angled Mountain-heather, *C. tetragona,* very similar but lvs grooved on back; Alas to NCas. Alaska Mountain-heather, *C. stelleriana,* similar but lvs alt, not flattened against stem; Alas s to Rainier.

COPPER BUSH, *Cladothamnus pyroliflorus.* Erect deciduous shrub 2′–7′ tall. Lvs spoon shaped, 1″–2″ long, sharply tipped, entire, pale green, hairless, occas with bloom. Flrs copper colored, to 1½″ diam. Bark peeling. Moist places, mont-subalp, Alas to n Ore, Cas to coast.

SALAL, *Gaultheria shallon.* Creeping or erect shrub gen 4″–80″ tall. Lvs thick, leathery, ovate, toothed, gen glossy, 2″–5″ long. Flrs bell shaped, white or pink, in sticky-haired inflor. Fruit a sweet, pungent black "berry." Com, forest, lowl-mont, E Cas to coast, BC to Cal.

ALPINE WINTERGREEN, *Gaultheria humifusa.* Prostrate shrublet scarcely 1¼″ tall. Lvs ± oval or round, to ¾″ long, entire or toothed. Flrs white, bell shaped, the calyx hairless. Fruit reddish. Subalp-alp, in all our mtns s to n Cal, e to RM. Slender Wintergreen, *G. ovatifolia,* similar but lvs larger and calyx red-hairy.

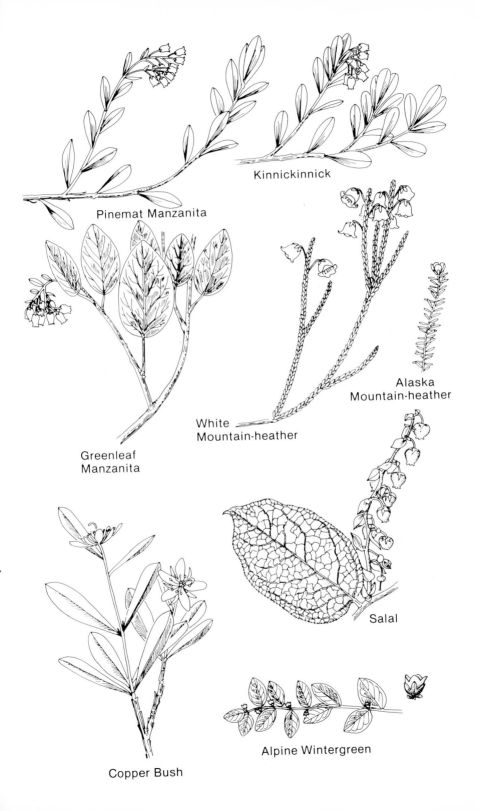

Kinnickinnick

Pinemat Manzanita

Alaska
Mountain-heather

White
Mountain-heather

Greenleaf
Manzanita

Salal

Copper Bush

Alpine Wintergreen

PLATE 44

Heath Family (Ericaceae)

ALPINE-LAUREL, *Kalmia microphylla.* Low, spreading shrub to 6″ tall. Lvs opp, dk green above, gray and downy beneath, ± oblong or elliptic, gen to ¾″ long. Flrs pink, saucer shaped, few in inflor. Wet mdws, bogs, subalp-alp, Alas to Cal, e to RM. Western Swamp-laurel, *K. occidentalis,* very similar but 4″–16″ tall and gen confined to low el sphagnum bogs.

MOUNTAIN LABRADOR-TEA, *Ledum glandulosum.* Erect shrub to ca 6½′ tall. Lvs ovate to elliptic, to 2″ long, dk green and smooth above, paler, mealy, and/or finely haired beneath. Moist, shady places. Flrs white. BC to Cal, e to RM. Bog Labrador-tea. *L. groenlandicum,* similar but lvs gen narrower and rusty-haired beneath.

FOOL'S HUCKLEBERRY (MENZIESIA), *Menziesia ferruginea.* Straggling deciduous shrub 1½′–6½′ tall. Lvs elliptic to obovate, 1½″–2½″ long, blue green and oft sticky above, whitish beneath, finely haired on both sides, alt but in whorllike groups. Flrs copper colored, urn shaped, with sticky calyx. Fruit a 4– 5-celled capsule. Com, moist places, lowl-subalp, Alas to Cal, e to RM.

RED MOUNTAIN-HEATHER, *Phyllodoce empetriformis.* Dwarf shrub 4″–16″ tall. Lvs needlelike, ca ½″ long, numerous on stems. Flrs pink, bell shaped, ca ¼″ long, single in lf axils near stem tips. Fruit a 5-celled capsule. Open places, gen subalp, Alas to Cal, e to RM. Brewer's Mountain-heather, *P. breweri,* with stamens extending beyond corolla, replaces this sp s of Shasta.

YELLOW MOUNTAIN-HEATHER, *Phyllodoce glanduliflora.* Shrub to 12″ tall. Lvs needlelike, ca ¼″ long, numerous on stems. Flrs yellow to greenish white, urn shaped, sticky-haired. Open places, gen subalp-alp, Alas to Ore, e to Can RM.

PACIFIC RHODODENDRON, *Rhododendron macrophyllum.* Evergreen, occas treelike shrub to 15′+ tall. Lvs leathery, oblong-elliptic, to 8″ long. Flrs white to rose purple, ca 1½″ long, tubular to bell shaped with flaring lobes, in dense, rounded, terminal inflor. Very showy. Drier woods, coastal forest, W Cas to coast, BC to nw Cal.

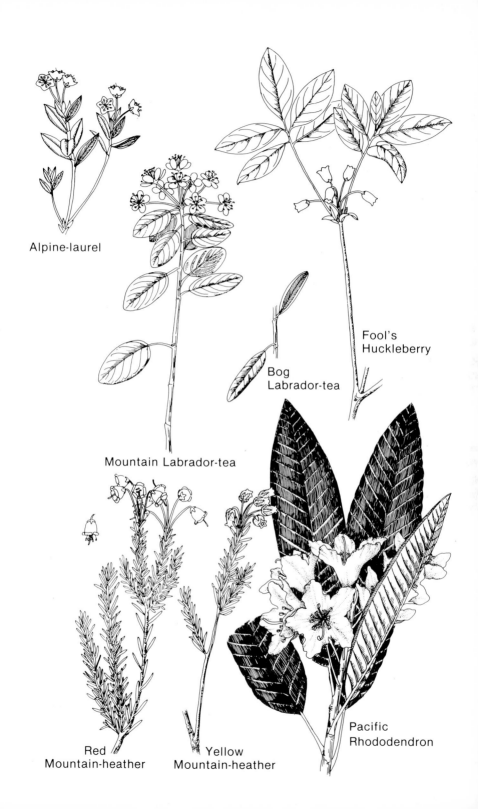

Alpine-laurel

Mountain Labrador-tea

Bog
Labrador-tea

Fool's
Huckleberry

Red
Mountain-heather

Yellow
Mountain-heather

Pacific
Rhododendron

PLATE 45

Heath Family (Ericaceae)

CASCADE AZALEA (WHITE RHODODENDRON), *Rhododendron albiflorum.* Deciduous shrub ca 3'–6½' tall. Twigs sticky haired. Lvs ± oval, dk green above, paler beneath, rusty-haired when young. Flrs white, ca ¾" diam, in axillary inflor. Moist places, mont-subalp, BC to Ore, e to Mont.

WESTERN AZALEA, *Rhododendron occidentale.* Deciduous shrub 3'–16' tall. Lvs elliptic to obovate, 1"–4" long, entire, slightly hairy. Flrs white, oft tinged pink or yellow at throat, ca 1½" long, 5–20 in terminal inflor. Moist places, low-mid el, Cas, s Ore to mtns of Cal.

ALASKA BLUEBERRY, *Vaccinium alaskense.* Deciduous shrub to 48" tall. Lvs ± elliptic, entire or minutely toothed, to 2⅜" long, dk green and slightly waxy above, paler beneath. Flrs urn shaped, bronzy pink, sharply constricted at mouth, with the pedicels straight, swollen just below flr. Fruit a choice, blue to black berry ca ¼" diam. Moist forest, lowl-mont, Alas to nw Ore, Cas to coast. Oval-leaved Blueberry, *V. ovalifolium,* is a com, very similar sp.

CASCADE BLUEBERRY, *Vaccinium deliciosum.* Low, oft matted deciduous shrub gen 6"–12" tall. Twigs greenish brown, circular in cross section. Lvs obovate, ⅝"–2⅜" long, thick, finely toothed above base, with powdery bloom beneath. Flrs pinkish, nearly spherical. Fruit a choice blue to black berry with bloom. Mont-alp, but esp subalp mdws, BC to n Ore, Cas to coast. Dwarf Bilberry, *V. caespitosum,* similar but lvs lack bloom beneath and flrs tubular.

THINLEAF BLUEBERRY, *Vaccinium membranaceum.* Shrub 3'–10' tall. Twigs slightly angled in cross section. Lvs ovate or oval, slender-pointed, 1"–2" long, toothed, bright green above, paler and sticky or with bloom beneath. Flrs yellowish pink, urn shaped. Fruit an extremely choice purplish berry. Com, open places, mont-subalp, BC to Cal, e to RM.

EVERGREEN HUCKLEBERRY, *Vaccinium ovatum.* Evergreen shrub 1½'–13' tall. Twigs hairy, branches very leafy. Lvs oval to ovate, leathery, glossy dk green above, sharply toothed. Flrs pink or white. Fruit a sweet purple or black berry. Coastal forest, lowl-low mont, W Cas to coast, BC to Cal.

RED HUCKLEBERRY, *Vaccinium parvifolium.* Open-branched deciduous shrub gen 3'–6' tall. Branches green, angled in cross section. Lvs oval to ± round, thin, entire, pale green, to 1" long. Flrs reddish or greenish. Fruit a red berry. Forest, esp on logs and stumps, lowl-low mont, BC to Cal, W Cas to coast.

GROUSEBERRY (WHORTLEBERRY), *Vaccinium scoparium.* Mat-forming shrub 4"–12" tall. Branches numerous, broomlike. Lvs ± ovate, gen smooth, finely toothed, ca ½" long. Flrs pink. Fruit a sweet, bright red berry. Woods, open places, subalp-alp, mostly E Cas, s BC to Cal; e to RM, S Dak. Dwarf Bilberry, *V. myrtillus,* similar but branches few and not broomlike.

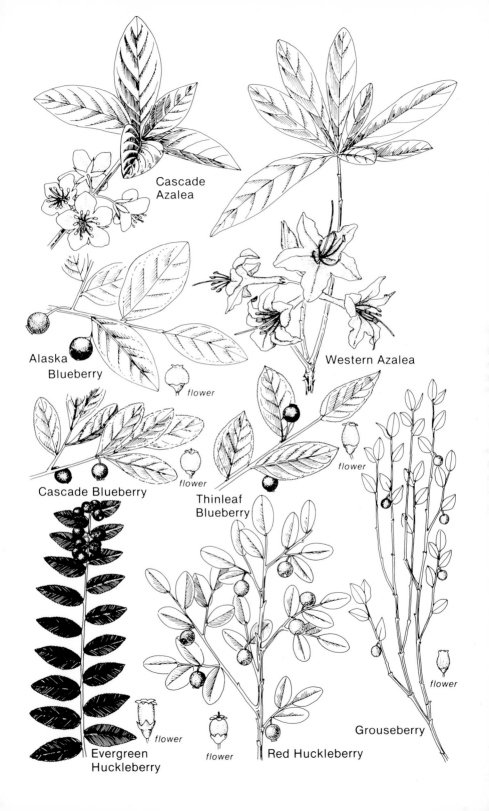

Cascade
Azalea

Western Azalea

Alaska
Blueberry

flower

Cascade Blueberry

flower

Thinleaf
Blueberry

flower

Evergreen
Huckleberry

flower

Red Huckleberry

flower

Grouseberry

flower

PLATE 46

Honeysuckle Family (Caprifoliaceae)

TWINFLOWER, *Linnaea borealis*. Creeping, herblike, evergreen shrublet with erect flr stalks to 4″ tall. Lvs opp, ± oval, to 1″ long, with a few shallow teeth or entire. Flrs pink, 2 on erect, forked stalk. Moist woods, N Amer s to Cal, Ariz, NMex, e to W Virginia.

ORANGE (TRUMPET, NORTHWEST) HONEYSUCKLE, *Lonicera ciliosa*. Trailing or twining woody vine with stems to 20′ long. Lvs opp, the upper pair perfoliate, ± oval, entire, with waxy bloom beneath. Flrs orange, funnel shaped, to 1¾″ long. Woods, thickets, low-mid el, s BC to n Cal, e to w Mont. Purple Honeysuckle, *L. hispidula*, also a woody vine but flrs pink to purple and some lvs have united stipules.

BLACK TWINBERRY (HONEYSUCKLE), *Lonicera involucrata*. Erect shrub 3′-13′ tall. Lvs opp, oval to spoon shaped, 2″-5″ long, abruptly pointed at tip. Flrs yellow, occas tinged red, ca 1″ long, in 2s from lf axils. Fruit a pair of black berries. Widespread in mtns of w N Amer. Utah Honeysuckle, *L. utahensis*, similar but lvs rounded at tip and berries red, ± united at base. Double Honeysuckle, *L. conjugalis*, has broadly elliptic to ovate lvs and pairs of red purple flrs.

BLUE ELDERBERRY, *Sambucus cerulea*. Shrub occas treelike, gen 6½′-13′ tall. Lvs opp, long petioled, pinnate, with 5-11 lancelike or elliptic, toothed, oft asymmetrical lflets to 6″ long. Flrs white or creamy, small, numerous in flat-topped inflor. Fruit a dk blue berry with whitish bloom. Open areas, lowl-mont, BC s to Mex, e to RM.

COAST RED ELDERBERRY, *Sambucus racemosa* var *arborescens*. Large, occas treelike shrub 10′-20′ tall. Lvs like those of Blue Elderberry. Flrs creamy white, in pyramidal inflor. Fruit a red berry without powdery bloom. Moist woods, open places, BC to Cal, e to Atl. Black Elderberry, *S. r.* var *melanocarpa*, similar to Blue Elderberry but fruit lacks bloom.

COMMON SNOWBERRY, *Symphoricarpos albus*. Erect shrub gen 3′-6½′ tall. Lvs opp, the blades gen ⅝″-2″ long, ± elliptic, entire or toothed, smooth above, smooth or sparsely hairy beneath. Flrs bell shaped, hairy inside, pinkish. Fruit a white berry, oft persisting after lvs. Woods, thickets, open areas, lowl-mont, widespread in N Amer. Western Snowberry, *S. occidentalis*, has style longer than petals. Mountain Snowberry, *S. oreophilus*, has funnel-shaped flrs. Creeping Snowberry, *S. mollis*, is a trailing shrub.

MOOSEWOOD VIBURNUM (HIGH-BUSH CRANBERRY, SQUASHBERRY), *Viburnum edule*. Straggling shrub 1½′-8′ tall. Lvs opp, the blades 2″-3″ long, gen 3-lobed and palmately veined. Flrs white, few per inflor. Fruit a smooth, sour, edible red berry. Moist places, Alas to e Can, s to n Ore and Colo. Snowball, *V. opulus*, has inflor with outer flrs much larger than inner ones. Oval-leaved Viburnum, *V. ellipticum*, has oval toothed lvs.

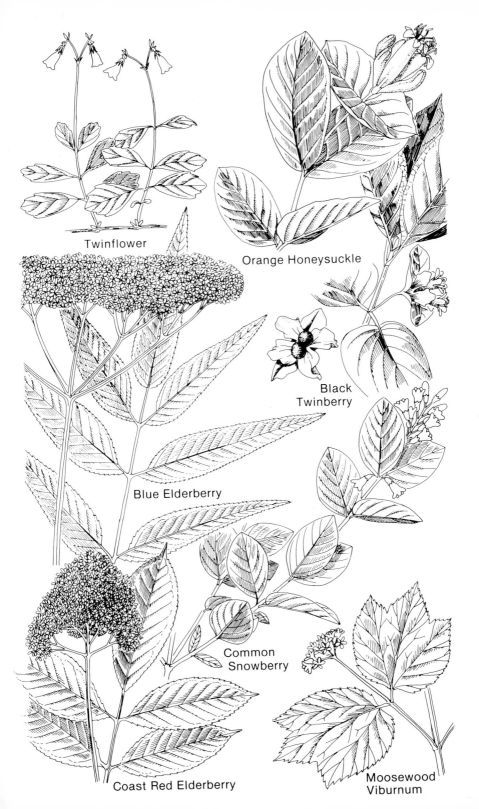

Twinflower

Orange Honeysuckle

Black
Twinberry

Blue Elderberry

Common
Snowberry

Coast Red Elderberry

Moosewood
Viburnum

TREES

This section includes only those native plants that characteristically occur as trees in our region. Woody plants that are normally shrubs, becoming tree-like in certain favored places, are discussed in the preceding section. These include Scouler's willow, Sitka alder, California hazelnut, black hawthorn, osoberry, vine maple, Douglas' maple, red-osier dogwood, blue elderberry, and coast red elderberry.

Roughly two-thirds of the more than 40 species of trees found in our mountains are conifers, which overwhelmingly dominate the forests. Although several broadleaf trees occur regularly in these forests, they form a distinctly minor element except where logging or fire has removed the conifers. Conifers have needlelike or scalelike leaves and bear naked seeds in cones. Native conifers in the region belong either to the pine family or the cypress family. Members of the pine family—pines, larches, true firs, Douglas-fir, hemlocks, and spruces—have needlelike leaves and woody cones with conspicuous scales. Members of the cypress family—incense-cedar, western red-cedar, Alaska yellow-cedar, and junipers—usually have overlapping, scale-shaped leaves. The single exception in our region is common juniper, a shrub that has awl-shaped leaves. Junipers have fleshy berrylike cones; other members of the cypress family have small, few-scaled woody cones.

Broadleaf trees have true flowers and bear their seeds in a fleshy capsule, or ovary, at the base of each flower. Most broadleaf trees in our region are deciduous, losing their leaves each autumn; a few are evergreen, retaining their leaves through the winters. Evergreens, it should be noted, lose their leaves, but not all at one time. Most broadleaf trees in the region have tiny, inconspicuous flowers, which may be borne singly or, more commonly, in elongated inflorescences called catkins.

Catkins consist entirely of either male or female flowers. Some trees, such as red alder, bear catkins of both sexes on the same plant; others, such as willows, bear male and female catkins on different plants. In identifying broadleaf trees, it is important to attend to leaves, flowers, and fruit (see figures 3 through 6).

For information on the organization and use of the species accounts and illustrations, as well as for a list of the abbreviations used in the accounts, see the Introduction.

PLATE 47

Pine Family (Pinaceae)

LODGEPOLE PINE, *Pinus contorta.* Evergreen conifer gen 30'–90' tall, 1'–3' diam, with slender, pyramidal crown. Needles 2 per bundle, 1¼"–2½" long, deep or yellow green, oft curved. Cones 1½"–2½" long, oft persistent on branches. Bark orange brown to dark gray, flaky. Poor or disturbed sites, all forest zones, in all our mtns but Vanc I; widespread in w N Amer. Shore Pine, *P. contorta* var *contorta,* gen 25'–30' tall, with rounded crown and crooked branches. Low el, W CMtns, also along coast s to Cal.

PONDEROSA (WESTERN YELLOW) PINE, *Pinus ponderosa.* Evergreen conifer gen 150'–180' tall, 3'–4' diam, with irreg crown. Needles 3 per bundle, ca 4½"–10" long, yellow green. Cones 3"–5½" long, ea scale ending in out-turned prickle. Bark reddish or golden brown, in large scaly plates; dk brown and furrowed on young trees. E CMtns-Cas s to Cal; W Cas, s Ore to Cal; widespread in w US s to Mex. Jeffrey Pine, *P. jeffreyi,* very similar but cones larger, with in-turned prickles. Cal Cas s in SNev to s Cal.

KNOBCONE PINE, *Pinus attenuata.* Evergreen conifer gen 30'–80' tall, 1'–2' diam, with sparse, irreg crown. Needles 3 per bundle, 3"–7" long, yellow green. Cones 3¼"–6" long, in persistent whorls on branches. Bark dk gray, fissured; smooth on young trees. Rare and local on poor soils and rocky sites in mtns of s Ore and Cal.

WHITEBARK PINE, *Pinus albicaulis.* Dwarfed or ± contorted evergreen tree gen 20'–50' tall, 1'–2' diam; or sprawling shrub near timberline. Needles 5 per bundle, usu 1½"–2¾" long, dull green, clustered at branchlet tips. Cones deep red to purple, 1½"–3¼" long, persistent on branches. Bark whitish gray, ± smooth. Subalp forest, CMtns-Cas s to SNev, e to RM.

SUGAR PINE, *Pinus lambertiana.* Evergreen conifer gen 175'–200' tall, 3'–5' diam, with irreg crown of long, spreading branches. Needles 5 per bundle, 2¾"–4" long, blue green. Cones 11"–18" long, without prickles. Bark brown or gray, furrowed on trunk, smooth on branches. Cas, cen Ore to Cal and Baja.

WESTERN WHITE (SILVER) PINE, *Pinus monticola.* Evergreen conifer gen 100'–175' tall, 3'–5' diam, with narrow crown. Needles 5 per bundle, 2"–4" long, blue green. Cones 5"–9" long, without prickles. Bark gray, thin, checked. All forest zones, esp W Cas, s BC to cen Cal, e to Idaho.

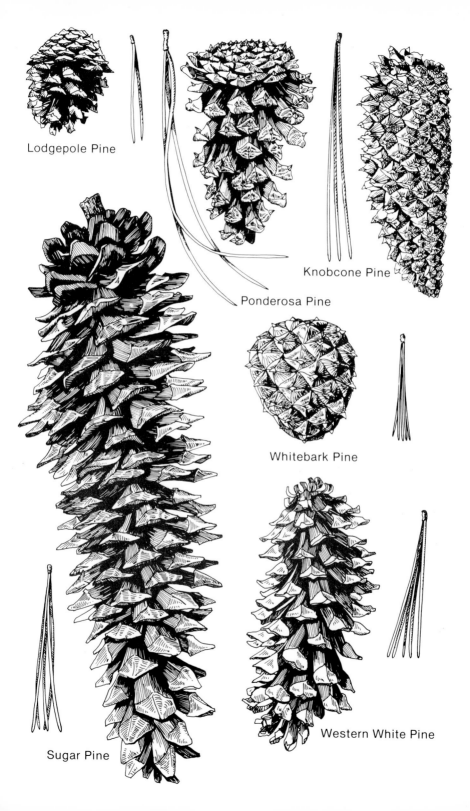

Lodgepole Pine

Knobcone Pine

Ponderosa Pine

Whitebark Pine

Western White Pine

Sugar Pine

PLATE 48

Pine Family (Pinaceae)

GRAND (LOWLAND) FIR, *Abies grandis.* Evergreen conifer to 290' tall, 1½'–3½' diam, with slender pointed crown. Needles 1¼"–2" long, flat, horizontal in 2 ranks, blunt or notched at tips, twisted at base, shiny dk green above, 2 silver lines beneath. Cones yellow green to green, ca 2"–4" long, erect on upper branches. Bark grayish to light brown, smooth or shallowly ridged. All forest zones, s BC to Cal.

WHITE FIR, *Abies concolor.* Evergreen conifer to 225'–260' tall, 1½'–4' diam, with slender, pointed crown. Needles 1½"–2¾" long, flat, twisted at base, blunt or pointed at tip, gen spreading in 2 ranks but upturned on cone-bearing branches, blue green with 2 silvery lines on both sides. Cones yellow to greenish purple, 3"–5" long, erect on upper branches. Bark dark gray or brownish furrowed. Cas, Ore to Cal; widespread in w US s to Mex.

SILVER (CASCADES, LOVELY) FIR, *Abies amabilis.* Evergreen conifer to 230' tall, 2'–4' diam, with spirelike crown of drooping branches. Needles ¾"–1½" long, flat, mostly notched at tip, shiny dk green and grooved above, striking silver and ridged beneath, crowded on stem, longer ones horizontal, shorter ones brushed forward. Cones gen dark purple, 3"–6" long, erect on upper branches. Bark gray, usu smooth. All forest zones, W CMtns-Cas, higher el, E CMtns-Cas, se Alas to n Cal.

NOBLE FIR, *Abies procera.* Evergreen conifer to 230' tall, 2½'–4' diam, with tapering, rounded crown and short horizontal branches. Needles 1"–1½" long, plump, blue green with whitish lines above and below, grooved above, notched or pointed at tip, brushed up and crowded on branchlets. Cones 4½"–7" long, with papery bracts extending beyond scales, erect on upper branches. Bark gray brown, readily flaking. Cas, cen Wn to s Ore; rare in n Cal.

RED FIR, *Abies magnifica* and SHASTA FIR, *A. m.* var *shastensis.* Evergreen conifers gen 60'–120' tall, 1'–4' diam, with open, tapering crown rounded at tip. Needles ¾"–1½" long, 4-sided, gen spreading in 2 ranks, blue green with whitish lines. Cones 6"–8" long, erect on upper branches, with bracts either inconspicuous (Red Fir) or extending beyond scale tips (Shasta Fir). Bark cinnamon red, deeply furrowed. Cas, cen Ore s to Shasta (Shasta Fir); Shasta s in SNev (Red Fir).

SUBALPINE (ALPINE) FIR, *Abies lasiocarpa.* Evergreen conifer gen 50'–100' tall, 1'–2½' diam, with slender, spirelike crown and short horizontal branches extending to base of tree; or prostrate shrub near timberline. Needles 1"–1¾" long, gen upturned, dk green with white lines on both sides. Cones dark purple, 2¼"–4" long, erect on upper branches. Bark gray, furrowed. Gen subalp forest, Alas s to s Ore and in RM to Ariz; e OMtns but not Vanc I.

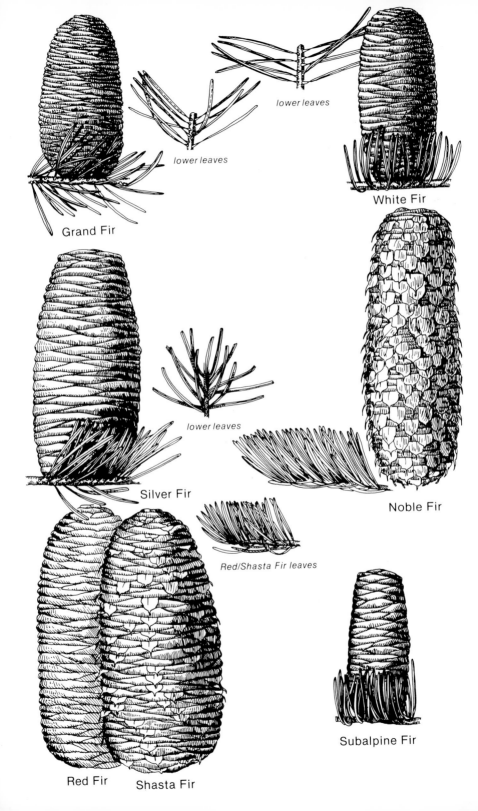

lower leaves

lower leaves

Grand Fir

White Fir

lower leaves

Silver Fir

Noble Fir

Red/Shasta Fir leaves

Red Fir Shasta Fir

Subalpine Fir

PLATE 49

Pine Family (Pinaceae)

SITKA SPRUCE, *Picea sitchensis.* Evergreen conifer to 230' tall, gen 3'-8' (to 16') diam, with open, conical crown. Needles to 1" long, pale to bluish green, stiff, sharp, flattened above, keeled beneath, on all sides of a twig from persistent woody pegs. Cones tan, 2"-3½" long, with papery scales. Bark grayish brown or purple-scaly; smooth and gray on young trees. Coast and low-mtns, Alas to nw Cal, e to Wn Cas.

ENGELMANN SPRUCE, *Picea engelmannii.* Evergreen conifer to 160' tall, 1'-3' diam, with narrow, pointed crown of short branches. Needles to 1" long, 4-sided, stiff, sharp, dk green, on all sides of a twig from persistent woody pegs. Cones 1½"-2½" long, tan, with papery scales. Bark brownish or reddish, scaly. All forest zones, mostly E CMtns-Cas, BC to s Ore; rare in n Cal; also RM s to Ariz, NMex.

WESTERN HEMLOCK, *Tsuga heterophylla.* Evergreen conifer gen 100'-160' tall, 3'-5' diam, with narrow crown and drooping leader. Needles to ¾" long, flat, rounded at tips, very short stalked, spreading in 2 rows, dk green with 2 white lines beneath, forming flat sprays. Cones to 1" long, hanging from twig ends. Bark brown, furrowed and cross-ridged. Low-mid el forests, W CMtns-Cas to coast, locally E CMtns, Cas s to Wn, s to cen Ore in Cas, to Cal along coast, n to Alas.

MOUNTAIN HEMLOCK, *Tsuga mertensiana.* Evergreen conifer gen 30'-100' tall, 1'-3' diam, with conical crown and drooping leader; or a sprawling shrub near timberline. Needles to ¾" long, curved, ½-round to nearly 4-sided, on all sides of twig, blue green with white lines on both sides. Cones 1"-3" long, purplish to brown. Bark dark, purplish- or reddish-scaly, furrowed; young twigs hairy. Gen subalp, all our mtns, Alas to Cal; also n RM.

ALPINE (SUBALPINE) LARCH, *Larix lyallii.* Deciduous conifer gen 30'-50' tall, 1' diam, with short branches and irreg crown. Needles gen 1"-1⅜" long, clustered on spur twigs and at cone bases or in spirals on leader twigs, 4-sided, stiff, pale blue green, gold in autumn. Cones to 2" long, upright, with hairy purplish scales and bracts extending well beyond scales. Bark thin, brown, scaly. Subalp, E Cas, BC to cen Wn; also n RM.

WESTERN LARCH, *Larix occidentalis.* Deciduous conifer to 260' tall, 1½'-3' diam, with narrow conical crown. Needles to 1¾" long, 3-sided, pale green, gold in autumn, clustered on spur twigs and at cone bases or in spirals on leader twigs. Cones to 1½" long, erect, with hairy scales and slender, pointed bracts extending beyond scales. Bark cinnamon brown, scaly, becoming furrowed and plated. E Cas, BC to n Ore; also n RM.

DOUGLAS-FIR, *Pseudotsuga menziesii.* Evergreen conifer to 290' tall, 2'-8' diam, with compact conical crown. Needles to 1⅜" long, flattened, roundly tipped, twisted at base, yellow green to dark or blue green, on all sides of twigs. Cones 2"-3½" long, pale brown, with 3-pointed bracts extending beyond scales. Bark dk brown, corky, furrowed. In all but highest forest zones, BC s in all our mtns to Cal, e to RM.

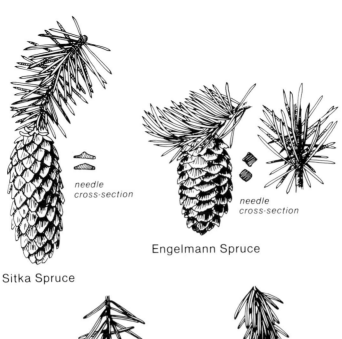

needle cross-section

needle cross-section

Sitka Spruce

Engelmann Spruce

Western Hemlock

Mountain Hemlock

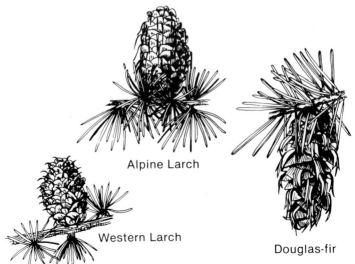

Alpine Larch

Western Larch

Douglas-fir

PLATE 50

Cypress Family (Cupressaceae)

WESTERN RED-CEDAR, *Thuja plicata.* Evergreen conifer gen 150'-200' tall, 2'-10' diam, with conical crown, downswept spraylike branches, deeply fluted and buttressed trunk. Lvs scalelike, to ⅛" long, shiny green, in alt pairs tightly pressed to stems, the lateral pair keeled. Cones ca ½" long, erect on curved stalks, in clusters, with 10-12 sharply pointed scales. Bark cinnamon red, fibrous, shreddy. Low-mid el forests, W CMtns-Cas to coast, Alas to nw Cal; also E CMtns-Cas in BC and Wn; e to n RM.

ALASKA YELLOW-CEDAR, *Chamaecyparis nootkaensis.* Evergreen conifer gen 65'-130' tall, 2'-3' diam, with droopy branches and leader and shaggy foliage; or a prostrate shrub at timberline. Lvs scalelike, sharp, ca ⅛" long, bluish green, in alt pairs loosely pressed to stems. Cones spherical, ½" diam, erect with 4 or 6 rounded, pointed scales. Bark gray, fibrous, shreddy. All our mtns, upper mont-subalp, Alas to n Cal.

INCENSE-CEDAR, *Calocedrus decurrens.* Evergreen conifer gen 60'-150' tall, 3'-4' diam, with columnar crown ± rounded at apex. Lvs scalelike, to ½" long, shiny green, in alt overlapping pairs tightly pressed to stems, the lateral pair keeled. Cones oblong, to 1" long, hanging from twig ends, with 6 opp woody scales. Bark cinnamon red, deeply furrowed, fibrous, shreddy. Mont forest, Cas from Hood s to Cal; Cal mtns to Baja.

WESTERN JUNIPER, *Juniperus occidentalis.* Evergreen conifer gen 13'-30' tall, 1'-3' diam, with short, thick trunk, open crown of spreading branches, oft twisted and gnarled. Lvs scalelike, tiny, mostly in 3s, ea with glandular dot, tightly pressed to stems, gray green. Cones berrylike, ca ¼" diam, soft and juicy, blue black with whitish bloom. Bark cinnamon red, fibrous, shreddy. Ponderosa Pine Zone and lower, E Cas, Ore to Cal; e Wn to Cal, e to Idaho, Nev.

ROCKY MOUNTAIN JUNIPER, *Juniperus scopulorum.* Evergreen conifer to ca 30' tall, 1½' diam, with short, oft divided trunk and rounded, bushy crown. Lvs scalelike, pointed, tiny, in alt overlapping pairs, forming 4-sided twigs. Cones berry-like, ¼" diam, soft and juicy, sweetish, bright blue with whitish bloom. Bark brown or reddish brown, fibrous, shreddy. Local in e OMtns, E Cas, Wn, elsewhere; BC and w US e to mid US and s to Mex. Baker Cypress, *Cupressus bakerii,* an open, conical tree to 100' tall, with small, gray green, scalelike lvs in alt pairs, with glandular dot exuding resin. Rare and local on rocky or poor soils in mtns of s Ore, n Cal.

Yew Family (Taxaceae)

PACIFIC (WESTERN) YEW, *Taxus brevifolia.* Evergreen tree or large shrub, gen 16'-30' tall, 2' diam, with rounded crown. Lvs needlelike, flat, sharply tipped, dk green above, pale green with 2 white lines beneath, spreading in 2 ranks. Seed brown, 1 borne in a scarlet gelatinous cup, resembling a berry. Bark purplish brown, thin, smooth, with papery scales. Lowl-mont forests, oft moist places, se Alas to cen Cal, also se BC and Idaho.

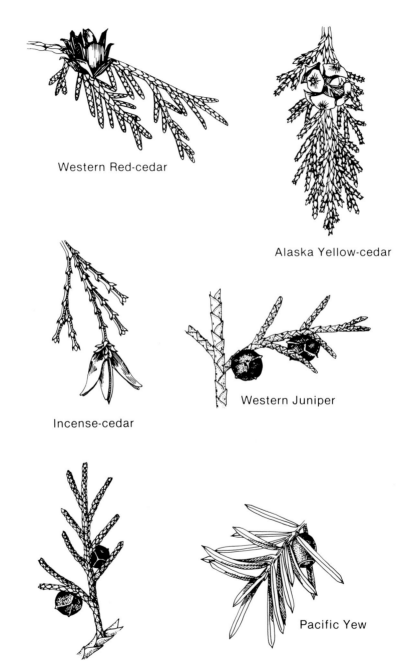

Western Red-cedar

Alaska Yellow-cedar

Incense-cedar

Western Juniper

Rocky Mountain Juniper

Pacific Yew

PLATE 51

Willow Family (Salicaceae)

QUAKING (TREMBLING) ASPEN, *Populus tremuloides.* Deciduous broadleaf tree gen to 50' tall, 1'-1½' diam, with narrow, open crown. Lvs 1¼"-3" long, nearly as wide, with short, pointed tip, shiny green above, dull below, yellow in fall, the margins toothed, on flat, twisted petiole. Flrs brownish catkins, M and F on separate trees. Fruit a small conical capsule. Bark pale gray to white, gen smooth, with black, warty blisters. Moist places, E CMtns-Cas s to Cal; widespread in Can and in n and w US.

BLACK COTTONWOOD, *Populus trichocarpa.* Deciduous broadleaf tree gen 60'-125' tall, 2'-4' diam, with open crown. Lvs long petioled, broadly ovate with rounded base and pointed tip, the blade 2"-8" long, 1¼"-4¾" wide, the margins wavy or toothed, dk green above, whitish, oft with rusty veins, beneath, yellow in fall. Flrs purplish catkins, M and F on separate trees. Fruit ca ¼" diam, round, hairy, 3-parted capsule. Bark dk gray, furrowed. Moist places, s Alas to s Cal, e to RM.

PACIFIC WILLOW, *Salix lasiandra.* Deciduous tree or shrub 6½'-40' tall, 1' diam, with broad irreg crown. Lvs narrowly lancelike, mostly 2½"-6" long, ½"-1¼" wide, shiny green above, paler below, toothed, short petioled. Flrs ± erect catkins 1½"-4" long. Fruit a reddish brown, hairless capsule ca ¼" long. Moist places, low-mid el, Alas to s Cal, NMex.

Birch Family (Betulaceae)

RED ALDER, *Alnus rubra.* Deciduous broadleaf tree gen 30'-60' tall, 1'-2' diam, with rounded crown. Lvs ovate to elliptic, 3"-6" long, 2"-3" wide, dk green and ± hairless above, gray green and rusty haired beneath, the margins double-toothed and slightly curled under, the veins parallel, straight. Flrs tiny, the M yellowish, in catkins, the F reddish, in woody cones. Bark pale gray or whitish, thin, ± smooth. Streamsides, damp places, low-mid el, W CMtns-Cas to coast, se Alas to Cal.

PAPER BIRCH, *Betula papyrifera.* Deciduous broadleaf tree to 65' tall, 1'-2' diam, with narrow, open crown. Lf blades ovate, 2"-4" long, 1½"-2" wide, double-toothed, smooth to hairy and dull dark green above, usu hairy and yellow green beneath, yellow in fall. Flrs tiny, M in droopy catkins, F in erect woody "cone." Bark chalky white with dk crosslines, thin, peeling, papery. Low el, Vanc I, CMtns, W Cas s to n Wn; widespread in n N Amer. Water Birch, *B. occidentalis,* a droopy shrub or small tree to 25' tall, with shiny, dk brown bark; local, rare, streamsides, E Cas s to Cal.

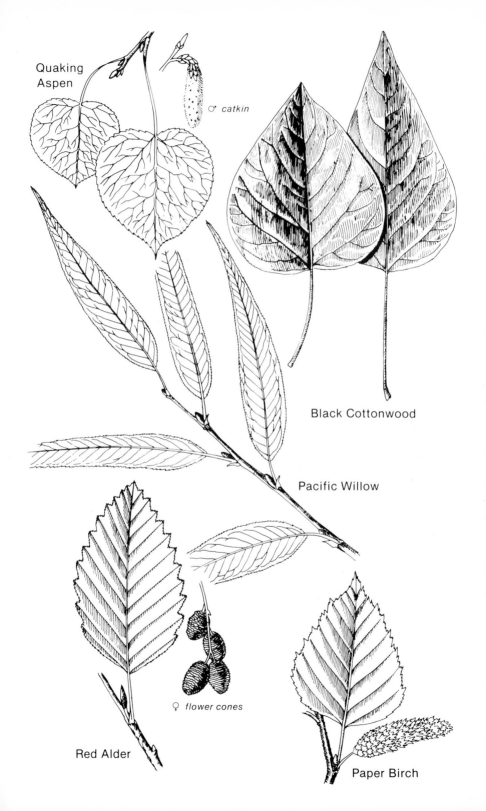

Quaking Aspen

♂ catkin

Black Cottonwood

Pacific Willow

Red Alder

♀ flower cones

Paper Birch

PLATE 52

Beech Family (Fagaceae)

GOLDEN (GIANT) CHINQUAPIN, *Castanopsis chrysophylla*. Evergreen broadleaf tree gen 20'–80' tall, with straight trunk and spreading crown; or a large shrub. Lvs lancelike or oblong, ca 2"–5" long, ½"–1½" wide, leathery, shiny dk green above, golden-scaly beneath, the margins entire, slightly curled under. Flrs tiny, white, in erect catkins near twig tips. Fruit a spiny bur. Bark reddish brown, deeply furrowed. Cas, Ore-Cal, n to sw Wn, s in mtns of Cal.

OREGON (WHITE, GARRY) OAK, *Quercus garryana*. Deciduous broadleaf tree gen 30'–70' tall, 1'–2½' diam, with rounded, spreading crown; occas shrubby. Lvs ± oblong, deeply lobed, leathery, shiny dk green above, pale and gen hairy beneath. Fruit an acorn to ¾" long. Bark gray, furrowed or scaly. Low el, oft with Ponderosa Pine, Cas, s Wn to Cal; s in SNev, w of Cas, BC to Cal.

BLACK (KELLOGG) OAK, *Quercus kelloggii*. Deciduous broadleaf tree gen 30'–80' tall, 1'–3' diam, with large branches and broad, irreg crown. Lvs ± oblong, deeply lobed, ea lobe with bristly teeth, shiny dk green above, paler and oft hairy beneath. Fruit an acorn to 1½" long. Bark dk brown, thick, furrowed. Low-mid el forests, with Ponderosa Pine, Cas, cen Ore s through SNev.

Rose Family (Rosaceae)

WESTERN (PACIFIC, OREGON) CRABAPPLE, *Pyrus fusca*. Deciduous broadleaf tree or shrub 10'–40' tall and to 1' diam. Lvs ovate, elliptic, or lancelike, the blade 1½"–3½" long, ¾"–1½" wide, occas 3-lobed at tip, shiny green above, paler and hairy beneath, orange or red in fall, the margins toothed. Flrs to 1" diam, white or pink. Fruit a sour yellow or red apple to ¾" diam. Bark gray, ± smooth. Mostly along coast, but in mtns to about 2500', se Alas to n Cal, CMtns-Cas to coast.

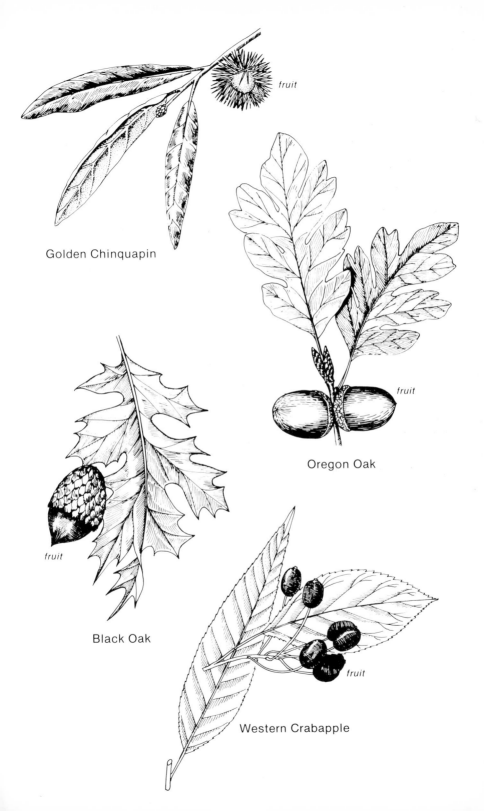

Golden Chinquapin

fruit

Oregon Oak

fruit

Black Oak

fruit

Western Crabapple

fruit

PLATE 53

Maple Family (Aceraceae)

BIGLEAF (BROADLEAF, OREGON) MAPLE, *Acer macrophylla*. Deciduous broadleaf tree to 100' tall, 1'–2½' diam, with broad, rounded crown. Lvs opp, deeply 5-lobed, 4"–12" long and wide, shiny green above, paler and hairy below, yellow in fall, with small lobes and teeth on margins, petioles to 10" long. Flrs fragrant, ¼" diam, yellow, in drooping inflor at twig ends. Fruit a brown, double samara, with stiff yellow hairs. Bark dk gray, furrowed. Moist places, low-mid el in all our mtns, BC to Cal. Cf shrubby maples, plate 41.

Buckthorn Family (Rhamnaceae)

CASCARA BUCKTHORN (CASCARA SAGRADA), *Rhamnus purshiana*. Small deciduous broadleaf tree or large shrub to 35' tall, 1' diam, with rounded crown. Lvs elliptic, finely toothed, the blade 2"–6" long, 1"–2½" wide, parallel veined, dull green and ± hairless above, paler and slightly hairy below, yellow in fall. Flrs bell shaped, greenish, ca ¼" diam. Fruit a small red to black, sweet, juicy "berry." Bark gray or brown, ± fissured and scaly, thin. Coast and lower mtns, BC to n Cal, also n RM.

Dogwood Family (Cornaceae)

PACIFIC (WESTERN FLOWERING) DOGWOOD, *Cornus nuttallii*. Deciduous broadleaf tree to 60' tall, 2' diam, with narrow to rounded crown. Lvs opp, elliptic, 2½"–4½" long, shiny green above, paler and woolly beneath, reddish in fall, with ± wavy margins. Flrs tiny, greenish, set amid 4–7 large, showy, white, petallike bracts. Fruit elliptic, ½" long, mealy, and bitter. Bark brown, scaly. Moist places, low-mid el, sw BC to s Cal.

Heath Family (Ericaceae)

MADRONE (MADRONA, ARBUTUS), *Arbutus menziesii*. Evergreen broadleaf tree gen 20'–80' tall, 1'–4' diam. Lvs elliptic, thick and leathery, glossy green above, 3"–6" long. Flrs urn shaped, creamy to pink, in branched inflor. Fruit a small, mealy red or orange "berry." Bark cinnamon red, very thin and smooth, peeling off in strips. Dry sites in forest, lowl-low mont, W CMtns-Cas, s BC to Cal.

Olive Family (Oleaceae)

OREGON ASH, *Fraxinus latifolia*. Deciduous broadleaf tree to 80' tall, 2'–3' diam, with slender trunk and narrow crown. Lvs opp, pinnately compound, 5"–14" long, with gen 5–7 lflets, ea 3"–6" long, obovate, pale green above, hairy below, yellow or brown in fall. Flrs tiny, greenish, in small inflor. Fruit a brown samara ca 1½" long. Bark dk gray or brown, furrowed. Locally along streams, low-mid el, Cas, s Wn to Cal, w to coast, s to cen Cal.

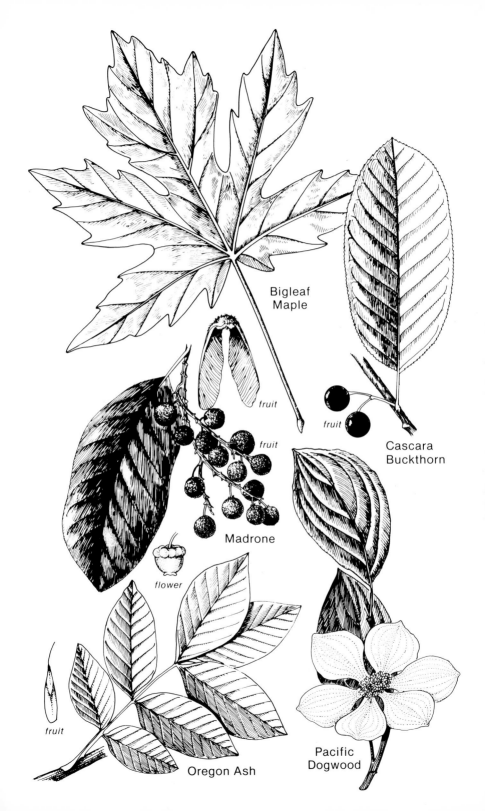

Bigleaf Maple

Cascara Buckthorn

fruit

fruit

fruit

Madrone

flower

Oregon Ash

fruit

Pacific Dogwood

Part III

THE ANIMALS

7

BUTTERFLIES

Butterflies are scaly-winged insects of the order Lepidoptera. They are divided into two major groups: true butterflies and skippers. Skippers are typically small, rather drab, mothlike butterflies with triangular wings and stout, hairy bodies. Though quite common, skippers on the whole are difficult to separate by species unless one is thoroughly familiar with their anatomy and behavior. They are represented in this chapter only by a few fairly common, more or less typical, examples.

Butterflies, like all insects, have bodies composed of three segmented sections: head, thorax, and abdomen. In adults the head includes two club-shaped antennae, two compound eyes, two sensory organs, or *palpi*, one on each side of the mouth, and a long, coiled, tubular proboscis for sipping flower nectar or other liquids. The thorax is the stout middle section of the body. It consists of three segments, each bearing a pair of five-jointed legs. In addition, the middle and rear segments each bear a pair of wings. The abdomen is the slender rear portion of the body. It consists of 11 segments, not all of which may be visible to the unaided eye. Butterflies breathe through *spiracles*, a series of minute openings located along the body. Attached to the end of the abdomen are the genitals: the ovipositor of the female and the claspers of the male.

Butterfly wings are membranous and densely coated with overlapping scales that come off as "dust" when the insect is carelessly handled. The scales determine the color and pattern of the wings either by pigmentation or light refraction. Some scales are modified into hairs. In male butterflies certain scales may also secrete *pheromones*, distinctly scented chemicals that probably play an important role in mate recognition and courtship.

After mating, female butterflies lay their eggs either singly or in rows or clusters, usually on the plants that will serve as food for the hatched larvae. The eggs of most species hatch within a few days. Certain species, however, overwinter in egg form, with the larvae emerging the following spring.

Butterfly larvae are caterpillars. They are smooth-skinned though often adorned with hairs, bristles, or horns. Caterpillars possess simple eyes, powerful mandibles for chewing vegetation, spinnerets for producing silky thread used to attach themselves to plants or to join leaves into shelters, three pairs of legs near the front, and five pairs of prolegs farther back.

As a caterpillar grows it molts several times, reaching full size in from a few days to several months, depending on the species. During the final molt it transforms into a pupa by developing a hard, mummylike case called a chrysalis. During the pupal stage, which also may last from a few days to several months, the caterpillar undergoes a radical anatomical reorganization, losing its jaws and wormlike body as it becomes an adult. Although various species may overwinter as eggs, larvae, or adults, most do so as pupae, emerging as adults in the spring.

The creature we normally think of as a butterfly is the adult insect. Upon emergence, its wings and legs are completely folded and shrunken, but they quickly expand as fluid is pumped throughout the body. While the role of the caterpillar is to eat and grow, that of the adult is reproduction. Its distinctive colors and patterns are probably important in mate recognition. The ability to fly allows the insects to track one another down over relatively large areas and assists the female in dispersing her eggs. Many species have elaborate courtship rituals featuring flight displays and other distinctive behavior. Copulation often lasts several hours, and fertilization is internal.

In warm regions most species produce several broods a year. At the other extreme, certain arctic and alpine species may require two years to produce a single brood, and adults may therefore be abroad only on alternating years.

Each species has a limited flight period during which most or all adults are abroad. The flight period for each species is fairly constant from year to year but may vary according to locale and weather. A long, cold winter can delay emergence of butterflies in the spring, and a mild winter followed by warmer weather can hasten their appearance. A cool, damp summer, as often occurs in our mountains, can inhibit a year's flight entirely.

As a rule the butterfly season begins in April or May on the west side of the Cascades and ends in September or October. On the warmer, drier east side of the range the season begins a month earlier and ends a month later. May and June are the best months for finding butterflies at lower elevations. July and August are best for seeking butterflies in the high country.

The most important factor influencing the distribution of butterflies is the presence of suitable food plants. The larvae of most butterfly species are limited to one plant or to a group of closely related plants. Some species tolerate a wider variety but still have certain preferences. Adult butterflies also prefer certain nectar plants but are generally less finicky. In their pursuit of nectar, butterflies perform the important function of cross-pollinating plants. Indeed, some plant species depend primarily on certain butterflies. Some adult butterflies, however, rarely visit flowers but instead relish such delicacies as tree sap, rotten fruit, dung, and aphid honeydew. Since most butterflies are rather weak fliers, they will normally occur only in the vicinity of both larval and adult food plants.

Butterfly habitats must also have adequate sunlight, moisture sources, suitable terrain for courtship, and appropriate conditions for overwintering eggs, larvae, pupae, or adults. In the mountains such places include sub-alpine parklands and the open pine forests of the eastern Coast Mountains and Cascades. Relatively few butterflies inhabit the shady conifer forests of the coastal region, where wildflowers and sunlight are both less common.

There are about 700 species of butterflies in North America north of Mexico, of which more than 130 occur in our mountains. The majority, however, are difficult to separate by species without collecting specimens for in-hand inspection. To discourage this practice simply for the purpose of identifying a species, this chapter focuses only on those species that are sufficiently large or distinct to allow identification "on the wing," as it were. The several groups of small or otherwise indistinct butterflies are therefore represented only by one or two common and rather typical species. Because careless handling will result in a butterfly's death, the casual observer, to whom this chapter is directed, should be content to identify difficult species by genus or family alone. If one wishes to pursue butterflies as a serious hobby, several excellent field guides are listed in the bibliography. No collecting, however, is allowed in national or provincial parks without special permit.

The term *food* as used in the species accounts, refers to larval food. The flight period for each species is given in months, and refers to the appearance of adults throughout the species' given range. The actual flight period at any given locale, however, may well be shorter than that indicated. As a rule butterflies appear earlier in the flight period at lower elevations and on the west side of the Coast Mountains-Cascade crest; later they appear at higher elevations and east of the mountains. The flight period will also vary from year to year and place to place, depending on local conditions.

Scientific names conform to "A Catalogue/Checklist of the Rhopalocera of North America North of Mexico" by Lee D. Miller and F. Martin Brown in *Memoir of the Lepidopterists' Society*, No. 2, 1981. For general information on the organization and use of the species accounts and illustrations, as well as for a list of the abbreviations used in the accounts, see the Introduction.

PLATE 54

Swallowtail Family (Papilionidae)

CLODIUS PARNASSIAN, *Parnassius clodius.* WS 2½"–3". Note gray-and-black-checked white butterfly with red spots on HW only. Food, mainly Bleeding Heart. Forest, mdws, lowl-subalp, se Alas to cen Cal, e to RM states. June-mid-Sept. Phoebus Parnassian, *P. phoebus,* very similar but red spots on *both* FW and HW.

ANISE SWALLOWTAIL, *Papilio zelicaon.* WS 2½"–3". Note broad yellow mid-wing band. Food, parsley family. All habitats but dense forest, lowl-alp, BC to Baja, e to mid US. May-Sept.

SHORT-TAILED BLACK SWALLOWTAIL, *Papilio indra.* WS 2"–3½". Note narrow yellow band on mostly black wings. Food, parsley family. Many habitats, lowl-subalp, widespread in w N Amer. Apr-Aug.

WESTERN TIGER SWALLOWTAIL, *Pterourus rutulus.* WS 2¾"–4". Note esp large size and black-striped yellow wings with 1 "tail" at tip of ea HW. Food, various hardwoods. Moist, wooded places, BC to Baja, e to RM and just beyond. May-Sept. Two-tailed Tiger Swallowtail, *P. multicaudatus,* very similar but larger, with 2 "tails" on ea HW; lower E Cas only.

PALE TIGER SWALLOWTAIL, *Pterourus eurymedon.* WS 3"–3¾". Note black stripes on white or creamy ground color. Food, alders, Chokecherry, Creambush, *Ceanothus.* Forest streams, brush, lowl-subalp, BC and Mont s to Baja and NMex. May-Aug.

Brush-footed Butterfly Family (Nymphalidae)

MOURNING CLOAK, *Nymphalis antiopa.* WS 3"–3½". Note chocolate brown butterfly with yellow wing margins. Food, willows, cottonwoods, other hardwoods. Open woods, forest openings, widespread in n hemis; also S Amer. All months.

LORQUIN'S ADMIRAL, *Basilarchia lorquini.* WS 2¼"–2¾". Note black wings with white midwing band and orange FW tips. Food, willows, cottonwoods, other hardwoods. Open places, streamsides, cen BC, Albta, s to Baja, Idaho, ne Nev. June-Sept.

Milkweed Butterfly Family (Danaidae)

MONARCH, *Danaus plexippus.* WS 3½"–4". Note large size and bright burnt orange wing with black veins and black margins with white dots. Food, milkweeds. Uncom in our range, esp w of CMtns-Cas; widespread in N Amer. June-Sept.

Clodius Parnassian

Phoebus Parnassian

Anise Swallowtail

Short-tailed Black Swallowtail

Western Tiger Swallowtail

Pale Tiger Swallowtail

Monarch

underside

upperside

Lorquin's Admiral

Mourning Cloak

PLATE 55

White Butterfly Family (Pieridae)

PINE WHITE, *Neophasia menapia*. WS ca 1¾". Note FW's black leading edge and white-spotted black tip; F's HW oft dark lined above; M's HW dark lined only beneath, F's orange- or red-lined beneath. Food, conifers. Forest, s BC, Albta, s to s Cal, NMex, e to mid US. Apr-Aug.

VEINED (MUSTARD) WHITE, *Artogeia napi*. WS ca 1½". Note wings ± clear white above, creamy to yellowish beneath with or without dk veins. Food, mustard family. Forest, woods, clearings, lowl-subalp, Alas to e Can, ne US, s to Ariz, n Cal; in our region mostly W CMtns-Cas. Several other similar whites in our area; difficult to distinguish in flight. Apr-Aug.

SARA'S ORANGE-TIP, *Anthocaris sara*. WS ca 1½". Note bright orange FW tips; F occas yellow above. Food, mustard family. Forest clearings, mdws, woods, se Alas to Baja, e to RM. Apr-Aug.

ALFALFA (ORANGE) SULPHUR, *Colias eurytheme*. WS 1½"-2⅜". Note orange wings with black borders. Food, pea family. Open places, low-high el, widespread in N Amer. Apr-Sept.

WESTERN SULPHUR, *Colias occidentalis*. Both sexes similar to Alfalfa Sulphur counterparts but lemon yellow above. Food, pea family. Mdws, clearings, low-high el, se Alas to SNev, in and w of W CMtns-Cas (only sulphur on Vanc I). Difficult to distinguish from several other very similar sulphurs in our range. June-Aug.

Satyr Family (Satyridae)

OCHRE (NORTHWEST) RINGLET, *Coenonympha ampelos*. WS 1"-2". Note clear buffy yellow to ochre color above. Food, grasses. Mdws, forest clearings, other grassy places, s BC to Ore, n Nev, Idaho; more com, E Cas. May-Sept.

LARGE WOOD NYMPH, *Cercyonis pegala*. WS 2"-2⅞". Note large size and 1 or 2 large eyespots on brown FW. Food, grasses. Wet grassy places, pine-oak woodlands and pine forest, lower E Cas, BC, Wn, n Ore, E and W Cas, s Ore, Cal; widespread in N Amer but gen absent from Northwest coast and Gulf Coast. Other wood nymphs in our range are much smaller. July-Aug.

ALPINES, *Erebia* spp. WS 1¾"-2". Note above dk brown wings with russet or orange band surrounding small dk eyespots. Food, grasses. Mdws, clearings, gen subalp-alp, all our mtns but Vanc I. June-Aug. Vidler's Alpine, *E. vidleri*, has broad, irreg orange bands above, checked wing fringes and grayish HW band beneath. Common Alpine, *E. epipsodea*, very similar but has smooth russet bands above; lacks checked wing fringes and gray HW band beneath; only alpine s of Snoqualmie Pass, Wn.

CHRYXUS ARCTIC, *Oeneis chryxus*. WS 1¾"-2". Above, note tan color and 2-3 eyespots; beneath, note broad dk band across HW. Food, grasses. Mdws, forest clearings, subalp-alp, in all our mtns, Alas s to Wn; in RM s to NMex. June-Aug. Nevada Arctic, *O nevadensis*, very similar but larger (WS 2"-2½") and lacks *broad* dk band across HW beneath. Melissa's Arctic, *O. melissa*, smaller (WS ±1¾"), gen lacks eyespots, smoky gray to dull tan (BC, N Cas).

♂ upperside

♂ upperside

upperside

♀ upperside   *♀ underside*

first brood   second brood
underside

underside

Pine White   **Veined White**   **Sara's Orange-tip**

♂ upperside   *♀ upperside*

Alfalfa Sulfur

♂ upperside

Western Sulfur

Ochre Ringlet

♀ upperside

♂ upperside

Large Wood Nymph

Vidler's Alpine   **Common Alpine**   **Chryxus Arctic**   **Melissa's Arctic**

PLATE 56

Brush-footed Butterfly Family (Nymphalidae)

LARGE FRITILLARIES, *Speyeria* spp. WS 1⅝"–3". Note orange wings (yellow only in F Great Spangled Fritillary, *S. cybele*) with black spots, bars, and chevrons; large, oft silver orbs beneath; and relatively large size (cf *Clossiana* Fritillaries below). 8 spp in our range, all very similar and ± variable in appearance. With some practice, 3 spp can gen be distinguished in the field, but beginners will do well to identify these insects by genus alone. Food, violets. Various habitats in all our mtns.

SMALL FRITILLARIES, *Clossiana* spp. WS 1⅛"–2". Smaller than *Speyeria* Fritillaries, but otherwise similar above. The 2 most common *Clossiana* Fritillaries in our mtns—Western Meadow Fritillary, *C. epithore,* and Titania's Fritillary, *C. titania*—may be distinguished by underside of wings (see illustrations). Mdws, clearings, low-high el, in all our mtns.

FIELD CRESCENTSPOT, *Phyciodes campestris.* WS ca 1¼". Above, wings black with orange and yellow marks; beneath, note orange FW, paler HW. Food, asters. Open places, mid-high el, Alas, n Can, s to Cal, Mex, mid US. July-Aug. Pearly Crescentspot, *P. tharos,* similar beneath but above, wings dk orange with dark marks and borders. Mylitta Crescentspot, *P. mylitta,* lighter, brighter, more banded above, and HW is white-banded, not yellow, beneath. Pallid Crescentspot, *P. pallida,* of E Cas foothills, like Mylitta but larger (WS 1¼"–1¾") and with large black spot on lower margin of FW beneath.

CHECKERSPOTS, *Occidryas* spp and *Charidryas* spp. WS ca 1½". 5 spp in our region, all so similar and variable as to defy identification in the field. Recognizable as a group by numerous red, orange, and/or yellow checks on dark field.

SATYR ANGLEWING, *Polygonia satyrus.* WS ca 2". Note ragged wings, lack of white spots above, pale mottled brown beneath. Food, stinging nettle. Various habitats, esp near water, BC to e Can, s in w US. All months. Similar spp are the Zephyr Anglewing, *P. zephyrus,* (mottled gray beneath), Faun Anglewing, *P. faunus* (mottled gray and dk brown beneath), and Oreas Anglewing, *P. oreas* (very dk brown to nearly black beneath).

MILBERT'S TORTOISESHELL, *Aglais milberti.* WS ca 2". Note distinctive vertical, red-orange, and yellow bands. Food, nettles. Most habitats, low-high el, n Can to s Cal, e US. All months.

CALIFORNIA TORTOISESHELL, *Nymphalis californica.* WS ca 2". Note broad, dk brown marginal bands across FW and HW. Food, *Ceanothus,* other shrubs. Open areas, BC to Cal, e to mid US. All months.

WESTERN PAINTED LADY, *Vanessa annabella.* WS 1¾"–2". Note above, orange bar near FW tip, blue eyes along HW margin; beneath, 5 eyes along HW margin. Food, mallows, nettles. CMtns-Cas crest to coast, BC to Baja. Painted Lady, *V. cardui,* has white, not orange, bar near FW tip and black dots along HW. American Painted Lady, *V. virginiensis,* similar to *V. annabella* above, but beneath has 2 large eyes on HW and large pink area on FW.

Mormon Fritillary
Speyeria mormonia

underside
Hydaspe Fritillary
Speyeria hydaspe

♀

LARGE FRITILLARIES

Great Spangled Fritillary
Speyeria cybele

upperside **W. Mdw. Fritillary** *underside*

und.
Titania's Fritillary

upperside
Field Crescentspot

Checkerspot

upperside *underside*
Mylitta Crescentspot

upperside
Pearly
Crescentspot

underside
Field

Satyr Anglewing

Milbert's Tortoiseshell

Calif. Tortoiseshell

upperside
W. Painted Lady

upperside
Painted Lady

underside
Amer. Painted Lady

PLATE 57

Metalmark Family (Riodinidae)

MORMON METALMARK, *Apodemia mormo.* WS ¾"-1¼". Note small size and bright checkered pattern. Food, wild buckwheats. Dry, open, rocky places, lower E Cas; widespread in w US s to Mex. July-Oct.

Gossamer Wing Butterfly Family (Lycaenidae)

BLUES, several genera. WS ca ½"-1"+. Tiny active butterflies, the M gen various shades of blue, the F usu brown or coppery; both gen white or pale beneath. More than a dozen spp in our range, most very difficult to distinguish on the wing.

COPPERS, several genera. WS ca ½"-1"+. Tiny active butterflies, the M gen coppery or gold above, the F drabber; both white, gray, orange, tan, or brown beneath. Ca a dozen spp in our range, most difficult to distinguish on the wing.

NELSON'S HAIRSTREAK, *Mitoura nelsoni.* WS ⅞"-1". Note dk gray brown or rusty brown color above, brown tinged with pink or lilac beneath, with ± distinct, light band on FW and HW. Food, Western red-cedar, Incense-cedar. Forest, BC to Baja, W CMtns-Cas to coast. May-June. Johnson's Hairstreak, *M. johnsonii,* very similar but rarer and not tinted with lilac or pink beneath. Several other hairstreaks in our range, most gen brown or coppery above, brown, gray, silvery, gold, or green beneath.

WESTERN PINE ELFIN, *Incisalia eryphon.* WS ¾"-1". Note chocolate brown to orange-brown color above; gray and brown beneath, with bands of black and white spots and chevrons. Food, pines. Mtn forests and clearings, BC to Cal and NMex; e to Albta, ne US. Apr-June. Brown Elfin, *I. augustinus,* is plain brown beneath. Moss Elfin, *I. mossii,* is two-toned brown and gray beneath.

Skipper Family (Hesperidae)

SILVER-SPOTTED SKIPPER, *Epargyreus clarus.* WS 1¾"-2⅜". Note above yellowish spots on FW; beneath, large silver spot on HW. Food, legumes. Most habitats, low-mid el, BC to e Can, s to Baja, Florida. May-July.

ARCTIC SKIPPER, *Carterocephalus palaemon.* WS ¾"-1¼". Note small size, brown and orange checkered pattern above, creamy spots on HW beneath. Food, grasses. Forest clearings, subalp-alp mdws, Alas, Can, n US s to cen Cal, Wyo, ne US. May-July.

ALPINE CHECKERED SKIPPER, *Pyrgus centaureae.* WS ⅞"-1¼". Note dk brown wings checked with white spots above. Food, unknown. Alp zone, CMtns, NCas; e to e Can, ne US. July. Common Checkered Skipper, *P. communis,* similar but not alp. Two-banded Checkered Skipper, *P. ruralis,* distinctly bluish.

ORANGE SKIPPERS, several genera. WS about 1". At least 7 spp of small orange skippers in our range, most very similar and difficult to identify.

NORTHERN CLOUDY-WING, *Thorbyes pylades.* WS ca 1½". Note 2 slim, triangular white bars on dark FW. Food, pea family. Dry open forest, E Cas, widespread in N Amer. One of nearly a dozen small- to medium-sized dark skippers in our range. May-July.

Mormon
Metalmark

♂ *upperside*
Northern Blue

♀ *upperside*
Northern Blue

underside

underside
Silvery
Blue

underside
Greenish
Blue

underside
High Mtn.
Blue

underside
Common
Western
Blue

upperside   *upperside*   *underside*
Lupine Blue
♂   ♀

underside
Spring
Azure

♂ *upperside*   *underside*
Lustrous Copper

upperside *upperside* *underside*
Mariposa Copper

underside
Purplish
Copper

underside
Lilac-
Bordered
Copper

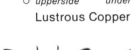

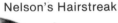

upperside   *underside*

Nelson's Hairstreak

und.
Gray
Hairstreak

und.
Johnson's
Hairstreak

und.
Calif.
Hairstreak

upperside   *underside*
Western
Pine Elfin

upperside   Silver-Spotted Skipper   *underside*

upperside

underside
Arctic Skipper

Alpine Checkered
Skipper

Orange Skipper

Northern Cloudy-wing

8

TROUT AND SALMON

Fish are cold-blooded aquatic vertebrates without legs but with fins, gills, and, usually, scales. Most are covered as well with a slimy coating of mucus, which reduces water resistance and protects against disease and parasites. Fins are extensions of the skin supported by soft or spiny rays. There are typically two sets of paired fins and three unpaired fins (see figure 17).

Fish breathe by taking water in through the mouth and passing it out through the gill openings. In the passage the water flows over numerous gill filaments, which are richly endowed with blood vessels. Dissolved oxygen in the water thereby passes into the bloodstream while dissolved carbon dioxide in the blood is released to the water.

Fish are able to see clearly for short distances and use their eyes for both navigation and orientation, as well as for spotting food. Internal ears — without external openings — serve both to transmit sound and maintain equilibrium. A special sense organ, the lateral line, consists of a series of minute pores extending from the gills to the base of the tail. It is sensitive both to temperature changes in the water and to vibrations from external objects, both moving and stationary.

Although a variety of species inhabits the lakes and streams of our mountains, this guide focuses on the popular sport fish of the family Salmonidae: Pacific salmon, trout, and char. For other species native to the mountain waters of our region, the reader is referred to the books listed in the bibliography.

Salmonids, which are native to cold waters of the northern hemisphere, are characterized by streamlined bodies, small round scales, soft-rayed fins, and a fatty, or *adipose*, fin. There are five species of Pacific salmon — pink, coho, chinook, sockeye, and chum — all native to our region. Our native trout are the rainbow (steelhead) and cutthroat. The Dolly Varden, though popularly considered a trout, is our only native char.

Species introduced to our region include the brook trout and lake trout (both chars), the brown trout, and the golden trout. Lake trout and golden trout, however, are present only in very limited numbers in a few widely scattered lakes or streams. Of these introduced species the brook trout is by far the most common and widespread in our region, having been stocked in lakes and streams both in the Cascades and Olympics, as well as on Vancouver Island.

All the salmon and some populations of rainbow, cutthroat, and Dolly Varden are anadromous, or seagoing, spawning in fresh water but thereafter migrating to the ocean. Sea-run rainbow are called steelhead and normally attain a much larger size than nonmigratory rainbows. Pacific salmon spend the greater part of their lives—from one to several years, depending on the species—at sea and are therefore generally classed as marine fish. At the end of their sojourn, however, they return to their home streams to spawn, after which they die. Since adult salmon cease feeding after entering their streams, they are only accidentally hooked by anglers at that time. They may sometimes be observed in fair numbers, however, either as they ascend the streams or upon their arrival at the spawning grounds.

Spawning behavior is similar for all five species of Pacific salmon. Upon or after entering the home stream, the males change radically in appearance, turning from silvery to various shades and combinations of red, green, and brown and developing pronounced hooked jaws and, in some cases, a humped back. Changes in the female are subtler, usually involving only a degree of alteration in color and pattern.

At the spawning ground the female digs a nest, or *redd*, in a gravel riffle, usually downstream from a pool. Several males congregate around the female, but one is dominant and keeps the rest at bay. When the female is ready to lay, she lowers her anal fin into the redd, whereupon the dominant male moves alongside and quivers. This behavior stimulates egg laying. After the dominant male has fertilized the eggs, the satellite males rush in to do so as well before the eggs are buried. The female moves upstream to dig another redd, burying her just-fertilized eggs in the process. The sequence repeats itself until the female is spent.

The time of year for spawning varies with each species and, to a lesser degree, with different populations of the same species. Eggs generally hatch in the spring, and the fry emerge from the gravel days or weeks later. Pink and chum salmon move downstream within days of emerging. Other species spend longer times in fresh water, in some cases as much as a year or two, before migrating to the ocean. Sockeye are unique among Pacific salmon in moving to fresh-water lakes before their journey to the sea. Landlocked populations of sockeye, known as kokanee or silver trout, spend their entire lives in fresh water and are often taken by anglers.

Salmon fry generally do not feed in fresh water. Juveniles, however, often congregate in estuaries before entering the ocean and during that time feed primarily on zooplankton. Mature salmon eat plankton, fish, and a variety of marine invertebrates.

Trout are the principal sport fish in our mountain waters and the only ones the vast majority of anglers ever lay eyes on in the course of fishing. Rainbow trout, cutthroat trout, and brook trout are the species most commonly encountered. Dolly Varden are somewhat less common, particularly south of Washington. Relatively few anglers will hook brown, golden, or lake trout in our waters. Large steelhead runs in the major streams provide a large, popular fishery throughout the region.

Most high glacial lakes in our mountains had no fish whatsoever prior to artificial stocking. Generally deficient in nutrients and lacking suitable spawning areas, those lakes are today stocked annually with brook trout, cutthroat, and rainbow. Golden trout, brown trout, or lake trout may also be present in some lakes.

Like salmon, trout and char spawn in gravel riffles in streams. Fish in lakes commonly move to tributary streams at spawning time and back into the lakes thereafter. Unlike salmon, trout and char do not die after spawning. Steelhead that survive the ordeal even return to the ocean. Seagoing Dolly Varden swim to the sea each spring and return in late summer or fall to spawn in headwater streams. Rainbow, steelhead, and cutthroat spawn from winter through late spring, depending on the species and particular population.

Trout fry feed on zooplankton and aquatic insect larvae. Adults, depending on the species and opportunities, take a variety of aquatic invertebrates, as well as terrestrial insects, fish, amphibians, and salmon eggs. Trout occupy a position near the top of the food chain in our mountain waters. As adults they are preyed upon mainly by humans, less commonly by mink, otter, bear, bald eagles, ospreys, and one another.

Our trout and salmon are indicators of water quality. Waters that maintain healthy populations of these magnificent fish, which require clear, well-aerated, unpolluted water, are in the main in good condition. Where salmon and trout populations have declined, water quality is suspect. The three principal threats to trout and salmon populations in our region are dam building, improper logging practices, and the release of toxic substances into the water. The last of these is a minor concern in the mountains but a major problem in the lowlands. Improper logging, however, is the chief destroyer of streams in the mountains. It results in stream siltation, destruction of spawning grounds, and possibly lethal changes in water chemistry and increases in water temperature. Losses of fish in some watersheds have been substantial as a result and are particularly regrettable because they are avoidable. Dam building has reduced or destroyed salmon runs, particularly in the upper Columbia River watershed, and locally has created detrimental changes in water flow, temperature, and chemistry.

Although most trout caught in our mountains are hatchery stock, there are still a few natives around. Among serious anglers, the philosophy of catch-and-release is widely practiced in the cases of large native trout. These fishermen keep the smaller fish for food but toss the big natives back for others or themselves to catch again. Undersized fish should be handled as little as possible to avoid injuring them.

The species descriptions to follow focus on gross characteristics that serve to distinguish *most* individuals of one species from those of another. In some cases, where the species may be very similar, more technical distinctions are cited. A great deal of variation in color and pattern exists among both individuals and populations of both salmon and trout. The descriptions provided are for typical specimens.

Popular and scientific names both conform to *A List of Common and Scientific Names of Fishes from the United States and Canada*, 3rd ed., American Fisheries Society, Special Publication 6, 1970. Other names in use are given in parentheses following the preferred name for each species. For general information on the organization and use of the species accounts and illustrations, as well as for a list of the abbreviations used in the accounts, see the Introduction.

PLATE 58

Trout and Salmon Family (Salmonidae)

PINK (HUMPBACK) SALMON, *Oncorhynchus gorbuscha*. L to 30″, wt to 10 lbs. Spawning M has pronounced dark, humped back, red sides blotched with brown; spawning F troutlike, olive green on sides; both sexes silvery upon entering spawning stream; note large oblong spots, the largest as long as eye diam, on back and *both* lobes of caudal fin. Spawn June-Sept, Alas to Cal; also ne Asia. Smallest, most abun Pacific salmon.

COHO (SILVER) SALMON, *Oncorhynchus kisutch*. L to 38″, wt to 31 lbs. Spawning M bluish green on back and head, with bright red stripe on ea side; spawning F drabber; note abun small black spots on back, dorsal fin, and *upper lobe only* of caudal fin, plus white gums of lower jaw. Spawn Sept-Dec (occas later), Alas to Cal; also ne Asia.

CHINOOK (KING) SALMON, *Oncorhynchus tshawytscha*. L to 60″, wt gen to ca 80 lbs. Largest Pacific salmon. Spawning M has slight hump; both sexes at that stage are dk olive green to maroon or nearly black, without conspicuous stripes or blotches on sides. Spawn gen May-Sept, esp in major rivers, Alas to Cal; also ne Asia.

SOCKEYE SALMON and KOKANEE, *Oncorhynchus nerka*. L to 33″, wt to 15½ lbs. Spawning M bright red on back and sides, with green head and white belly; spawning F similar, darker on sides; note lack of distinct spots on backs and fins; also note 28–40 *long, slender* gill rakers on first gill arch (cf Chum Salmon). Landlocked Sockeye or Kokanee silvery in nonbreeding stage. Spawn Aug-Dec, streams tributary to lakes, Alas to Cal; also ne Asia. Fry migrate to lakes after hatch, spending 1–2 years before migrating to ocean.

CHUM (DOG) SALMON, *Oncorhynchus keta*. L to 38″, wt to 45 lbs. Spawning adults nearly black on back, brick red on sides with vertical greenish bars or mottling; note lack of distinct spots on back and fins; also note 19–26 *short, stout* gill rakers on first gill arch (cf Sockeye Salmon). Spawn Aug-Jan, Alas to Cal, Arctic coast e to Mackenzie R; also ne Asia.

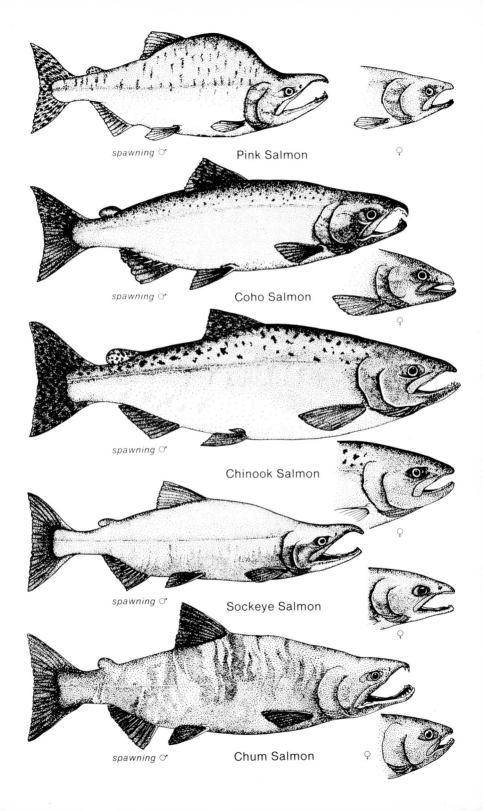

spawning ♂   Pink Salmon   ♀

spawning ♂   Coho Salmon   ♀

spawning ♂   Chinook Salmon   ♀

spawning ♂   Sockeye Salmon   ♀

spawning ♂   Chum Salmon   ♀

PLATE 59

Trout and Salmon Family (Salmonidae)

BROWN TROUT, *Salmo trutta*. L to 32½". Golden brown with dark spots surrounded by pale halos on sides of body. Secretive, wary, difficult to catch. Tolerates warmer waters (68°–75°F) than other trout. Native n Europe; uncom and local, Cas.

CUTTHROAT TROUT, *Salmo clarki*. Both sea-run and nonmigratory populations in our range. L gen to 19", occas larger. Fresh sea-run fish bluish with silvery sides; nonmigratory fish gen green above, olive green on sides, silvery below, with pinkish sheen on gill covers. Note numerous dark spots on back and sides, extending below lateral line, and red orange slash marks on underside of lower jaw (sometimes missing in sea-run fish). Lacks red side stripe or fins with colored borders; 150–180 scales in lateral line. Coastal fish spawn in smallest headwater streams, Alas to Cal; inland fish introduced to lakes and streams in Cas.

RAINBOW TROUT and STEELHEAD, *Salmo gairdneri*. Steelhead is the sea-run form of Rainbow Trout, both occurring throughout our range. Inland Rainbows known as Kamloops Trout in BC. L gen to 30" (nonmigratory) or 45" (Steelhead). Color variable, gen bluish or greenish on back and upper sides, usu with broad red lateral band on each side, plus numerous dark spots. Lacks red slashes beneath lower jaw; less than 150 scales in lateral line. Steelhead uniformly silver. Native n Mex to Alas, e to Albta, Idaho, Nev; widely planted in mtn lakes and streams throughout our range. Steelhead runs in coastal streams Dec-Feb and Aug-Sept.

BROOK TROUT (CHAR), *Salvelinus fontinalis*. L gen 8"–16" in our area. Gen olive green with small greenish spots—some with red centers—surrounded by blue halos on sides of body; wavy marks on back and dorsal fin; white front margins on lower fins; caudal and lower fins gen pinkish. Native e N Amer; widely planted in lakes and streams, Cas and OMtns; Cowichan drainage, Vanc I.

DOLLY VARDEN, *Salvelinus malma*. L gen to 20". Olive green with numerous creamy to red spots ca size of eye or slightly smaller. Spawning M has orange belly and red lower fins. Both sea-run and nonmigratory populations in our range. Sea-run fish silvery with indistinct spots. Cold-water lakes and streams, Alas to n Cal, inland to RM; uncom s of Wn. Interior Dolly Varden, or Bull Trout, similar in appearance but treated by some authorities as a separate species; local and uncom, Cas, Wn to n Cal.

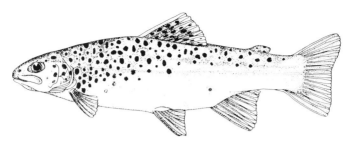

Brown Trout

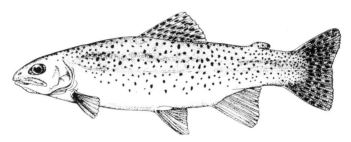

Cutthroat Trout

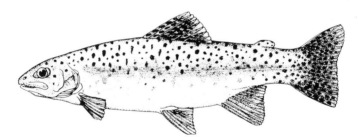

Rainbow Trout

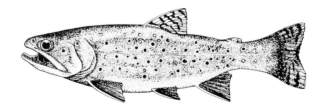

Brook Trout

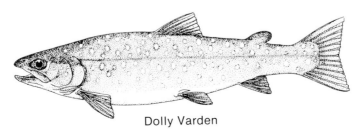

Dolly Varden

9

AMPHIBIANS

Amphibians occurring in our region include salamanders, tailed frog, treefrog, toads, and true frogs. All are partly aquatic, partly terrestrial vertebrates that regulate their body temperatures through behavior. Such behavior includes spending a good deal of time in especially favored environments—in animal burrows, under rocks and logs, in the water—where changes in temperature and humidity are less pronounced than in the open. Frogs rarely venture far from water even as adults and may be seen abroad during the day along the margins of lakes and streams. Toads, tree frogs, and salamanders are more terrestrial, returning to water to spawn, but otherwise spending most of their time on land. Salamanders hole up in various damp retreats, emerging mainly at night for short periods during or after rains. Toads and tree frogs are chiefly nocturnal but also may be about during the day.

At higher elevations in the mountains the spawning season begins early to mid-summer and ends in the fall. During the remainder of the year amphibians hibernate beneath the insulating blanket of snow. At lower elevations,however, the period of activity is longer.

Most amphibians have moist skin produced by a thin coating of mucus secreted from numerous glands. Toads also secrete a toxic milky fluid that repels some predators. By secreting mucus, terrestrial amphibians in a sense are able to carry the aquatic environment of their youth around with them. The mucus retards moisture loss and aids in respiration. (Though most amphibians possess lungs, all breathe to some extent through their skin.) The slippery coating may also assist them in eluding predators.

Amphibians begin life as larvae—i.e., tadpoles—equipped with gills and fins, as well as a streamlined shape, for successful existence in an aquatic environment. The larvae gradually transform into adults, losing gills and fins, developing lungs (in most cases) and limbs (which are absent in the larvae of frogs and toads, rudimentary in the larvae of salamanders).

Usually this transformation, or metamorphosis, occurs in a single season, but at high elevations two years may be required, with the larvae overwintering beneath the ice surface of frozen lakes. Some salamanders never transform into adults but grow in size and breed in the larval state.

Salamanders superficially resemble lizards but are readily distinguished by their smooth, moist, scaleless skin and clawless toes. Toads and frogs also have moist skin, which is smooth in frogs and warty in toads. Both have enlarged hind legs, webbed feet, and clawless toes.

Amphibians will eat almost any creature they can capture and swallow, including small vertebrates such as fish or tadpoles. In practice, however, their principal food is insects, worms, centipedes, spiders, and other invertebrates. They are preyed upon in turn by various birds and mammals and thus occupy a middle position in the food chain. The greatest threat to amphibians, however, is human activity, particularly habitat destruction such as the draining of marshes and clearcutting.

Because they are largely nocturnal and rather reclusive as a group, amphibians often go unseen even where they are abundant. Frequently they can be located only by lifting up logs, rocks, or loose bark to reveal their dens. If done carefully, this is a permissible activity that will not unduly disturb the animals. Further disturbance, however, should be avoided, and when observation is complete the cover materials should be carefully replaced.

All but one of the 18 species of amphibians found in our mountains are depicted in this chapter. The exception, a small salamander restricted to the Columbia River Gorge, is described briefly in the account of the western red-backed salamander, plate 61.

Common and scientific names conform to *Standard Common and Current Scientific Names for North American Amphibians and Reptiles*, Society for the Study of Amphibians and Reptiles, Committee on Common and Scientific Names, 1978. For information on the use of the species accounts and illustrations, as well as for a list of the abbreviations used in the accounts, see the Introduction.

PLATE 60

Newt Family (Salamandridae)

ROUGH-SKINNED NEWT, *Taricha granulosa*. L 5″–8½″. Skin warty, not slimy, light brown to black above, yellow or orange beneath, with or without black spots on belly. Breeding M has smooth skin. Only newt in our range. Ponds, lakes, slow-moving streams, adjacent forest, grassy places, se Alas s in W CMtns-Cas, Vanc I, OMtns to nw Cal.

Mole Salamander Family (Ambystomatidae)

NORTHWESTERN SALAMANDER, *Ambystoma gracile*. L 5½″–8½″. Brown above with or without light flecks, light brown beneath, with conspicuous parotoid glands and thick tail. Moist places, beneath logs, rocks, near water, lowl-subalp, se Alas s in all our mtns to sw Ore, nw Cal.

LONG-TOED SALAMANDER, *Ambystoma macrodactylum*. L 4″–6½″. Dk brown to black above, oft with lighter flecks and ± blotchy yellow or greenish stripe down back. Moist woods, mdws, near water, under logs, rocks, n BC s in all our mtns to Cal, e to RM.

PACIFIC GIANT SALAMANDER, *Dicamptodon ensatus*. L 7″–12″. Skin smooth, mottled brown or purplish above, paler beneath. Rivers, streams, moist forest under bark, rocks, logs, even walking or climbing about, extreme s BC s to cen Cal; also Idaho. Cope's Giant Salamander, *D. copei*, similar to larvae of Pacific Giant Salamander, but never transforms to adult. Streams, OPen.

OLYMPIC SALAMANDER, *Rhyacotriton olympicus*. L 3″–4½″. Brown above, yellow orange beneath, or mottled olive and brown above, yellow green with black mottling beneath. Cold, shady streams, seeps, springs in coastal forest, OMtns s along coast to nw Cal, W Cas of Wn, Ore.

Lungless Salamander Family (Plethodontidae)

CLOUDED SALAMANDER, *Aneides ferreus*. L 3″–5¼″. Plain brown or mottled with green, gray, or copper above; whitish, or brown speckled with white, beneath. Coastal forest, oft near clearings under bark, Vanc I, w Ore (including Cas) s to nw Cal.

OREGON SLENDER SALAMANDER, *Batrachoseps wrighti*. L 3¼″–4¼″. Slim, short legged, wormlike; dk brown above with back stripe of gold or reddish blotches; black spotted with white beneath. Coastal forest, Ore Cas, CRGorge to cen Ore.

ENSATINA, *Ensatina eschscholtzi*. L 3″–6″. Brown to nearly black above; whitish or yellowish, with black speckles, beneath; tail swollen, constricted at base. Forest, under rocks, logs, bark, W Cas to coast (Vanc I but not CMtns), extreme s BC to s Cal.

Rough-skinned Newt

Northwestern Salamander

Long-toed Salamander

Pacific Giant Salamander

Olympic Salamander

Clouded Salamander

Oregon Slender Salamander

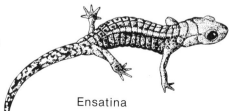

Ensatina

PLATE 61

Lungless Salamander Family (Plethodontidae)

DUNN'S SALAMANDER, *Plethodon dunni.* L 4″–6″. Dk brown or black above, with tan spots white flecks, and mottled yellowish or greenish stripe down back (not reaching tip of tail); dk gray brown with yellowish spots beneath. Moist, shady rocks near water in coastal forest, W Cas in Ore, sw Ore to nw Cal.

WASHINGTON SALAMANDER, *Plethodon vandykei* sbsp *vandykei.* L 3¾″–5″. Black above with yellowish stripe down back and pale yellow throat; some individuals uniformly tan. Under rocks and logs near water, OMtns, W Cas of s Wn to coast.

WESTERN RED-BACKED SALAMANDER, *Plethodon vehiculum.* L 2¾″–4½″. Dusky, speckled with white, on sides; back stripe gen reddish or tan, occas yellowish, distinct, extending to tip of tail; blue gray beneath flecked with yellow or orange. Moist places, low-mid el, W Cas to coast, extreme sw BC (including Vanc I), to s Ore. Larch Mountain Salamander, *P. larselli,* similar but belly reddish, only in and near CRGorge.

Tailed-frog Family (Ascaphidae)

TAILED FROG, *Ascaphus truei.* L 1″–2″. Skin rough, gen olive or gray, occas darker, oft with black stripe through eye; M with taillike copulatory organ; pupils vertical; no external eardrum. Cold, swift streams, in all our mtns but Vanc I, s BC to nw Cal, e to Idaho, Mont.

Toad Family (Bufonidae)

WESTERN TOAD, *Bufo boreas.* L 2½″–5″. Gray to green with ± white stripe and many dk blotches. Forest, mdws, near water, lowl-subalp, in all our mtns, se Alas to Baja, Colo, Nev.

Treefrog Family (Hylidae)

PACIFIC TREEFROG, *Hyla regilla.* L ¾″–2″. Color variable and changeable but note black eyestripe and pale underside. Amidst vegetation near water, low-high el, in all our mtns, s BC to Baja, e to Mont, Idaho, Nev.

Frog Family (Ranidae)

RED-LEGGED FROG, *Rana aurora.* L 2″–3″. Brownish or reddish above with black flecks and blotches, red behind legs and on belly. Damp forest near water, sw BC to Baja, W Cas to coast. Spotted Frog, *R. pretiosa,* very similar but dark spots oft have light centers, hind legs are shorter, and skin has more warts.

CASCADES FROG, *Rana cascadae.* L 1¾″–2¼″. Brown or olive above with distinct black spots on back and legs; yellowish beneath. Moist mdws near water, montsubalp, OMtns, Cas, Wn to Cal. Foothill Yellow-legged Frog, *R. boylei,* lacks distinct black spots but is ± gray-mottled above and yellow beneath. W Cas, s Ore and Cal, w to Coast, s to s Cal.

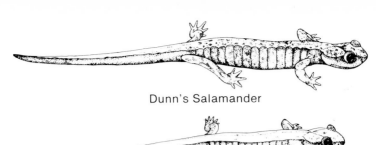

Dunn's Salamander

Washington Salamander

Western Red-backed Salamander

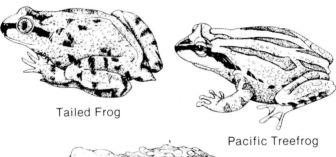

Tailed Frog

Pacific Treefrog

Western Toad

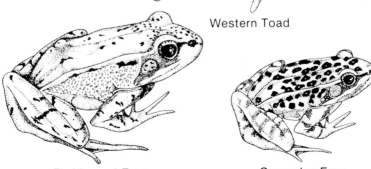

Red-legged Frog

Cascades Frog

10

REPTILES

Reptiles are represented in our region by turtles, lizards, and snakes. The painted turtle and western pond turtle, confined largely to ponds and slow-moving streams at low elevations, are not included in this guide. Approximately six species of lizards and twelve species of snakes inhabit our mountains, and these are most numerous in the southern portion of the Cascade Range. The cool, humid climate of our northern mountains is particularly inhospitable to most reptiles. In western British Columbia and Washington, one is likely to encounter only two species of lizards (western fence lizard and northern alligator lizard) and four species of snakes (rubber boa, common garter snake, western terrestrial garter snake, and northwestern garter snake). Along the east slope of the Cascade Range the number increases somewhat but still is not large. There is only one poisonous snake in our region, the Northern Pacific rattlesnake, and it is absent from western Washington, much of western Oregon, and all but extreme south-central British Columbia.

Most reptiles hatch from hard- or leathery-shelled eggs that are buried in warm, sandy ground. Some garter snakes and rattlesnakes, however, are born live. In either case fertilization is internal, and the young are born fully active and alert.

Reptiles maintain remarkably constant body temperatures by moving back and forth between sunny and shady locations. During the morning hours many snakes and lizards warm up by basking on rocks or open ground. At dusk they commonly seek out rocks, which retain the day's heat after sundown. In cool, cloudy weather, they may remain in their dens or burrows even during the day. Reptiles tend to be intolerant of cold weather, and our species either hibernate or at least temporarily den up during cold spells. The only reptiles apt to be found at high elevations in our region are the garter snakes.

The appreciation of reptiles seems to be an acquired taste. The great majority of humankind has a deep-seated, time-honored, and ultimately irrational aversion to lizards and, in particular, snakes. Presumably, many readers share this feeling. On behalf of reptiles, however, it should be noted that many species boast patterns and colors that rival those of birds in beauty, and all display modes of behavior that, precisely because they are alien to those of warm-blooded creatures such as ourselves, are just that much more interesting. Moreover, reptiles are voracious feeders upon insects, spiders, and other invertebrates and thus play an important role in keeping populations of those creatures in check. True, reptiles may also feed upon birds, amphibians, small mammals, and fish, but in this they are no different than any other predators. Finally, the great majority of reptiles are harmless to humans, and in our region only the Northern Pacific rattle-snake poses a potential—and vastly overrated—threat. The rattlesnake is by nature retiring and, if unmolested, will quickly retreat upon encountering a human. Anyone tramping through rattlesnake country should feel fortunate even to get a glimpse of the animal. To actually get bitten requires either monumental bad luck or carelessness. Moreover, even if one sustains a bite, it is rarely fatal—despite popular notions to the contrary—to a normally healthy adult. Visitors who can learn to regard reptiles with an objective eye will find much to repay their attention.

Common and scientific names conform to *Standard Common and Current Scientific Names for North American Amphibians and Reptiles,* Committee on Common and Scientific Names, 1978. For information on the use of the species accounts and illustrations, as well as for a list of the abbreviations used in the accounts, see the Introduction.

PLATE 62

Iguana Family (Iguanidae)

SAGEBRUSH LIZARD, *Sceloporus graciosus.* L 5″–6¼″. Gray or brown above, with darker spots and bars and pale stripes down body; blue belly patches and throat patch in M; orange throat in F; rusty behind forelegs; no yellow or orange on back of legs; smaller scales than Western Fence Lizard. Sagebrush, dry woods, lower E Cas of Wn, Cas of Ore and Cal; widespread in w US s to s Cal, e to RM.

WESTERN FENCE LIZARD, *Sceloporus occidentalis.* L 6″–9¼″. Brown, gray, or black above with darker spots, bars, occas paler stripes; orange or yellow behind legs, blue belly patches, blue throat patch in M; scales larger, spinier than Sagebrush Lizard. Rocky places, low-high el, E Cas of Wn, Cas of Ore and Cal, local on OPen; Wn to Baja, e to Idaho, Utah.

Alligator Lizard Family (Anguidae)

NORTHERN ALLIGATOR LIZARD, *Gerrhonotus coeruleus.* L 8¾″–13″. Large, short legged, dark eyed; olive to bluish above with indistinct crossbars or blotches on back and tail. Moist woods to high el, s BC to Cal, e to n RM.

SOUTHERN ALLIGATOR LIZARD, *Gerrhonotus multicarinatus.* L 10″–17″. Similar to above sp, but eyes yellow, body rusty to yellowish above with distinct crossbars on back and tail. Moist places, woods and forest, Cas, Wn (E Cas only) to Cal, s to Baja.

Skink Family (Scincidae)

WESTERN SKINK, *Eumeces skiltonianus.* L 6½″–9¼″. Boldly black, cream and brown striped; tail indistinctly striped in adults, blue in juveniles. Gen rocky places, Cas, Ore to Cal, lower E Cas in Wn.

Whiptail Family (Teiidae)

WESTERN WHIPTAIL, *Cnemidophorus tigris.* L 8″–12″. Gen 8 light stripes separated by black, but side stripes oft blotchy and indistinct. Oak and oak-pine woods, low el, Cas of s Ore and Cal; widespread in arid, semiarid places in sw US, s to n Mex.

Sagebrush Lizard

Western Fence Lizard

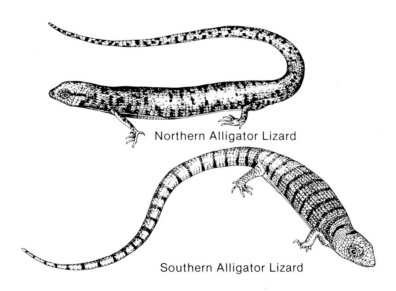

Northern Alligator Lizard

Southern Alligator Lizard

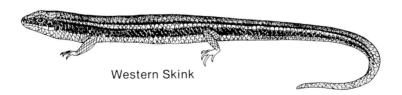

Western Skink

PLATE 63

Boa Family (Boidae)

RUBBER BOA, *Charina bottae*. L 14"–29". Plain brown above, yellowish beneath, without pattern; scales small, smooth, shiny; tail ± shaped like head. Damp places, oft near water, in forest, also mdws, in all our mtns but Vanc I, s BC s to Cal, e to RM.

Racer Family (Colubridae)

RACER, *Coluber constrictor*. L 22"–78". Plain olive or brown above, yellow beneath; slender, whiplike, with large eyes. Dry forest, woods, Cas from Wn (E Cas only) to Cal; widespread in w US, s Can to Mex.

SHARP-TAILED SNAKE, *Contia tenuis*. L 8"–18". Rusty brown or gray above, grading to red near tail; distinct yellow and black crossbars beneath; tail sharply pointed. Forest, grassy places, oft near water, low-mid el, W Cas, mostly Ore to Cal (local in s Wn Cas); s along coast and in SNev to cen Cal.

RINGNECK SNAKE, *Diadophus punctatus*. L 12"–30". Olive or bluish above, red or yellow beneath and extending in ring around neck. Moist woods, W Cas, Ore to Cal; also CRGorge; widespread but spotty throughout US.

COMMON KINGSNAKE, *Lampropeltis getulus*. L 30"–82". Dk brown or black rings alternating with pale yellow or white. Various habitats, Cas, s Ore to Cal; widespread in N Amer. California Mountain Kingsnake, *Lampropeltis zonata*, with White and red bands bordered with black, occurs locally in extreme s Wn Cas and in mtns of sw Ore and Cal, including the Cas.

STRIPED WHIPSNAKE, *Masticophis taeniatus*. L 30"–72". Gray to olive above, with creamy stripe bisected by black line on ea side; whiplike. Dry woods, sagebrush, E Cas, Ore to Cal; e Wn and Idaho s to e Cal, Ariz, NMex, Mex.

Rubber Boa

Racer

Sharp-tailed Snake

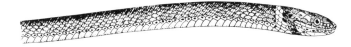

Ringneck Snake

Common Kingsnake

Striped Whipsnake

PLATE 64

Racer Family (Colubridae)

GOPHER SNAKE, *Pituophis melanoleucus*. L 36″–100″. Yellowish or creamy with black spots and blotches. Grassland, brush, open woods, Cas, Wn (E Cas only) to Cal.

COMMON GARTER SNAKE, *Thamnophis sirtalis*, 3 sbsp: L 18″–51″.
Red-Spotted Garter Snake, *T. s.* sbsp *concinnus*. Black with yellowish stripe down back, reddish spots on sides and gen red on head, black extending onto belly, lateral stripes oft obscured. Damp places, W Cas of Ore; sw Wn and w Ore.
Puget Sound Garter Snake, *T. s.* sbsp *pickeringi*. Similar to Red-spotted but yellowish back stripe confined to only one scale row and top of head gen black. Wet places, sw CMtns, Vanc I, OMtns, W Cas of Wn.
Valley Garter Snake, *T.s.* sbsp *fitchi*. Dk gray or brown with broad back stripe, no reddish side spots, black on top of head. Moist places, CMtns, Cas, BC to Cal, e to RM.

WESTERN TERRESTRIAL GARTER SNAKE, *Thamnophis elegans*, 2 sbsp. L 18″–57″.
Wandering Garter Snake, *T. e.* sbsp *vagrans*. Gray or olive above (occas black near Puget Sound), with distinct yellowish or tan stripes and black spots between stripes; no reddish spots. Moist places near water, lowl-subalp, CMtns, OMtns, Cas, BC to Ore; s in e Ore to Cal, e to RM.
Mountain Garter Snake, *T. e.* sbsp *elegans*. Blackish above, pale beneath, with yellow back stripe and pale yellow side stripes; no reddish spots. Moist places near water, Cas, Ore to Cal; s in Cal mtns.

NORTHWESTERN GARTER SNAKE, *Thamnophis ordinoides*. L 15″–26″. Brown, greenish, bluish, or black above, yellow beneath, with distinct red, yellow, or orange back stripe, and lateral stripe occas obscure or absent. Moist mdws, thickets, low-mid el, W CMtns, Vanc I, OMtns, Cas to s Ore; also nw Cal.

Viper Family (Viperidae)

NORTHERN PACIFIC RATTLESNAKE, *Crotalus viridis* sbsp *oreganus*. L 15″–62″. Note triangular head and rattles on tail; olive, gray, or brownish, with large dk brown or black blotches. Dry brushy or rocky places, low-mid el, Cas, Wn to Cal; E Cas only in BC, Wn, n Ore; s to s Cal, e to Idaho.

Gopher Snake

Puget Sound Garter Snake

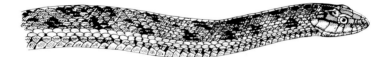

Wandering Garter Snake

Mountain Garter Snake

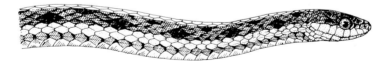

Northwestern Garter Snake

Northern Pacific Rattlesnake

11

BIRDS

Birds attract our attention by their sheer numbers, variety, beauty, and bold, lively behavior. Mammals, reptiles, and amphibians are not only less numerous, both in species and absolute numbers, but are less obvious, tending more often to be reclusive or nocturnal. An observant visitor to the mountains can expect to encounter many species of birds but may not see a single mammal, reptile, or amphibian. To a greater degree than these other vertebrates, birds rely heavily on visual cues for choosing mates and recognizing members of their own species. As a result most species have evolved distinctive, often striking plumages, which allow us to identify them with relative ease.

Feathers, which distinguish birds from all other animals, provide excellent insulation against cold, a smooth outer surface to reduce air resistance during flight, and—through various types of pigmentation and structure—aid in recognition and courtship. Flight is made possible by the specialized flight feathers of the wings, as well as by other anatomical features, such as hollow bones and enlarged breast bones to which the relatively huge flight muscles are attached.

Flight provides birds a degree of mobility denied to other terrestrial vertebrates. As a result birds are able to a greater extent than other land animals, including the insects, to move rapidly into newly available habitats and to avoid shortages of food or water—as well as other problems—by utilizing different, often widely separated habitats during different seasons of the year. More than half the species nesting in our mountains during the summer migrate southward in the fall and winter from the southern United States to South America, depending on the species. Many other species simply move downslope to spend the winter in the milder climes of the lowlands. A small number spends the entire year in the mountains.

The best places to look for birds are near water and along habitat boundaries. For example, far more species will be seen along the margins of the forest than deep within its interior. As a matter of fact, dense conifer forests, contrary to popular belief, support relatively few species of birds compared to adjacent meadows, brush, and woodlands, where food is available in greater variety. Moreover, observing the birds that do live in the forest is often difficult because many species spend the greater part of their time foraging high in the trees. The best times to look for birds other than owls, which are largely nocturnal, are shortly after dawn, when activity is at its daily maximum, and near dusk, when activity increases after a midday hiatus. Few birds may be in evidence in the afternoon.

Approximately 120 species of birds are depicted in this guide, including all the common nesting species. Omitted for reasons of space are uncommon or rare visitors, migrants, and casual nesters, which even experienced birders are unlikely to encounter. This guide, however, is not intended for serious birders, who will be able to recognize virtually all these species without recourse to a field guide, but for the casual observer who wants to identify the birds seen on the trail or in camp.

Birds are grouped on the plates by family, though for entirely practical reasons the taxonomic order preferred by most ornithologists is not strictly followed. If male and female differ greatly in appearance, usually both are shown. If the difference is minor, the showier of the two (nearly always the male) is shown, and the female's plumage is described in the species account. Several species either occur in more than one color phase or exhibit markedly different plumages during different times of the year. Such species are shown only in the plumages they most commonly exhibit during their sojourn in our mountains. Finally, birds, like people, exhibit individual differences, and their markings and colors may seem to change somewhat according to available light. Such variations should be considered when your specimens do not exactly match the illustrations, which depict typical individuals seen at close range in a direct, bright light.

Common and scientific names conform to the American Ornithologists Union's *Checklist of North American Birds*, 5th ed., 1957; 32nd supplement, 1973; 33rd supplement, 1976. For information on the use of the species accounts and illustrations, as well as for a list of the abbreviations used in the accounts, see the Introduction.

PLATE 65

Loon Family (Gaviidae)

COMMON LOON, *Gavia immer*. L 28″-36″. Ducklike bird with long, pointed bill; rides low in the water; neck and legs droop in flight. Uncom sum res, lakes, Vanc I, CMtns, Cas s to n Cal; breeds Alas e to Iceland, s to n US.

Waterfowl Family (Anatidae)

BARROW'S GOLDENEYE, *Bucephala islandica*. L 16½″-20″. Note M's white crescent on head; F's brown head, white collar. Uncom sum res, lakes and streams, CMtns, Cas s to Cal; breeds Alas, n Can, s in mtns to US; winters along coasts; Eurasia.

HARLEQUIN DUCK, *Histrionicus histrionicus*. L 14½″-21″. Note M's rusty sides and harlequin pattern; F's 3 white spots on head. Uncom-rare sum res, mtn streams in all our mtns; breeds Alas, n Can, s in mtns to US; winters along coasts; ne Asia, Greenland.

COMMON MERGANSER, *Mergus merganser*. L 22″-27″. Note M's white body, green head; F's rusty head and crest; narrow, hooked, serrated bill. Com sum res, lakes and streams, in all our mtns; Alas, n Can s in mtns to s US; winters along coasts; Eurasia.

Plover Family (Charadriidae)

KILLDEER, *Charadrius vociferus*. L 9″-11″. Note 2 black breast bands, reddish rump. Nests on ground. Fairly com to rare sum res or vis, open places near water, in all our mtns s to Cal; Can to cen Mex and Caribbean, also Peru.

Sandpiper Family (Scolopacidae)

COMMON SNIPE, *Capella gallinago*. L ca 11″. Note extremely long bill, white belly, zigzag flight. Uncom sum res, wet mdws, bogs, mtn marshes, in all our mtns, BC to Cal; N Amer and Eurasia.

SPOTTED SANDPIPER, *Actitis macularia*. L 7″-8″. Note round black spots on white breast, bobbing walk; smaller than snipe, with much shorter bill. Com sum res, mtn lakes and streams in all our mtns, BC to Cal; Alas, Can to US; winters s US to S Amer.

Kingfisher Family (Alcedinidae)

BELTED KINGFISHER, *Ceryle alcyon*. L 11″-14½″. Note large, crested head; long, pointed bill; broad, gray breastband; F's rusty breastband. Com sum res near water, in all our mtns; N Amer s to s US; winters s to cen Amer.

Common Loon *x1/6*
breeding plumage

Barrow's Goldeneye *x1/6*

♂ ♀

♀ ♂

Harlequin Duck *x1/6*

♀ ♂

Common Merganser *x1/6*

Common Snipe *x1/4*

Kildeer *x1/4*

♀

Spotted Sandpiper *x1/4*

Belted Kingfisher *x1/4*

PLATE 66

Hawk Family (Accipitridae)

GOSHAWK, *Accipiter gentilis.* L 20″-26″. Note gray back; light, barred breast; barred tail; young, brown with spotted breast. Uncom-rare res, forest, in all our mtns s to Cal; Eurasia, N Amer.

COOPER'S HAWK, *Accipiter cooperii.* L 14″-20″. Note contrasting rusty-barred breast and gray back. Com to rare sum res, forest and broadleaf woods, esp near clearings, in all our mtns s to Cal. Sharp-shinned Hawk, *A. striatus,* very similar but smaller and tip of tail notched, not rounded as in Cooper's Hawk.

RED-TAILED HAWK, *Buteo jamaicensis.* L 19″-25″. Gen seen soaring. Clear rusty tail is diagnostic. Some birds darker than shown. Com sum res, in all our mtns s to Cal; widespread in N Amer s to Panama. Ferruginous Hawk, *B. regalis,* is white beneath except for rusty legs; vis or rare res in our mtns. Rough-legged Hawk, *B. lagopus,* has white tail with black band near tip; migr.

SWAINSON'S HAWK, *Buteo swainsonii.* L 19″-22″. Gen seen soaring. From below note white wing linings with darker flight feathers and white tail (dark forms—not shown—lack white wing linings and have narrowly banded tails). Uncom-rare sum res and vis, Wn Cas s to Cal; N Amer to n Mex.

GOLDEN EAGLE, *Aquila chrysaetos.* L 30″-40″. Note large size and uniformly dk color. Rare-com res, rough, open country, mostly E Cas, BC to Cal; widespread in N Amer; Eurasia.

BALD EAGLE, *Haliaetus leucocephalus.* L 33″-43″. Note large size, white head and tail of adult; patches of white in young. Rare or locally com res near water, BC to Cal; com win vis to lowl rivers, lakes, bays; rare post-nesting wanderer s in Cas; N Amer s to s US. Endangered sp.

Osprey Family (Pandionidae)

OSPREY, *Pandion haliaetus.* L 21″-24½″. Note white underparts and white head with black through cheek. Local, rare-com res near lakes, BC to Cal; widespread in N Amer; worldwide.

Falcon Family (Falconidae)

PEREGRINE FALCON, *Falco peregrinus.* L 15″-21″. Note gray back, black and white head, long pointed wings, lack of black patches in wingpits when in flight. Rare and local res or vis, in all our mtns; widespread but rare (endangered) in N Amer; worldwide. Prairie Falcon, *F. mexicanus,* is sandy colored, with black wingpits; casual or rare vis. Gyrfalcon, *F. rusticolus,* much larger, grayer, less distinctly marked; casual win vis.

AMERICAN KESTREL (SPARROW HAWK), *Falco sparverius.* L 9″-12″. Note small size, pointed wings, rusty color; F similar but wings rusty and tail banded. Fairly com sum res, open places, mostly E Cas, but also w to coast, BC to Cal; most of N and S Amer.

Goshawk *x1/10*

Cooper's Hawk *x1/10*

Red-tailed hawk *x1/10*

Swainson's Hawk *x1/10*

Golden Eagle *x1/10*

Bald Eagle *x1/10*

Osprey *x1/10*

Peregrine Falcon *x1/10*

American Kestrel *x1/6*

PLATE 67

Grouse and Ptarmigan Family (Tetraonidae)

BLUE (DUSKY, SOOTY) GROUSE, *Dendragapus obscurus*. L 15½"–21". Note M's dk gray plumage and paler band at tip of tail; F brownish with dk tail. Com res, forest, BC to Cal; Alas, n Can, s to Cal, Ariz, NMex.

SPRUCE (FRANKLIN'S) GROUSE, *Canachites canadensis*. L 15"–17". Note M's blackish plumage with white spots on sides and tail; F rusty brown, barred, with tail like M's. Fairly com res, forest, esp mont-subalp, CMtns, Cas, BC and n Wn; Alas, Can, n US.

RUFFED GROUSE, *Bonasa umbellus*. L 16"–19". Note barred breast and sides, barred tail with black band. Most birds rusty brown, some gray brown. Com, lowl-mont forest in all our mtns s to s Ore; Alas, most of Can, s in mtns of US.

WHITE-TAILED PTARMIGAN, *Lagopus leucurus*. L 12"–13". Note short white tail; in win note *lack* of black eye mark. Com res, alp, Alas s in mtns to Wn, e to RM. Rock Ptarmigan, *Lagopus mutus*, has short black tail, darker summer plumage, and a black eye mark in winter. Uncom res in CMtns of s BC n to Alas, n Can.

Pheasant Family (Phasianidae)

MOUNTAIN QUAIL, *Oreortyx pictus*. L ca 11". Note long, erect head plume, chestnut throat, sides, and belly, vertical white streaks on sides. Rare-com local res, brushy places, OMtns, Cas, n Wn to Cal. California Quail, *Lephortyx californicus*, has comma-shaped head plume, black throat, golden-scaled belly, and horizontal side streaks; lowl-low mtn only. Bobwhite, *Colinus virginianus*, has white throat and eye line; E Cas foothills. Chukar, *Alectoris graeca*, has black necklace, eye stripe, and dk stripes on flanks; rare introduced res, E Cas, Wn to Cal.

Pigeon Family (Columbidae)

BAND-TAILED PIGEON, *Columba fasciata*. L ca 15". Similar to domestic pigeon (Rock Dove), but slimmer; note white crescent on nape of neck and light band on tail. Com sum res, woods and forest, low-mid el, in all our mtns s to Cal. Mourning Dove, *Zenaida macroura*, is much slimmer and has a long, pointed tail bordered in white; rare res and vis, mostly lower el, E Cas.

Blue Grouse

Spruce Grouse

Ruffed Grouse

White-tailed Ptarmigan

winter

summer

Mountain Quail

Band-tailed Pigeon

224

PLATE 68

Owl Family (Strigidae)

SCREECH OWL, *Otus asio.* L 8″–10″. Note small size and prominent ear tufts; gray, brown, and rusty phases. Nocturnal. Open forest, oft near water, gen low-mid el, in all our mtns s to Cal; coastal BC throughout all of US to cen Mex.

FLAMMULATED OWL, *Otus flammeolus.* L 6″–7″. Note small size, dk eyes, tiny ear tufts. Nocturnal. Uncom res, dry forest, E Cas s to Cal; extreme s BC s in mtns of w US to Cen Amer.

GREAT HORNED OWL, *Bubo virginianus.* L 18″–25″. Note large size, prominent ear tufts, barred underparts. Nocturnal. Fairly com res, various habitats in all our mtns s to Cal; widespread in w hemis.

SAW-WHET OWL, *Aegolius acadicus.* L 7″–8½″. Note songbird size, lack of ear tufts, streaked underparts; white V over eyes of young birds. Nocturnal. Com-uncom res, forest in all our mtns s to Cal; se Alas s through most of Can and US to cen Mex.

PYGMY OWL, *Glaucidium gnoma.* L ca 7″. Note songbird size, black patches at nape of neck, streaked sides. Nocturnal/diurnal. Rare-uncom res, forest, Vanc I, CMtns, Cas s to Cal; Alas s in w Can and w US to cen Mex.

SPOTTED OWL, *Strix occidentalis.* L 16½″–19″. Note large size, dk eyes, lack of ear tufts, heavily spotted and streaked undersides. Nocturnal. Rare res, forest in all our mtns s to Cal; Pac coast, BC to Cal, e to s RM.

Goatsucker Family (Caprimulgidae)

POOR-WILL, *Phalaenoptilus nuttalli.* L 7″–8½″. Note rounded wings without white bars and short rounded tail with white outer corners. Nocturnal. Seldom noticed. Rare res, mostly E Cas, Wn s to Cal; e to mid US, s to cen Mex.

COMMON NIGHTHAWK, *Chordeiles minor.* L 8½″–10″. Note pointed sweptback wings with white crossbar on ea. Gen seen flying at twilight. Utters a distinctive metallic-sounding call during flight. Com-rare res, open areas, pine forest, in all our mtns s to Cal; widespread in N Amer in sum; winters in S Amer.

Screech Owl x1/5

gray phase

Flammulated Owl x1/5

Great Horned Owl x1/8

Saw-whet Owl x1/5

Pygmy Owl x1/5

Poor-will x1/5

Spotted Owl x1/8

Common Nighthawk x1/8

PLATE 69

Woodpecker Family (Picidae)

COMMON (RED-SHAFTED) FLICKER, *Colaptes auratus*. L 12½″–14″. Note orange on underside of wings and tail, heavily spotted breast and belly, M's red streak on gray cheek (lacking in F). Com res, open forest, clearings, in all our mtns s to Cal. The Yellow-shafted race, with yellow on underside of wings and tail, is an uncom-irreg win vis in our area. Widespread in N Amer.

PILEATED WOODPECKER, *Dryocopus pileatus*. L 16″–19½″. Note large size, red crest, white wing patches in flight. Uncom res, forest, in all our mtns s to Cal; Can s to nw and e US.

LEWIS' WOODPECKER, *Melanerpes lewis*. L ca 11″. Note red face, pink underparts, green head and back. Com res, open woods, clearings, in all our mtns s to Cal, breeds cen Can s in w US to s Cal, NMex; winters widely.

YELLOW-BELLIED SAPSUCKER, *Sphyrapicus varius*. L 8″–9″. Note red crown and chin (partly white in F), black bib, barred back, pale yellow belly. Com res, forest, riparian woods, in all our mtns s to Cal; widespread in N Amer.

RED-BREASTED SAPSUCKER, *Sphyrapicus ruber*. L 8″–9″. Note bright red head and breast and lemon yellow belly. Com res, mixed conifer and broadleaf forest, in all our mtns, se Alas to Cal.

WILLIAMSON'S SAPSUCKER, *Sphyrapicus thyroideus*. L 8¼″–9½″. Note M's black back and breast, black crown and red chin, white wing patch; F's brown head, barred back and wings, yellow belly. Uncom res, open forest, mostly mid-high el, gen E Cas, s BC to Cal; widespread in mtns of w US.

HAIRY WOODPECKER, *Picoides villosus*. L 8½″–10½″. Note clear white back and large black bill; F lacks red on head. Com res, forest, in all our mtns s to Cal; widespread in US s to Cen Amer.

DOWNY WOODPECKER, *Picoides pubescens*. L 6″–7″. Very similar to above sp but noticeably smaller in most cases and with slimmer bill; F lacks red on head. Com res, broadleaf woods, in all our mtns s to Cal; Alas s in w and se Can through most of US.

WHITE-HEADED WOODPECKER, *Picoides albolarvatus*. L 7¾″–9″. Note white head; red nape absent in F. Uncom res, dry forest, E Cas, Wn to Cal, s in SNev.

BLACK-BACKED THREE-TOED WOODPECKER, *Picoides arcticus*. L 9″–10″. Note black back, barred sides, yellow cap. Rare res, open forest, mont-subalp, mostly E Cas, BC s to Cal; Alas s in mtns of Pac states, e to n RM, ne US.

NORTHERN THREE-TOED WOODPECKER, *Picoides tridactylus*. L 8″–9½″. Note barred back and sides and yellow cap. Uncom-rare res, forest, upper mont-subalp, in all our mtns s to Cal; widespread in Can and n US.

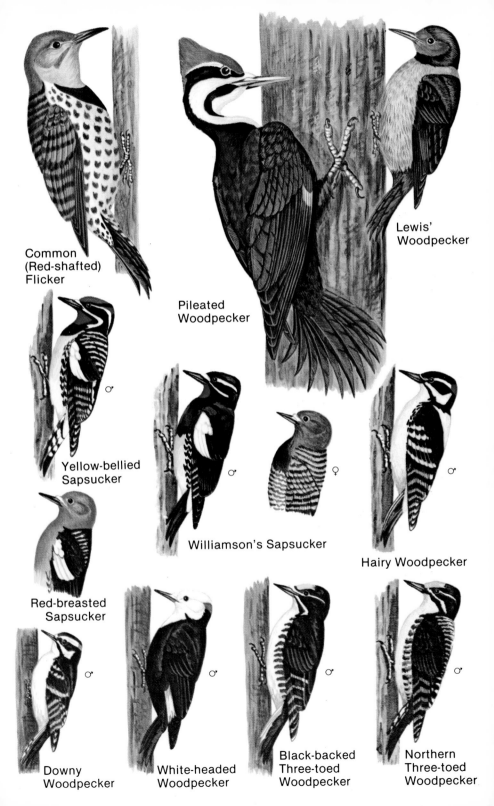

Common
(Red-shafted)
Flicker

Pileated
Woodpecker

Lewis'
Woodpecker

Yellow-bellied
Sapsucker

♂

Williamson's Sapsucker

♂   ♀

Hairy Woodpecker

♂

Red-breasted
Sapsucker

Downy
Woodpecker

♂

White-headed
Woodpecker

♂

Black-backed
Three-toed
Woodpecker

♂

Northern
Three-toed
Woodpecker

♂

PLATE 70

Hummingbird Family (Trochilidae)

RUFOUS HUMMINGBIRD, *Selasphorus rufus.* L 3¼"–4". Note M's rusty head, back, sides, and tail, metallic red throat; F green above, ± white below, buffy on sides, with rust in tail. Cf following sp. Com sum res, mdws, clearings, low-high el, in all our mtns s to Cal; breeds se Alas to nw Cal, e to n RM; winters in Mex.

CALLIOPE HUMMINGBIRD, *Stellula calliope.* L 2¾"–3½". Note M's green head, back, and tail, reddish- purple-streaked throat; F smaller than but nearly identical to F Rufous. Local, occas com sum res, clearings, mdws, mostly E CMtns-Cas s to Cal; breeds cen BC s to Colo and s Cal; winters in Mex.

Swift Family (Apodidae)

BLACK SWIFT, *Cypseloides niger.* L ca 7¼". Note narrow sweptback wings, black underparts, forked tail; larger than following sp. Local sum res, near waterfalls, se Alas s in mtns to Mex, e to RM.

VAUX'S SWIFT, *Chaetura vauxi.* L 4"–4½". Note dark but not black underparts, stubby tail, narrow sweptback wings. Sum res, forest, se Alas s in BC and Pac states to Mex.

Swallow Family (Hirundinidae)

VIOLET-GREEN SWALLOW, *Tachycineta thalassina.* L 5"–5½". Note white rump patches and eye patch, green head and back, purple at nape and tail. Com sum res, various habitats, in all our mtns s to Cal; breeds Alas s in BC and w US to Mex; winters Mex and Cen Amer.

TREE SWALLOW, *Iridoprocne bicolor.* L 5"–6¼". Note solid blue green head and back, white underparts, no purple or white near eye or on rump. Com sum res, forest, oft near water, in all our mtns s to Cal; breeds widely in N Amer; winters s US to Cen Amer.

ROUGH-WINGED SWALLOW, *Stelgidopteryx ruficollis.* L 5"–5¾". Note brown back and white underparts without dk band. Com sum res near water, mostly lowl, but also mont, in all our mtns s to Cal; breeds s Can through all of US to n Mex; winters s of US. Bank Swallow, *Riparia riparia,* similar but brown band across breast; sum vis and res, low-mid el.

BARN SWALLOW, *Hirundo rustica.* L 5¾"–7¾". Note blue back, orange underparts, deeply forked tail. Com sum res near habitations, in all our mtns s to Cal; widespread sum res, N Amer and Eurasia; winters s hemis.

CLIFF SWALLOW, *Petrochelidon pyrrhonota.* L 5"–6". Note rusty throat and rump, pale underparts, unforked tail. Com, irreg sum res near cliffs and water, low-mid el in all our mtns s to Cal; widespread sum res in N Amer; winters in S Amer.

Calliope
Hummingbird

Rufous
Hummingbird

Black Swift

Vaux's Swift

Violet-green Swallow

Tree Swallow

Cliff Swallow

Rough-winged
Swallow

Barn Swallow

PLATE 71

Tyrant Flycatcher Family (Tyrannidae)

EASTERN KINGBIRD, *Tyrannus tyrannus*. L 8″–9″. Note white underparts, black head and back, black tail with white band at tip. Rare-com sum res, open woods, gen near water, low el, Vanc I, CMtns, Cas s to n Ore; breeds s Can, nw and e US; winters in S Amer.

EMPIDONAX FLYCATCHERS, *Empidonax* spp. L 5″–6¾″. Note dk green, olive, or gray back, white to yellowish underparts, 2 white wingbars, light eye ring. 6 spp in our area, very difficult to distinguish, esp during migration. Hammond's Flycatcher, *E. hammondii,* is the most com in the mtns. All told from kinglets and vireos by habit of repeatedly sallying forth from same perch to catch flying insects.

WESTERN WOOD PEWEE, *Contopus sordidulus*. L 6″–6½″. Similar to *Empidonax* flycatchers but gen larger, lacks eye ring, wings much longer. Uncom-com sum res, forest, broadleaf woods, esp near water, low-mid el, in all our mtns s to Cal; breeds Alas s to n Mex, e to RM; winters Cen and S Amer.

OLIVE-SIDED FLYCATCHER, *Nuttallornis borealis*. L 7″–8″. Note olive "vest," lack of wingbars. Uncom-com sum res, forest, lowl-subalp in all our mtns, s to Cal; breeds Alas s to n Mex, e to RM and ne US; winters S Amer.

Old World Warbler Family (Sylviidae)

GOLDEN-CROWNED KINGLET, *Regulus satrapa*. L 3¼″–4″. Note black and yellow (and red in M) crown and white eyestripe. Com res, forest; com win vis, woods; in all our mtns s to Cal; breeds widely in Can, n US, mtns of west; winters widely s Can to Mex.

RUBY-CROWNED KINGLET, *Regulus calendula*. L 3¾″–4½″. Note M's red crown patch (oft not seen), M and F's broken eye ring, habit of continually fluttering wings. Com sum res, forest; win vis other wooded areas; Vanc I, CMtns, Cas s to Cal; widespread in N Amer.

Vireo Family (Vireonidae)

SOLITARY VIREO, *Vireo solitarius*. L 5″–6″. Note white "spectacles," 2 white wingbars, white throat. Com sum res, gen forest, low-mid el, in all our mtns s to Cal; breeds in Can, w US, ne US s in Appalachians; winters from s US south.

RED-EYED VIREO, *Vireo olivaceus*. L 5½″–6½″. Note black and white eyebrow stripes, red eye, lack of spectacles or wingbars. Com sum res, broadleaf woods, low-mid el, CMtns, OMtns, Cas s to n Ore; breeds in Can, n and e US; winters S Amer.

WARBLING VIREO, *Vireo gilvus*. L 4½″–5½″. Note plain, unmarked, dull greenish plumage. Com sum res, broadleaf woods, low-mid el, in all our mtns s to Cal; widespread sum res in N Amer; winters in Mex and Cen Amer.

Hammond's Flycatcher
Empidonax hammondii

Western Wood Pewee

Eastern Kingbird

Olive-sided Flycatcher

Solitary Vireo

Golden-crowned Kinglet

♂
♀

Red-eyed Vireo

Ruby-crowned Kinglet

♂

Warbling Vireo

PLATE 72

Crow Family (Corvidae)

GRAY JAY, *Perisoreus canadensis*. L 10″–13″. Note fluffy gray plumage, white forehead, black across back of head. Young are slate gray. Com res, forest, lowl-subalp, in all our mtns to Shasta; Alas across Can to ne US, s in RM and Pac mtns.

STELLER'S JAY, *Cyanocitta stelleri*. L 12″–13½″. Note dk blue body and black, crested head. Com res, conifer forest, lowl-subalp, in all our mtns s to Cal; Alas s in mtns and forests w of RM to Cen Amer. Two other blue jays occas range into the Cas of Ore and Cal. Scrub Jay, *Aphelocoma coerulescens,* a bird of oak woodland and chaparral, may range upslope into pine-fir forests. Pinyon Jay, *Gymnorhinus cyano-cephalus,* inhabits juniper woods e of the Cas from Ore to Cal. Both birds lack crests.

COMMON RAVEN, *Corvus corax*. L 21½″–27″. Note large size, thick bill, shaggy throat feathers, wedge-shaped tail, deep, harsh, croaklike call. Com res, forest, woodland, in all our mtns s to Cal; widespread in n hemis.

COMMON CROW, *Corvus brachyrhynchos*. L 17″–21″. Note smaller size than raven, thinner bill, lack of shaggy throat feathers, fan-shaped tail (in flight), higher-pitched call. Com res, various habitats, low-mid el, in all our mtns s to Cal; wide-spread in Can and US.

CLARK'S NUTCRACKER, *Nucifraga columbiana*. L 12″–13″. Note black and white wings and tail, gray body, long, black, awl-shaped bill. Com res, subalp forest where pines, esp Whitebark Pine, occur, CMtns, OMtns, Cas s to Cal.

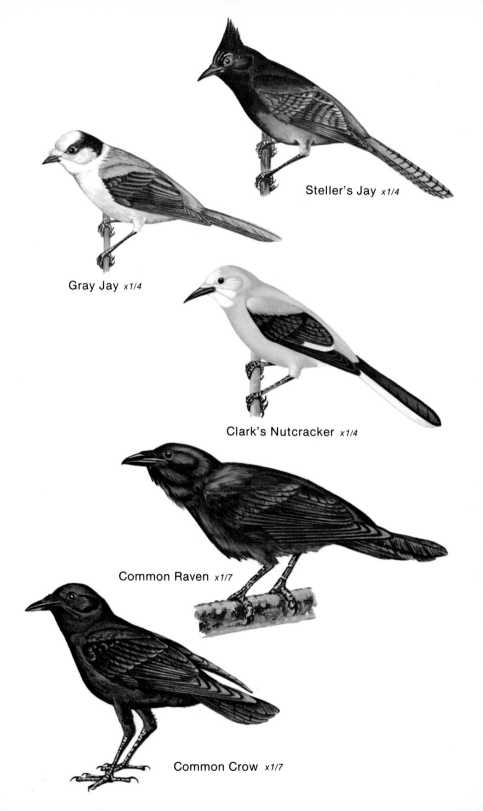

Steller's Jay *x1/4*

Gray Jay *x1/4*

Clark's Nutcracker *x1/4*

Common Raven *x1/7*

Common Crow *x1/7*

PLATE 73

Chickadee (Tit) Family (Paridae)

BLACK-CAPPED CHICKADEE, *Parus atricapillus*. L 4¾"–5¾". Note solid black cap, gray back, buffy sides. Com res, broadleaf and mixed woods, low-mid el, CMtns, OMtns, Cas s to n Cal; widespread, Alas, Can, n US.

MOUNTAIN CHICKADEE, *Parus gambeli*. L 5"–5¾". Note white eyebrow and black line through eye. Com res, open-semiopen forest, gen upper mont-subalp, CMtns, OMtns, Cas s to Cal; mtns of w US and Can.

BOREAL CHICKADEE, *Parus hudsonicus*. L 5"–5½". Note dull brown cap, rich brown sides. Com-rare res, open-semiopen forest, CMtns, Cas of BC and extreme n Wn; Alas, Can, ne US.

CHESTNUT-BACKED CHICKADEE, *Parus rufescens*. L 4½"–5". Note reddish brown back and sides. Com res, moist coastal forest, lowl-mont, in all our mtns s to Ore; along coast s to Cal, n to Alas.

Nuthatch Family (Sittadae)

WHITE-BREASTED NUTHATCH, *Sitta carolinensis*. L 5"–6". Note black cap, gray back, white face and underparts. Com-rare res, open forest, mostly E Cas (uncom W Cas), lowl-subalp, BC to Cal; res in much of US.

RED-BREASTED NUTHATCH, *Sitta canadensis*. L 4½"–4¾". Note reddish underparts, white eyebrow stripe, black line through eye. Com res, conifer forest, mostly mont-subalp, lower in winter, in all our mtns s to Cal; widespread in s Can, US.

PYGMY NUTHATCH, *Sitta pygmaea*. L 3¾"–4½". Note white underparts, black eyestripe, gray head and back. Com res, pine forests, E Cas, BC to s Ore; both sides Cas in s Ore and Cal; western US s into Mex, n just barely into BC.

Creeper Family (Certhiidae)

BROWN CREEPER, *Certhia familiaris*. L 5"–5¾". Note curved bill, rusty, pointed tail, streaked brown back, habit of spiraling up tree trunks. Easily overlooked but com res, forest, in all our mtns s to Cal; widespread in w and s Can and in US s to Mex.

Black-capped Chickadee

Mountain Chickadee

Boreal Chickadee

Chestnut-backed Chickadee

White-breasted Nuthatch

Brown Creeper

Red-breasted Nuthatch

Pygmy Nuthatch

236

PLATE 74

Lark Family (Alaudidae)

HORNED LARK, *Eremophila alpestris*. L 7″–8″. Note black bib, face patch, "horns," yellow face, pale underparts. Young lack horns and show little or no black. Rare-com sum res, dry mdws, subalp-alp, lower in win, CMtns, OMtns, Cas s to Cal; widespread in N Amer s to S Amer.

Dipper Family (Cinclidae)

DIPPER (WATER OUZEL), *Cinclus mexicanus*. L 7″–8½″. Note bobbing motion, chunky build, uniform slate gray color, short tail, habit of entering water. Com res, mtn streams, less oft near lakes, in all our mtns s to Cal; Alas to Mex w of RM.

Wren Family (Troglodytidae)

HOUSE WREN, *Troglodytes aedon*. L 4½″–5¼″. Note plain gray brown plumage, dusky, faintly barred underparts. Rare-uncom res or vis, CMtns, OMtns, Cas s to Cal; widespread in US, n to s Can; winters s US, Mex. Bewick's Wren, *Thryomanes bewickii*, an occas vis from lowl, has white underparts, prominent white eyestripe.

WINTER WREN, *Troglodytes troglodytes*. L 4″–4½″. Note small size, short tail, faint eyestripe, heavily barred flanks. Com res, moist coastal forest, broadleaf woods, Alas s in all our mtns to Cal; e US, Eurasia.

ROCK WREN, *Salpinctes obsoletus*. L 5″–6¼″. Note buffy corners of tail, lightly streaked breast, faint white stripe over eye. Uncom-fairly com res, rocky places, Cas, BC to Cal; sum res in nw US and extreme sw BC; res in sw US s to Cen Amer.

Wagtail Family (Motacillidae)

WATER PIPIT, *Anthus spinoletta*. L 6″–7″. Sparrowlike bird, but slimmer, with more slender bill; note streaked, buffy underparts, white outer tail feathers. Com sum res, alp and arctic tundra, N Amer, Eurasia; winters along shores and in fields, s US to Cen Amer, N Africa, s Asia.

Waxwing Family (Bombycillidae)

CEDAR WAXWING, *Bombycilla cedrorum*. L 6½″–8″. Note crest, fawn color, black mask and chin, yellow band on tail. Com sum res, broadleaf and riparian woods, low-mid el, fall vis at higher el; breeds across s Can and n US; winters widely in s US s to Cen Amer. Bohemian Waxwing, *B. garrulus*, very similar but note white and yellow marking on wings, rusty under-tail coverts, absence of yellow tint on belly.

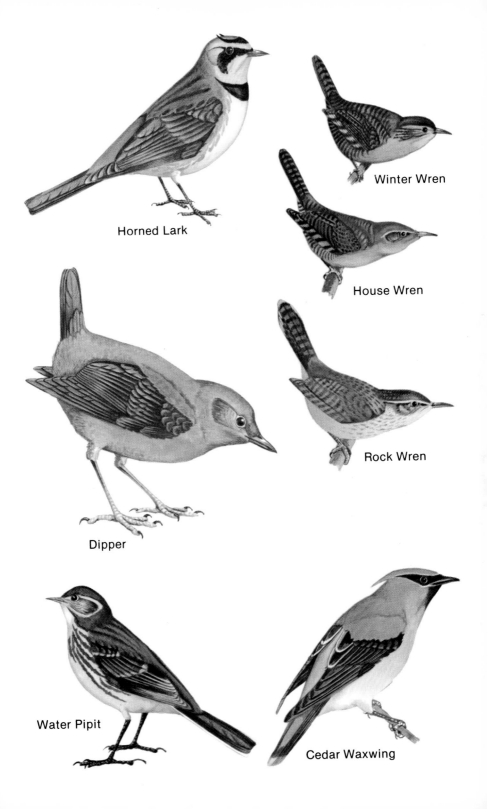

Horned Lark

Winter Wren

House Wren

Rock Wren

Dipper

Water Pipit

Cedar Waxwing

PLATE 75

Mimic-thrush Family (Mimidae)

CATBIRD, *Dumetella carolinensis.* L 8″–9¼″. Note black cap, long tail, rusty under-tail coverts. Fairly com sum res, riparian woods, low el, E Cas of Wn; breeds s Can, n and e US; winters s US to Cen Amer.

Thrush Family (Turdidae)

AMERICAN ROBIN, *Turdus migratorius.* L 9″–11″. Note rusty breast, dk grayish black back. Com res, areas with grassy openings for feeding, trees for nesting, in all our mtns s to Cal; widespread in N Amer.

VARIED THRUSH, *Ixoreus naevius.* L 9″–10″. Robinlike, but note black breast band, rusty eyebrow stripe and wing markings. Com res, forest, in all our mtns (gen W CMtns-Cas), BC to Ore; breeds n to Alas; winters s to s Cal.

HERMIT THRUSH, *Catharus guttatus.* L 6½″–7¾″. Note spotted and rusty tail. Com sum res, upper mont-subalp forest, in all our mtns s to Cal; breeds Alas, Can, n US; winters along Pac coast, in s US, s to Cen Amer.

SWAINSON'S THRUSH, *Catharus ustulatus,* L 6½″–7¾″. Note spotted breast, dull brown back and head, buffy cheek and eye ring. Com res, forest and broadleaf woods, lowl-mont, in all our mtns s to Cal; breeds widely in n US, Can, Alas; winters Mex s to Peru.

VEERY, *Catharus fuscescens.* L 6½″–7¾″. Note uniformly warm brown upper-parts, buffy spotted breast, white (not buffy) eye ring. Fairly com sum res, riparian woods, low-mid el, E CMtns-Cas, BC and Wn; breeds n US, s Can, s in RM; winters S Amer.

WESTERN BLUEBIRD, *Sialia mexicana.* L 6½″–7″. Note M's bright blue head, wings, tail; rusty back and breast, white belly; F gen similar but paler. Com res, dry conifer forest, pine-oak woods, mostly E Cas in BC, Wn; both sides Cas, Ore and Cal.

MOUNTAIN BLUEBIRD, *Sialia currucoides.* L 6½″–7¾″. Note M's uniform turquoise color; F resembles F Western Bluebird but has gray (not rusty) breast. Com sum res, upper mont-subalp forest near mdws, clearings; lower in win, CMtns, OMtn, Cas, BC to Cal; breeds Alas s in mtns of w Can and US; winters widely in lowl s to Mex.

TOWNSEND'S SOLITAIRE, *Myadestes townsendi.* L 8″–9½″. Note white eye ring, white tail margins, buffy wing patches. Com sum res, pine-fir forest, E CMtns-Cas s to Cal; breeds Alas s in mtns of w Can, US to Mex; winters in lowl.

Catbird

American Robin

Hermit Thrush

Varied Thrush

Swainson's Thrush

Veery

Western
Bluebird

Mountain
Bluebird

Townsend's
Solitaire

PLATE 76

Wood Warbler Family (Parulidae)

ORANGE-CROWNED WARBLER, *Vermivora celata*. L 4½"–5½". Note olive green above, yellow green beneath, lack of distinctive markings; orange crown patch oft not apparent. Com-uncom sum res, brushy slopes, lowl-subalp, in all our mtns s to Cal; widespread sum res, w N Amer; winters s US to Cen Amer.

NASHVILLE WARBLER, *Vermivora ruficapilla*. L 4"–5". Note white eye ring, blue-gray head, yellow throat, no wingbars. Com sum res, pine forest, gen E Cas, BC to Cal; breeds s Can, w and n US; winters s US to Cen Amer.

YELLOW WARBLER, *Dendroica petechia*. L 4½"–5¼". Note M's yellow breast with faint rusty streaks (oft not apparent), yellow in tail, absence of white markings; F similar but paler, oft without rusty streaks. Com sum res, riparian woods, wet thickets, low el in all our mtns s to Cal; widespread sum res in N Amer; winters from Mex to S Amer.

YELLOW-RUMPED (AUDUBON'S) WARBLER, *Dendroica coronata*. L 5"–5½". Note yellow throat and rump, black breast, white wing patches; F brown with 2 white wingbars; win birds brownish, streaked, white below with yellow throats. Com res or sum res, forest, low-high el, in all our mtns s to Cal; breeds widely in w N Amer; winters s to Cen Amer. The Myrtle race, an uncom migr in mtns, win vis in lowl w of mtns, is similar but has a white throat.

BLACK-THROATED GRAY WARBLER, *Dendroica nigrescens*. L 4½"–5". Note M's black crown, cheeks, throat; F duller, lacks black throat. Com-uncom sum res, forest, in all our mtns, gen W CMtns-Cas, BC to Cal; breeds widely in w US; winters sw US, Mex.

TOWNSEND'S WARBLER, *Dendroica townsendi*. L 4½"–5". Note black and yellow head, yellow underparts, striped sides; F lacks black throat. Com sum res, conifer forest, in all our mtns (W CMtns-Cas) s to Cal; breeds s Alas to Wn, Idaho, Wyo; winters Ore s to Cen Amer.

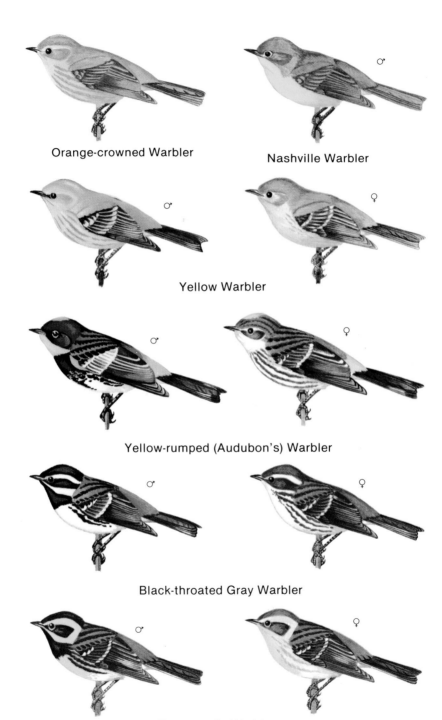

Orange-crowned Warbler

Nashville Warbler ♂

Yellow Warbler ♂

♀

Yellow-rumped (Audubon's) Warbler ♂ ♀

Black-throated Gray Warbler ♂ ♀

Townsend's Warbler ♂ ♀

PLATE 77

Wood Warbler Family (Parulidae)

HERMIT WARBLER, *Dendroica occidentalis.* L 4½"–4¾". Note yellow head, white breast and belly, M's black throat. Uncom-com sum res, forest, Cas, s Wn to Cal; also breeds s in coast ranges to nw Cal and in SNev; winters Mex, Cen Amer.

NORTHERN WATERTHRUSH, *Seiurus noveboracensis.* L 5½"–6½". Note brown back, streaked underparts, white eyebrow stripe. Uncom sum res, riparian woods, bogs, E CMtns-Cas to n Wn; breeds Alas s in Can and n US; winters Cen and S Amer.

MACGILLIVRAY'S WARBLER, *Oporornis tolmiei.* L 4¾"–5½". Note olive back, gray head, black and gray throat, yellow belly. F lacks black on throat. Com sum res, damp, dense brush, lowl-subalp, in all our mtns s to Cal; breeds in w US, mtns of BC; winters Mex to S Amer.

COMMON YELLOWTHROAT, *Geothlypis trichas.* L 4½"–5¾". Note M's black mask, yellow throat; F's white belly, buffy sides. Com sum res, fresh-water marshes, low el, in all our mtns s to Cal; widespread in N Amer; winters s US to Cen Amer.

WILSON'S WARBLER, *Wilsonia pusilla.* L 4¼"–5". Note M's black cap, F's yellow eyebrow and lack of wingbars. Com sum res, broadleaf or mixed forest, thickets, low-mid el, in all our mtns s to Cal; breeds widely in w and n N Amer; winters Mex to Cen Amer.

AMERICAN REDSTART, *Setophaga ruticilla.* L 4½"–5¾". Note M's bold black and orange pattern, F's white underparts, yellow patches in wings and tail. Mixed woods with willows, alders, E CMtns-Cas to n Ore; breeds widely in n and e N Amer; winters Mex to S Amer.

Hermit Warbler ♂ ♀

Northern Waterthrush   Macgillivray's Warbler ♂

Common Yellowthroat ♂ ♀

Wilson's Warbler ♂ ♀

American Redstart ♂ ♀

PLATE 78

Troupial Family (Icteridae)

RED-WINGED BLACKBIRD, *Agelaius phoeniceus.* L 7″–9½″. Note M's red shoulder patches, F's streaked underparts. Com-uncom sum res, mtn marshes; res in lowl; in all our mtns s to Cal; widespread in N Amer.

BREWER'S BLACKBIRD, *Euphagus cyanocephalus.* L 8″–10″. Note M's iridescent black plumage, yellow eye; F's gray plumage, dk eye; win M ± browner, lacks iridescence. Occas vis, mtns of BC, Wn (res in lowl); com sum res, mdws, Cas, Ore-Cal; widespread w US, sw Can.

NORTHERN (BULLOCK'S) ORIOLE, *Icterus galbula.* L 7″–8½″. Note M's black and orange plumage, white wing patch, long pointed bill; F dull olive above, paler, buffy beneath. Local sum res, riparian woods, low el valleys, Cas, Wn to Cal; breeds widely in w US; winters Mex to Cen Amer.

Tanager Family (Thraupidae)

WESTERN TANAGER, *Piranga ludoviciana.* L 6¼″–7½″. Note M's red head, yellow breast and belly, black back, wings, tail; F's green back, yellow breast and belly, black wings, tail. Com sum res, forest, in all our mtns s to Cal; breeds widely in forests of sw Can and w US; winters Mex to Cen Amer.

Finch Family (Fringillidae)

BLACK-HEADED GROSBEAK, *Pheucticus melanocephalus.* L 6½″–7¾″. Note M's black head, ochre breast, white wing spots; F's striped head, large bill, tan breast. Uncom-com sum res, pine forest, broadleaf woods, low-mid el, in all our mtns s to Cal; breeds widely in s Can, w US; winters mainly in Mex.

EVENING GROSBEAK, *Hesperiphona vespertina.* L 7″–8½″. Note very large, pale, conical bill; M's yellow brow, black back and belly, black and white wings; F's gray plumage, white wingbars. Com res mont-subalp forest, in all our mtns s to Cal; breeds widely in Can and n US, s in mtns; winters widely in lowl in all but se US.

RUFOUS-SIDED TOWHEE, *Pipilo erythrophthalmus.* L 7″–8½″. Note white underparts, rusty sides, black head, breast, back, tail; F very similar but head and back dk brown. Com res, mixed or broadleaf woods, mostly lowl, but also low el, in all our mtns (mostly W CMtns-Cas) s to Cal; widespread in N Amer.

GREEN-TAILED TOWHEE, *Pipilo chlorurus.* L 6¼″–7″. Note rusty cap and white throat. Local sum res, mtn brush, mostly E Cas of Ore and Cal; sum res w US; winters in Mex.

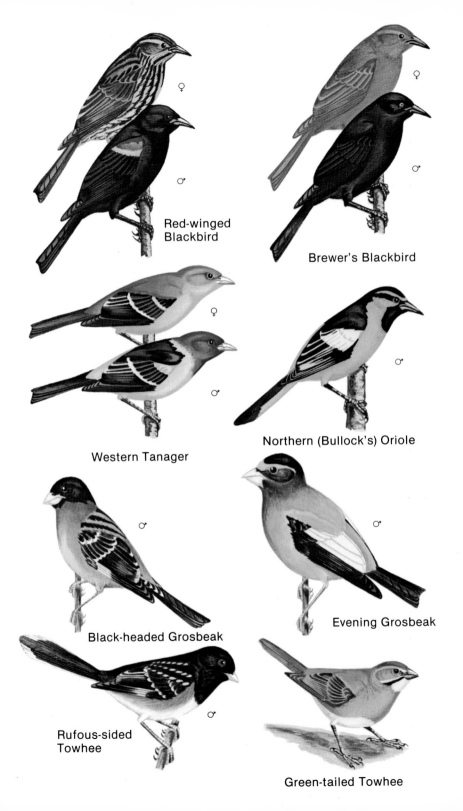

Red-winged
Blackbird

Brewer's Blackbird

Western Tanager

Northern (Bullock's) Oriole

Black-headed Grosbeak

Evening Grosbeak

Rufous-sided
Towhee

Green-tailed Towhee

PLATE 79

Finch Family (Fringillidae)

LAZULI BUNTING, *Passerina amoena.* L 5″–5½″. Note M's rusty breast, white belly, white wingbars, bright turquoise head and back; F's unstreaked underparts, white wingbars. Com sum res, woods, thickets, esp E Cas, BC to Cal, mostly low-mid el; breeds sw Can, s in w and mid US; winters Ariz, Mex.

PURPLE FINCH, *Carpodacus purpureus.* L 5½″–6¼″. Note M's rosy head, breast, rump, white belly, unstreaked flanks; F much streaked beneath, very similar to F Cassin's Finch. Com res, coastal forest, riparian woods, lowl-low mont, mostly W Cas, in all our mtns s to Cal; widespread in N Amer. The familiar House Finch, *C. mexicanus,* of parks and gardens, very similar but more red than rose and has streaked flanks; rarely in mtns.

CASSIN'S FINCH, *Carpodacus cassinii.* L 6″–6½″. Very similar to Purple Finch, but note M's paler pink breast and contrast between rosy crown and brown nape of neck; F very similar to F Purple Finch. Com sum vis (res at lower el), forest to timberline, mostly E CMtns, Cas s to Cal; widespread in mtns of w US.

PINE GROSBEAK, *Pinicola enucleator.* L 8″–10″. Note large size, M's dull rosy color, F's yellow green color; both M and F's black wings with white wingbars. Uncom-rare res, mont-subalp forest, in all our mtns s to Cal; breeds Alas s in mtns of w Can, US, e in Can to ne US; winters widely in lowl of Can and US.

GRAY-CROWNED ROSY FINCH, *Leucosticte tephrocotis.* L 5¾″–6¾″. Note pinkish wash on wings and rump, gray patch on back of head. Com sum res, alp, lower in win, in all our mtns s to Cal; Alas s in mtns to SNev, n RM.

PINE SISKIN, *Carduelis pinus.* L 4½″–5¼″. Note heavy streaking and yellow in wings and at base of tail. Very com res, forest, lowl-subalp, in all our mtns s to Cal; breeds Can, n US, s in mtns of w N Amer; winters widely in lowl.

AMERICAN GOLDFINCH, *Carduelis tristis.* L 4½″–5½″. Note M's black cap, wings, tail, yellow body; win birds buffy to pale yellow, without black cap. Com res, broadleaf woods, open brushy areas, mostly lowl, also low mtn, in all our mtns s to Cal; widespread in s Can, US.

RED CROSSBILL, *Loxia curvirostra.* L 5¼″–6½″. Note crossed bill, M's brick red color, F's olive gray color. Fairly com but irreg res, forest, in all our mtns s to Cal; widespread in conifer forests of N Amer.

WHITE-WINGED CROSSBILL, *Loxia leucoptera.* L 6″–6¾″. Note crossed bill, M's rosy pink color and 2 white wingbars, F's 2 white wingbars. Rare res, conifer forest, mont-subalp, in all our mtns s to Wn; conifer forests of Can, n US.

Purple Finch

Lazuli Bunting

Cassin's Finch

Pine Grosbeak

American Goldfinch

Pine Siskin

Gray-crowned Rosy Finch

Red Crossbill

White-winged Crossbill

PLATE 80

Finch Family (Fringillidae)

LARK SPARROW, *Chondestes grammacus*. L 5½"–6¾". Note bold head stripes, black spot on pale breast. Sum res, uncom in pine forest, com in brushy open areas, E Cas, BC to Cal; breeds widely in US; winters s US to Cen Amer.

DARK-EYED (OREGON) JUNCO, *Junco hyemalis*. L 5"–6". Note M's black head, rusty back, pink or buffy sides; F similar but paler; young birds have gray head. Com res, forest, lowl-subalp, in all our mtns s to Cal; breeds Alas to Baja, e to RM; winters in lowl. The Slate-colored race is a rare win vis, gen in lowl.

CHIPPING SPARROW, *Spizella passerina*. L 5"–5¾". Note rusty crown and white eyebrow stripe. Com sum res, forest, woods, lowl-subalp, in all our mtns s to Cal; breeds widely in N Amer; winters s US south.

WHITE-CROWNED SPARROW, *Zonotrichia leucophrys*. L 5½"–7". Note black and white stripes on head, gray throat, pink bill; young birds have gray-and-brown-striped crowns. Rare-com sum res, conifer forest, brushy places, near mdws, low-subalp, in all our mtns s to Cal; breeds Alas, Can, s in US to Cal, cen RM; winters w US s to Cen Amer.

GOLDEN-CROWNED SPARROW, *Zonotrichia atricapilla*. L 6"–7". Note dull yellow crown bordered with black. Res, thickets, subalp-alp, CMtns; com migr and win vis southward; breeds Alas to BC; winters s BC to s Cal, Baja.

FOX SPARROW, *Passerella iliaca*. L 6¼"–7¼". Note dk or rusty brown back, pale, blotchy underparts, rusty tail. Uncom-com sum res, brushy thickets, lowl-subalp, in all our mtns s to Cal; breeds widely in Alas, n Can, w US; winters coastal and s US.

LINCOLN'S SPARROW, *Melospiza lincolnii*. L 5"–6". Note streaked, buffy breast. Com sum res, moist thickets, mid-high el, CMtns, Cas s to Cal; breeds widely Alas, Can, mtns of w US; winters Ore, s US south.

SONG SPARROW, *Melospiza melodia*. L 5"–6". Note heavily streaked breast with central spot. Com res or sum res (higher el), riparian woods, moist thickets, in all our mtns s to Cal; breeds widely in N Amer; winters s US south.

Lark Sparrow

Dark-eyed (Oregon) Junco

Chipping Sparrow

White-crowned Sparrow

Golden-crowned Sparrow

Fox Sparrow

Lincoln's Sparrow

Song Sparrow

12

MAMMALS

Mammals are four-legged, fur-bearing animals that suckle their young. Body temperature is regulated internally, but protection from extreme cold is provided by their fur, or pelage, which consists of durable outer guard hairs and short, soft inner fur for insulation. The young are born live and are thereafter nourished by milk secreted from the mother's mammary glands. The young of some species, notably rodents and carnivores, are born naked, blind, and helpless. Young deer, elk, mountain goat, and snowshoe hare, however, are fully active and alert shortly after birth. Most mammals have acute senses of smell, hearing, and vision. Many also possess sensitive facial whiskers that convey information through touch. Bats possess a type of sonar that enables them to locate flying insects at night.

Small mammals tend to be nocturnal, active at a time when they are least conspicuous to predators. In response, however, most predators are at least partly nocturnal as well. Large mammals such as deer, elk, mountain goat, bear, coyote, and others are abroad both day and night. Among the smaller mammals that are active during the day are squirrels, marmots, pikas, and hares.

During the winter, mammals must contend with food shortages occasioned by cold weather and deep snow. Though some of the larger species—notably deer and elk, along with their predators—migrate downslope in the fall, the great majority of mammals remain in the mountains all year long. Of these only marmots truly hibernate. Chipmunks and bears sleep soundly for much of the season, but awaken from time to time and may even be seen abroad. They do not experience the deep coma of true hibernation, and their body temperatures and metabolisms do not reach extremes of depression. Most carnivores are active throughout the winter, though some migrate downslope if food becomes too scarce. Even at higher elevations, however, many small mammals and birds remain active throughout the winter, holing up only during nasty weather.

Some small mammals, such as voles and pocket gophers, spend the winter foraging under the protective insulation of the snow cover. They generally encounter difficulty only when extreme cold combined with a lack of snow cover prevents them from foraging without expending a great deal of energy. Tree squirrels cope with winter food shortages by living off caches of seeds stored up during the summer. Many small rodents subsist largely on bark during the winter months, as does the larger porcupine.

Approximately 75 species of mammals occur in our mountains. These include: typically northern species, such as the wolverine, fisher, and bog-lemming; southern species, such as the western gray squirrel and western jumping mouse; and numerous species of widespread distribution, such as the mule deer, black bear, coyote, and mountain lion. The Coast Mountains–Cascade crest, separating the humid coastal region from the drier interior, has formed a geographic barrier to some species. The mountain-beaver, hoary marmot, and Townsend's chipmunk, for example, occur mainly west of the crest, while the yellow-bellied marmot, least chipmunk, and badger occur mainly on the east. A number of species—the California ground squirrel, for example—that are found on both sides of the Cascades in Oregon and California are restricted to the east slope of the range in Washington and British Columbia. Water has also presented a barrier to many animals that might otherwise occur on Vancouver Island but do not. These include moles, pika, snowshoe hare, mountain-beaver, pocket-gophers, chipmunks, Douglas' squirrel, northern flying squirrel, and porcupine. The Olympic Mountains also lack several species that occur or once occurred in the nearby Cascades—the pika and grizzly bear, for example.

The more than 50 species of mammals depicted in this chapter include all those that one is likely to see, as well as a few of the rarer and more reclusive types. A few groups of mammals, such as the shrews, bats, and voles, which are extremely difficult or impossible for most people to distinguish by species in the field, are treated generically.

The best times to see mammals are at dawn and dusk, when both nocturnal and diurnal types may be abroad. The worst time is midday, when even diurnal mammals may be resting. The most likely places to encounter mammals are near water sources, in open areas, or near nesting sites. An observer who waits patiently and quietly downwind from a prospective observation area stands the best chance of success. More often than not, however, one sees not the mammal itself but only signs of the beast, such as tracks, scat, and nests. Tracks are shown on plates 88 and 89. Distinctive signs and voice are mentioned in the species accounts.

Common and scientific names conform to the *Revised Checklist of North American Mammals North of Mexico* by Jones, Carter, and Genoways, published in 1979 by Texas Tech University, Lubbock, Texas. Alternate common names in wide use are sometimes given in parentheses. For information on the use of the species accounts and illustrations, as well as for a list of the abbreviations used in the accounts, see the Introduction.

PLATE 81

Shrew Family (Soricidae)

SHREWS, *Sorex* spp. H/B 2″–3¾″; T 1¼″–3¼″. 7 spp in our range, all very difficult to separate. 2 spp partly aquatic. Tiny mouselike insectivores, pale brown or gray to nearly black, with narrow, pointed snout and inconspicuous, beady eyes. Gen moist places in all our mtns. Nocturnal/diurnal.

Mole Family (Talpidae)

MOLES, *Scapanus* spp. H/B 5″–7″; T 1¼″–2″. 3 spp in our range, all very difficult to separate. Small, tunneling insectivores with dk brown or black fur (our spp), naked, pointed snout, large out-turned foreclaws for digging. Rich, workable soils, in all our mtns but Vanc I. Sign: soil ridges. Nocturnal/diurnal; mostly subterranean.

SHREW-MOLE, *Neurotrichus gibbsii*. H/B 2½″–3″; T 1″–1½″. Tiny shrewlike mole with gray fur, scaly hairy tail. Moist, dense forest undergrowth, W Cas to coast, s BC (not Vanc I) to Cal. Nocturnal/diurnal; oft above ground.

Bat Family (Vespertilionidae)

BATS, several genera. L 3″–5½″. Flying mammals with hands formed into wings, the digits elongated and connected by membranous skin, the thumbs exposed and clawed. Ca 12 spp in our range, all difficult to separate when in flight. Most habitats, gen seen overhead at dusk or night. Nocturnal; roost by day gen in caves or trees.

Pika Family (Ochotonidae)

PIKA, *Ochotona princeps*. H/B 6¼″–8½″; no visible tail. Grayish to buffy brown, with large rounded ears. Rockslides, subalp-alp, CMtns s in Cas to SNev, e to RM. Sign: black pelletlike scat; "haystacks" of vegetation left in sun to cure. Voice: a shrill whistle or squeak. Diurnal; hibernates.

Hare Family (Leporidae)

SNOWSHOE HARE, *Lepus americanus*. H/B 13″–18″. In sum, brown above, white or buffy beneath; in win, white with black-tipped ears. Forest, thickets, in all our mtns but Vanc I; Alas, Can, s in mtns of US. Nocturnal; rests beneath brush during the day.

Mountain-beaver Family (Aplodontidae)

MOUNTAIN-BEAVER, *Aplodontia rufa*. H/B 12″–17″; T ca 1″. Dk brown, stocky; not a true beaver (cf plate 83). Moist woods, thickets, oft near water, W Cas to coast, s BC (not Vanc I) to Cal. Sign; large burrow openings, runways, "haystacks," earth cores to 6″ diam. Mostly nocturnal; reclusive.

Pocket-gopher Family (Geomyidae)

POCKET-GOPHERS, *Thomomys* spp. H/B ca 5″–6½″; T ca 2½″. 2 spp in our range, both very similar. Tunneling rodents with long incisors and foreclaws; brown to gray or nearly black. Mdws, grassy places in all our mtns but Vanc I. Nocturnal/diurnal; mostly subterranean.

Shrew x1/2

Pocket Gopher x1/2

Shrew-mole x1/2

Mole x1/2

Little Brown Bat x1/3

Snowshoe Hare x1/6

Mountain-beaver x1/6

Pika x1/4

PLATE 82

Squirrel Family (Sciuridae)

LEAST CHIPMUNK, *Eutamias minimus.* H/B 3"–4½"; T 3"–4½". Yellowish gray above with distinct black and white stripes. Sagebrush, dry forest, E Cas, s Wn to Cal; widespread Can, w US. Diurnal; hibernates.

YELLOW-PINE CHIPMUNK, *Eutamias amoenus.* H/B 4½"–5½"; T 3"–4½". Bright golden or reddish brown above with distinct black and white stripes. Forest (esp pine), CMtns, Cas s to n Cal; also RM. Diurnal; hibernates.

TOWNSEND'S CHIPMUNK, *Eutamias townsendi.* H/B 5¼"–6½"; T 3"–4½". Dk brown above with ± indistinct black and creamy or grayish stripes; distinctly larger than preceding spp. Dense woods, forest, Cas to coast, extreme s BC (not Vanc I) to SNev, nw Cal. Diurnal; hibernates.

GOLDEN-MANTLED GROUND SQUIRREL, *Spermophilus lateralis.* H/B 6"–8"; T 2½"–4¾". Told from chipmunks by larger size and lack of facial stripes; head and shoulders ("mantle") a bright reddish or golden brown. Open forest, rocky places, brush, mont-subalp, Cas, s Wn to Cal, e to RM. Diurnal; hibernates. Cascade Golden-mantled Ground Squirrel, *S. saturatus,* very similar but duller, with fainter stripes; Cas of BC and n Wn. Diurnal; hibernates.

CALIFORNIA GROUND SQUIRREL, *Spermophilus beecheyi.* H/B 9"–11"; T 5"–9". Brown grizzled with white or buff, neck and shoulders whitish, dk V between shoulders, buffy beneath. Open forest, rocky places, mdws, Cas, s Wn to Cal. Diurnal; hibernates.

WESTERN GRAY SQUIRREL, *Sciurus griseus.* H/B 9"–12"; T 10"–12". Gray above, white beneath, with very bushy tail. Oak woods, pine forest, low-mid el, Cas, s Wn to Cal. Sign: gnawed nuts, large twiggy nests in trees. Diurnal.

DOUGLAS' SQUIRREL (CHICKAREE), *Tamiasciurus douglasii.* H/B 6"–7"; T 4¾"–5". Reddish olive above (grayer in win), yellowish or rusty beneath. Forest, in all our mtns but Vanc I, s BC to Cal. Sign: dismantled cones, nests in trees. Voice: scolding chatter, trilling whistle. Diurnal. Red Squirrel, *T. hudsonicus.* Very similar to Douglas' Squirrel but white beneath. Forest, E CMtns-Cas to n Wn; Vanc I; Alas s to Wn, e to RM, ne US, e Can. Sign and voice similar to Douglas' Squirrel's. Diurnal.

NORTHERN FLYING SQUIRREL, *Glaucomys sabrinus.* H/B 5½"–6½"; T 4¼"–5½". Brown above, white beneath, with loose fold of skin between legs forming a "cape" for gliding from tree to tree. Forest, Alas e across Can to ne US, s in mtns of w US; in all our mtns but Vanc I. Sign: nut caches. Voice: birdlike chirps. Nocturnal; seldom seen but fairly com.

Least Chipmunk

Yellow Pine Chipmunk

Townsend's Chipmunk

Golden-mantled Ground Squirrel

California
Ground Squirrel

Western Gray Squirrel

Douglas'
Squirrel

Northern
Flying Squirrel

256

PLATE 83

Squirrel Family (Sciuridae)

YELLOW-BELLIED MARMOT, *Marmota flaviventris*. H/B 14″–19″; T 4½″–9″. Frosted golden brown above, yellowish beneath, with dk brown — not black — feet, dk head, white between eyes. Rocky places, gen subalp, Cas, BC to Cal, e to RM. Voice: loud chirps or whistles. Diurnal; hibernates.

HOARY MARMOT, *Marmota caligata*. H/B 18″–21″; T 7″–10″. Silvery gray above, white beneath, with brown rump and tail, black feet and black and silver head. Rocky places, gen subalp, CMtns-Cas; Alas s to Wn. Voice: similar to above sp. Diurnal; hibernates.

OLYMPIC MARMOT, *Marmota olympus*. H/B 18″–21″; T 7″–10″. Grizzled brown, with brown feet, white muzzle. Rocky places, mdws, subalp-alp, OMtns only (and only marmot in OMtns). Voice: similar to above spp. Diurnal; hibernates.

VANCOUVER MARMOT, *Marmota vancouverensis*. H/B 16″–18″; T 8″–12″. Gen rich dk brown, with gray on muzzle, white patches on belly, black rump. Rocky places, subalp-alp, Vanc I Range only (and only marmot on Vanc I). Voice: similar to above spp. Diurnal; hibernates.

Beaver Family (Castoridae)

BEAVER, *Castor canadensis*. H/B 25″–30″; T 9″–10″. Large rodent with rich brown fur, naked, scaly, paddlelike tail, huge incisors, webbed hind feet. Streams and beaver ponds, gen near aspen or alder, in all our mtns; widespread in N Amer. Sign: dammed streams, beaver lodges, gnawed and cut trees, sound of tail slapping on water, 1″-long oval pellets in which woody materials are apparent. Diurnal/nocturnal.

Porcupine Family (Erethizontidae)

PORCUPINE, *Erethizon dorsatum*. H/B 18″–22″; T 7″–9″. Yellowish brown, with long guard hairs near shoulders and sharp quills on rump and tail. Forest in all our mtns but Vanc I; widespread in Alas, Can to ne US, mtns of w US. Diurnal/nocturnal.

Hoary Marmot

Yellow-bellied Marmot

Olympic Marmot

Vancouver Marmot

Beaver

Porcupine

258

PLATE 84

New World Mice Family (Crecitidae)

WESTERN HARVEST MOUSE, *Reithrodontomys megalotis.* H/B ca 3"; T 2¼"–3¼". Brownish above, white beneath, buffy on sides. Gen dense vegetation near water, low el, Cas, s Ore to Cal; widespread in w US. Nocturnal.

DEER MOUSE, *Peromyscus maniculatus.* H/B 2¾"–3¾"; T 2"–5". Brown above, white beneath, with bicolored tail. Most habitats, in all our mtns; widespread in N Amer. Nocturnal. Forest Deer Mouse, *P. oreas* of some authorities, is treated here as a larger, darker race of *P. maniculatus.*

BUSHY-TAILED WOOD RAT, *Neotoma cinerea.* H/B 7"–9¾"; T 5¼"–7½". Gray brown above, white beneath, with bushy, squirrellike tail. Rocky places, in all our mtns but Vanc I; widespread in w N Amer. Sign: stick nests in rock crevices. Nocturnal.

SOUTHERN RED-BACKED VOLE, *Clethrionomys gapperi.* H/B 3¾"–4¾"; T 1¼"–1¾". Reddish on back, buffy to gray on sides, gray or whitish beneath, with short tail. Damp, wooded areas, CMtns-Cas, BC to Wn; widespread in Can, s to n US, RM, Appalachians. Sign: runways, perhaps littered with vegetation. Diurnal/nocturnal. Western Red-backed Vole, *C. occidentalis,* is dk brown above, the back not contrasting sharply with sides; OMtns, s W CMtns.

MEADOW VOLES (MICE), *Microtus* spp., Heather Vole, *Phenacomys intermedius,* and Water Vole, *Arvicola richardsonii.* H/B ca 3½"–6½"; T ca 1"–3½". All these spp very difficult to separate without in-hand specimens. Note stout bodies, blunt snouts, small, ± obscure ears, beady eyes. Fur thick, gray or brown to black. Mdw Voles most com in wet mdws or grassy places near water; Heather Vole, in subalp heather mdws; Water Vole, near water; in all our mtns. Sign: runways, oft littered with vegetation. Diurnal.

NORTHERN BOG-LEMMING, *Synaptomys borealis.* H/B 4"–4¾"; T ¾"–1". Brown above, gray beneath, with short bicolored tail. Mtn bogs, wet mdws, heather mdws, CMtns, Cas of BC and extreme n Wn; Alas, Can, s to n US. Diurnal/nocturnal.

Jumping Mice Family (Zapodidae)

PACIFIC JUMPING MOUSE, *Zapus trinotatus.* H/B 3⅝"–3¾"; T 5"–6"+. Back dusky, sides yellowish, underparts white, with long tail and large hind feet. Marshes, mdws, moist woods, in all our mtns but Vanc I, BC to s Ore, s along coast to cen Cal. Nocturnal; hibernates. Replaced in northern CMtns and in Cas of s Ore and Cal by the very similar Western Jumping Mouse, *Z. princeps.*

Western Harvest Mouse

Deer Mouse

Bushy-tailed
Wood Rat

Southern Red-backed Vole

Meadow Vole

Northern Bog Lemming

Pacific Jumping Mouse

PLATE 85

Dog Family (Canidae)

COYOTE, *Canis latrans.* H/B 32″–37″; T 11″–16″. Grizzled gray above, buffy beneath, legs reddish, tail black tipped. Like wolf but carries tail low while running. All habitats in all our mtns but Vanc I; widespread N Amer. Sign: doglike scat, large dens. Voice: howls, barks. Diurnal/nocturnal.

GRAY WOLF, *Canis lupus.* H/B 43″–48″; T 12″–19″. Color varied but gen grizzled gray to blackish above, lighter on sides and belly. Like coyote but larger and carries tail high while running. All habitats, Vanc I, CMtns; rare or absent, NCas; formerly widespread in N Amer. Diurnal/nocturnal. Endangered sp.

RED FOX, *Vulpes vulpes.* H/B 22″–25″; T 14″–16″. Color variable: rusty red; black grizzled with silver; reddish with dk cross on shoulders and back; black (the most com in our range). Most habitats, CMtns, Cas s to Cal; widespread N Amer. Nocturnal.

GRAY FOX, *Urocyon cinereoargenteus.* H/B 21″–29″; T 11″–16″. Forehead, back, upper sides, top of tail all grizzled gray; rusty around head, throat, lower sides, legs, underside of tail; throat and belly white. Most habitats, Cas, Ore to Cal; widespread in s US, Mex. Mostly nocturnal.

Raccoon Family (Procyonidae)

RACCOON, *Procyon lotor.* H/B 18″–28″; T 8″–12″. Grizzled gray with black and white rings on tail, black mask on whitish face. Brushy or wooded areas near water, gen lowl-lower mont, sw CMtns, Vanc I, OMtns, Cas s to Cal; widespread in N Amer. Mostly nocturnal.

Weasel Family (Mustelidae)

WESTERN SPOTTED SKUNK, *Spilogale gracilis.* H/B 9″–13½″; T 4½″–9″. Black with irreg white spots and stripes. Brushy or rocky places, open woods, oft near water, low-mid el, CMtns, OMtns, Cas, s BC to Cal; widespread in w US s to Mex. Nocturnal.

STRIPED SKUNK, *Mephitis mephitis.* H/B 13″–18″; T 7″–10″. Black with white cap and 2 broad white stripes down back. Open woods, brush, oft near water, lowl-low mtn, all our mtns but Vanc I; widespread in N Amer. Mostly nocturnal.

Coyote
x1/13

Gray Wolf
x1/13

Red Fox
black phase
x1/10

Gray Fox
x1/10

Raccoon
x1/10

Western
Spotted
Skunk
x1/10

Striped
Skunk
x1/10

PLATE 86

Weasel Family (Mustelidae)

WOLVERINE, *Gulo gulo.* H/B 29″-32″; T 7″-9″. Dk brown with 2 broad yellowish stripes down back; bearlike but smaller, with blunt face. Forest, mdws, rocky areas, upper mont-alp, in all our mtns but OMtns; nowhere com. Sign: ± cylindrical scat oft 5″+ long. Nocturnal/diurnal.

PINE MARTEN, *Martes americana.* H/B 16″-17″; T 8″-9″; F slightly smaller. Various shades of brown above, paler beneath and on head, darker on legs; throat orange or buffy. Forest, oft near talus in sum, mid-high el, in all our mtns; widespread in Alas, Can, n US, s in mtns. Nocturnal/diurnal.

FISHER, *Martes pennanti.* H/B 20″-25″; T 13″-15″. Frosted dk brown to ± black; much larger, darker than marten. Forest, in all our mtns but Vanc I, nowhere com; widespread in Can, s in mtns of US; NEng. Nocturnal/diurnal.

SHORT-TAILED WEASEL (ERMINE), *Mustela erminea.* H/B 6″-9″; T 2½″-4″; F slightly smaller. In sum, dk brown above, white beneath, feet white; in win, white with tail black tipped. Wooded or open places, oft near water, in all our mtns; widespread in Alas, Can, n US, mtns of w US. Diurnal/nocturnal. Long-tailed Weasel, *M. frenata,* very similar but slightly larger and feet brown, not white; in all our mtns but Vanc I.

MINK, *Mustela vision.* H/B 13″-17″; T 7″-9″; F slightly smaller. Dk brown to black, white chin patch. Near and in water in all our mtns; widespread in N Amer except sw US. Mostly nocturnal.

BADGER, *Taxidea taxus.* H/B 18″-22″; T 4″-6″. Body ± flattened, grizzled gray to brown, face black and white, tail yellowish, legs short and with long foreclaws. Grassy places, mdws, mostly foothills E CMtns-Cas, BC to Cal; widespread w N Amer. Nocturnal/diurnal.

RIVER OTTER, *Lutra canadensis.* H/B 26″-30″; T 12″-17″. Dk brown above, pale beneath, oft silvery at throat, feet webbed, tail long and pointed. Near or in water in all our mtns; widespread in N Amer. Nocturnal/diurnal.

Pine Marten x1/8

Fisher x1/8

Wolverine x1/8

Short-tailed
Weasel (summer)
x1/4

Mink x1/8

Badger x1/8

River Otter x1/8

PLATE 87

Bear Family (Ursidae)

BLACK BEAR, *Ursus americanus.* L 5′–6′; ht 3′–3½′ at shoulders. Color variable, gen black or brown in our mtns. Most habitats in all our mtns; widespread in N Amer. Sign: clawed or chewed "bear trees," various feeding signs, large doglike scat. Nocturnal/diurnal; hibernates.

GRIZZLY BEAR, *Ursus arctos.* L 6′–7′; ht 3′–4½′ at shoulders. Color variable, yellowish brown to black, oft grizzled with white hairs; hump over shoulders, face dished. Most habitats, mtns of BC; rare straggler NCas; Alas, Can, s in US to Wyo; formerly widespread in N Amer. Sign: remains of a kill, excavated areas, same signs as for Black Bear. Nocturnal/diurnal; hibernates. Unpredictable, can be dangerous.

Cat Family (Felidae)

MOUNTAIN LION, *Felis concolor.* H/B 42″–54″; T 30″–36″. Tawny with dark-tipped tail. Various habitats in all our mtns; formerly widespread in N Amer, range now much reduced. Sign: scratching trees, remains of a kill, copious catlike scat. Nocturnal/diurnal.

LYNX, *Felis lynx.* H/B 32″–36″; T 4″. Buffy or tawny, mixed with darker hairs above, rusty beneath, with long, black ear tufts, long cheek ruffs, stubby tail entirely tipped with black. Forest, CMtns–Cas s to n Ore; Alas, Can, s in mtns of US. Nocturnal.

BOBCAT, *Felis rufus.* H/B 25″–30″; T 5″. Tawny or grayish above, indistinctly spotted, cheek ruffs short, tail stubby and only partly tipped in black. Various habitats in all our mtns but Vanc I; widespread in N Amer. Nocturnal/diurnal.

Grizzly Bear

Black Bear

Mountain Lion

Lynx

Bobcat

PLATE 88

Deer Family (Cervidae)

ELK (WAPITI), *Cervus elaphus*. L 81″–117″; ht 4½′–5′ at shoulders. Brown or reddish brown, darker beneath and on neck, head; yellowish on rump, tail; large many-tined antlers to 5′ long on M. In sum, subalp mdws; in win, lowl, esp river valleys. In all our mtns s to Cal; also RM, Can. Voice: a bugling call. Most active mornings and evenings.

MULE DEER (including BLACK-TAILED DEER), *Odocoileus hemionus*. L 3¾′–6½′; ht 3′–3½′ at shoulders. In sum, reddish to golden brown; in win, grayish above, throat, rump, insides of legs and ears white; tail either white above and tipped in black (Mule Deer) or black above (Black-tailed Deer). Most habitats in all our mtns; widespread in w N Amer. Nocturnal/diurnal.

MOOSE, *Alces alces*. L 81″–108″; ht 78″–90″ at shoulders. Dark brown with palmate antlers gen 4′–5′ across, overhanging muzzle and dewlap on throat. Lakes, bogs, CMtns; Alas and n Can s to BC, n RM, NEng. Voice: a low moo or grunt, seldom heard. Mostly nocturnal but also active by day.

Cattle Family (Bovidae)

MOUNTAIN GOAT, *Oreamnos americanus*. L 4′–5¾′; ht 3′–3½′ at shoulders. White, shaggy, goatlike, with smooth, black, curved horns. Rocky slopes, cliffs, gen subalp-alp, in all our mtns s to Wn; se Alas to Wn and RM. Nocturnal/diurnal.

BIGHORN SHEEP, *Ovis canadensis*. L 5¼′–6′; ht 2½′–3½′ at shoulders. Brown to grayish, rump white; horns of M massive and coiled; F's horns shorter, not coiled. Rough, rocky terrain, high mdws, cliffs; local bands in CMtns, e NCas; mtns of w N Amer. Sign: bell-shaped scat; day beds littered with scat. Diurnal.

Black-tailed Deer

♂ in velvet

Mule Deer

Elk

Moose

♂

Bighorn Sheep

Mountain Goat

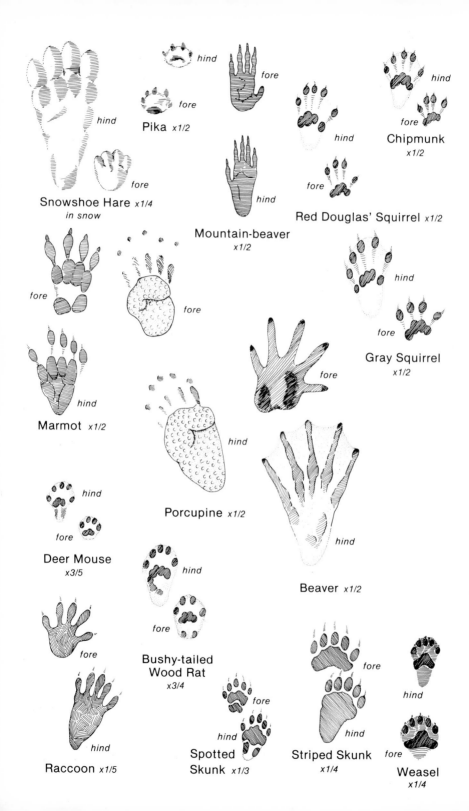

Snowshoe Hare x1/4
in snow

hind

fore

Pika x1/2

hind

fore

fore

hind

Mountain-beaver
x1/2

hind

fore

Chipmunk
x1/2

fore

hind

Red Douglas' Squirrel x1/2

fore

hind

Marmot x1/2

fore

Porcupine x1/2

hind

fore

hind

Gray Squirrel
x1/2

hind

fore

Deer Mouse
x3/5

hind

fore

Bushy-tailed
Wood Rat
x3/4

fore

hind

Beaver x1/2

fore

hind

Raccoon x1/5

fore

hind

Spotted
Skunk x1/3

fore

hind

Striped Skunk
x1/4

hind

fore

Weasel
x1/4

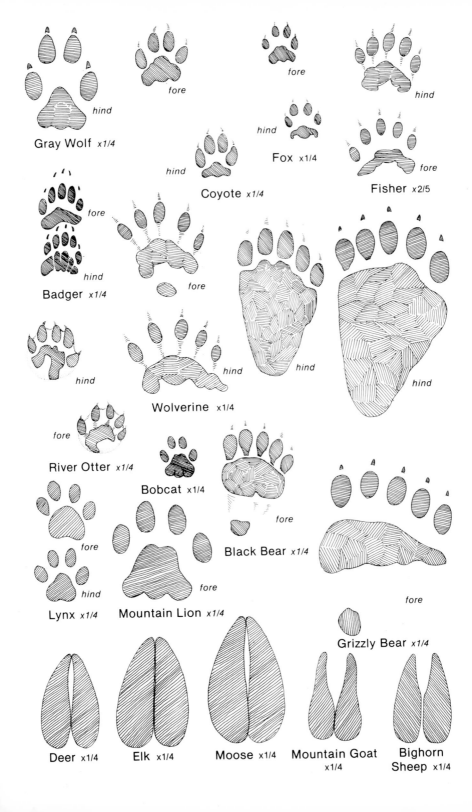

Gray Wolf *x1/4* — fore, hind

Coyote *x1/4* — fore, hind

Fox *x1/4* — fore, hind

Fisher *x2/5* — fore, hind

Badger *x1/4* — fore, hind

Wolverine *x1/4* — fore, hind

River Otter *x1/4* — fore

Bobcat *x1/4*

Black Bear *x1/4* — fore, hind

Grizzly Bear *x1/4* — fore, hind

Lynx *x1/4* — fore, hind

Mountain Lion *x1/4* — fore

Deer *x1/4*

Elk *x1/4*

Moose *x1/4*

Mountain Goat *x1/4*

Bighorn Sheep *x1/4*

SELECTED REFERENCES

GENERAL

Atkeson, Ray, 1969. *Northwest Heritage: The Cascade Range.* Graphic Arts, Portland, Oregon.

Barbour, Michael G. and Jack Major, eds., 1977. *Terrestrial Vegetation of California.* John Wiley and Sons, New York.

Evans, Brock, E. Cooper and R. Gunning, 1971. *The Alpine Lakes.* The Mountaineers, Seattle.

Fagerlund, Gunnar O., 1955. *Olympic National Park, Washington.* U.S. Government Printing Office, Washington, D.C.

Franklin, Jerry F. and C.T. Dyrness, 1973. *Natural Vegetation of Oregon and Washington.* U.S. Forest and Range Experiment Station, USDA, Portland, Oregon.

Grinnell, J., J. Dixon and J. Linsdale, 1936. *Vertebrate Natural History of a Section of Northern California through the Lassen Peak Region.* University of California Press, Berkeley.

Highsmith, Richard M. and A. Jon Kimerling, 1979. *Atlas of the Pacific Northwest,* 6th ed. Oregon State University Press, Corvallis.

Kirk, Ruth, 1968. *Exploring Mount Rainier.* University of Washington Press, Seattle.

———, 1964. *Exploring the Olympic Peninsula.* University of Washington Press, Seattle.

———, 1966. *The Olympic Rain Forest.* University of Washington Press, Seattle.

Kozloff, Eugene N., 1976. *Plants and Animals of the Pacific Northwest.* University of Washington Press, Seattle.

Manning, Harvey, 1965. *The Wild Cascades, Forgotten Parkland.* Sierra Club, San Francisco.

Manning, Harvey and Tom Miller, 1964. *The North Cascades.* The Mountaineers, Seattle.

Peattie, Roderick, ed., 1949. *The Cascades: Mountains of the Pacific Northwest.* The Vanguard Press, New York.

Schaffer, Jeffrey P., 1983. *Crater Lake and Vicinity.* Wilderness Press, Berkeley, California.

———, 1981. *Lassen Volcanic National Park and Vicinity.* Wilderness Press, Berkeley, California.

Schwartz, Susan, 1976. *Cascade Companion.* Pacific Search Press, Seattle.

Taylor, Walter P. and William T. Shaw, 1927. *Mammals and Birds of Mount Rainier National Park.* National Park Service, U.S. Department of the Interior, Washington, D.C.

Yocom, Charles and Vinson Brown, 1971. *Wildlife and Plants of the Cascades.* Naturegraph Publishers, Healdsburg, California.

Zwinger, Ann H. and Beatrice E. Willard, 1977. *Land Above the Trees: A Guide to American Alpine Tundra.* Harper and Row, New York.

GEOLOGY

Baldwin, Ewart M., 1976. *Geology of Oregon,* rev. ed. Kendall-Hunt Publishing Company, Dubuque, Iowa.

Campbell, C.D., 1962. *Introduction to Washington Geology and Resources.* Washington Division of Mines and Geology, Olympia, Washington.

Cannon, Bart, 1975. *Minerals of Washington.* Cordilleran, Mercer Island, Washington.

Crandell, Dwight R., 1969. *The Geologic Story of Mt. Rainier.* U.S. Geological Survey Bulletin 1292, Washington, D.C.

Crandell, Dwight R. and Donal R. Mullineaux, 1967. *Volcanic Hazards at Mt. Rainier, Washington.* U.S. Geological Survey Bulletin 1238, Washington, D.C.

Danner, W.R., 1955. *Geology of Olympic National Park.* University of Washington Press, Seattle.

Easterbrook, Don J. and David A. Rahm, 1970. *Landforms of Washington: The Geologic Environment.* Union Printing Company, Bellingham, Washington.

Ekman, L.C., 1962. *Scenic Geology of the Pacific Northwest.* Binfords and Mort, Publishers, Portland, Oregon.

Harris, Stephen L., 1980. *Fire and Ice: The Cascade Volcanoes,* rev. ed. The Mountaineers and Pacific Search Press, Seattle.

Livingston, Vaughn E., Jr., 1969. *Geologic History and Rocks and Minerals of Washington.* Division of Mines and Geology Information Circular 45, Olympia, Washington.

McKee, Bates, 1972. *Cascadia: The Geologic Evolution of the Pacific Northwest.* McGraw-Hill Book Company, New York.

Schulz, Paul E., 1959. *Geology of Lassen's Landscape.* Loomis Museum Association, Lassen Volcanic National Park, Mineral, California.

Tabor, Rowland W., 1975. *Guide to the Geology of Olympic National Park.* University of Washington Press, Seattle.

CLIMATE

Reifsnyder, William F., 1980. *Weathering the Wilderness: The Sierra Club Guide to Practical Meteorology.* Sierra Club, San Francisco.

Rue, Walter, 1978. *Weather of the Pacific Coast: Washington, Oregon, British Columbia.* The Writing Works, Mercer Island, Washington.

Schaefer, Vincent J. and John A. Day, 1981. *A Field Guide to the Atmosphere.* Houghton Mifflin Company, Boston.

GENERAL FLORAS

Abrams, L., 1940–1960. *An Illustrated Flora of the Pacific States,* 4 vols. Stanford University Press, Stanford, California.

Brockman, C.F., 1947. *Flora of Mt. Rainier National Park.* U.S. Government Printing Office, Washington, D.C.

Enari, Leonid, 1956. *Plants of the Pacific Northwest.* Binfords and Mort, Publishers, Portland, Oregon.

Gilkey, H.M. and L.R.J. Dennis, 1967. *Handbook of Northwestern Plants.* Oregon State University, Corvallis.

Henry, J.K., 1915. *Flora of Southern British Columbia and Vancouver Island.* W.J. Gage, Toronto.

Hitchcock, C. Leo and Arthur Cronquist, 1973. *Flora of the Pacific Northwest.* University of Washington, Seattle.

Hitchcock, C. Leo, Arthur Cronquist, Marion Ownbey, and J.W. Thompson, 1955–1969. *Vascular Plants of the Pacific Northwest,* 5 vols. University of Washington Press, Seattle.

Lyons, C.P., 1956. *Trees, Shrubs and Flowers to Know in Washington.* J.M. Dent and Sons, Ltd., Toronto.

Munz, Philip A. and David D. Keck, 1973. *A California Flora and Supplement.* University of California Press, Berkeley.

Peck, M.E., 1941. *A Manual of the Higher Plants of Oregon.* Binfords and Mort, Publishers, Portland, Oregon.

WILDFLOWERS

Clark, Lewis J., 1976.*Wild Flowers of the Pacific Northwest from Alaska to Northern California.* Grays Publishing, Ltd., Sidney, British Columbia.

Fries, Mary A., 1970. *Wildflowers of Mount Rainier and the Cascades.* Mount Rainier Natural History Association and The Mountaineers, Seattle.

Haskin, Leslie H., 1959. *Wildflowers of the Pacific Coast.* Binfords and Mort, Publishers, Portland, Oregon.

Horn, Elizabeth L., 1972. *Wildflowers of the Cascades.* The Touchstone Press, Beaverton, Oregon.

Larrison, E.J., G.W. Patrick, W.H. Baker, and J.A. Yaich, 1974. *Washington Wildflowers.* Seattle Audubon Society, Seattle.

Manning, Harvey, 1979. *Mountain Flowers.* The Mountaineers, Seattle.

Niehaus, Theodore F. and Charles L. Ripper, 1976. *A Field Guide to Pacific States Wildflowers.* Houghton Mifflin Company, Boston.

Rickett, Harold W., 1970. *Wildflowers of the United States,* vol. 5, *The Northwestern States.* McGraw-Hill Book Company, New York.

Sharpe, Grant and Wenonah, 1954. *101 Wildlflowers of Olympic National Park.* University of Washington Press, Seattle.

Spellenbery, Richard, 1979.*The Audubon Society Field Guide to North American Wildflowers: Western Region.* Alfred A. Knopf, New York.

Stewart, Charles, 1972. *Wildflowers of the Olympics.* Nature Education Enterprises and Olympic Natural History Association, San Francisco.

Taylor, Ronald J. and George W. Douglas, 1975. *Mountain Wild Flowers of the Pacific Northwest.* Binfords and Mort, Publishers, Portland, Oregon.

TREES AND SHRUBS

Arno, Stephen F. and Ramona P. Hammerly, 1977. *Northwest Trees.* The Mountaineers, Seattle.

Brockman, C. Frank, 1949. *Trees of Mount Rainier.* University of Washington Press, Seattle.

————, 1968. *Trees of North America.* Golden Press, New York.

Garman, Eric H., 1963. *Pocket Guide to the Trees and Shrubs of British Columbia,* 3rd rev. ed. British Columbia Forest Service Publication B.28, Victoria.

Hosie, R.C., 1979. *Native Trees of Canada,* 8th ed. Fitzhenry and Whiteside, Ltd., Don Mills, Ontario.

Little, Elbert J., Jr., 1971. *Atlas of U.S. Trees,* vols. 1 and 3. Miscellaneous Publications 1146 and 1314, Forest Service, USDA, Washington, D.C.

————, 1980. *The Audubon Society Field Guide to North American Trees: Western Region.* Alfred A. Knopf, New York.

————, 1978. *Important Forest Trees of the United States.* Agriculture Handbook 519, Forest Service, USDA, Washington, D.C.

McMinn, Howard E. and Evelyn Maino, 1967. *An Illustrated Manual of Pacific Coast Trees.* University of California Press, Berkeley.

Sudworth, George B., 1967. *Forest Trees of the Pacific Slope.* Dover Publications, Inc., New York.

Underhill, J.E., 1974. *Wild Berries of the Pacific Northwest.* Superior Publishing Company, Seattle.

BUTTERFLIES

Christensen, James R., 1981. *A Field Guide to Butterflies of the Pacific Northwest.* University Press of Idaho, Moscow.

Dorfeld, Ernst J., 1980. *The Butterflies of Oregon.* Timber Press, Forest Grove, Oregon.

Erlich, Paul and Anne Erlich, 1964. *How to Know the Butterflies.* W.C. Brown, Dubuque, Iowa.

Howe, William H. et al., 1975. *The Butterflies of North America.* Doubleday and Company, Garden City, New York.

Neill, W.A. and D.J. Hepburn, 1976. *Butterflies Afield in the Pacific Northwest.* Pacific Search Press, Seattle.

Pyle, Robert Michael, 1981. *The Audubon Society Field Guide to North American Butterflies.* Alfred A. Knopf, New York.

————, 1974. *Watching Washington Butterflies.* Seattle Aububon Society, Seattle.

TROUT AND SALMON

Bond, C.E., 1973. *Key to Oregon Freshwater Fishes,* rev. ed. Oregon Agriculture Experiment Station, Technical Bulletin 58.

Carl, G. Clifford, W.A. Clemens, and C.C. Lindsey, 1967. *The Fresh-water Fishes of British Columbia,* 4th ed. British Columbia Provincial Museum, Victoria.

McAllister, D.E. and E.J. Crossman, 1973. *A Guide to the Freshwater Sport Fishes of Canada*. National Museum of Natural Sciences, Ottawa.

Moyle, Peter B., 1976. *Inland Fishes of California*. University of California Press, Berkeley.

Wydoski, Richard S. and Richard R. Whitney, 1978. *Inland Fishes of Washington*. University of Washington Press, Seattle.

AMPHIBIANS AND REPTILES

Behler, John L., 1979. *The Aubudon Society Field Guide to North American Reptiles and Amphibians*. Alfred A. Knopf, New York.

Brown, Vinson, 1974. *Reptiles and Amphibians of the West*. Naturegraph Publishers, Healdsburg, California.

Carl, G.C., 1966. *The Amphibians of British Columbia*. British Columbia Provincial Museum, Victoria.

————, 1968. *The Reptiles of British Columbia*, 2nd ed. British Columbia Provincial Museum, Victoria.

Cochran, Doris M. and Colman J. Goin, 1970. *New Field Book of Reptiles and Amphibians*. Putnam, New York.

Leviton, Alan, 1972. *Amphibians and Reptiles of North America*. Doubleday and Company, Garden City, New York.

Stebbins, Robert C., 1954. *Amphibians and Reptiles of Western North America*. McGraw-Hill Book Company, New York.

————, 1966. *A Field Guide to Western Reptiles and Amphibians*. Houghton Mifflin Company, Boston.

BIRDS

Alcorn, G.D., 1978. *Northwest Birds: Distribution and Eggs*. Western Media, Tacoma, Washington.

Campbell, R.W. and H. Hosford, 1979. *Attracting and Feeding Birds in British Columbia*. British Columbia Provincial Museum, Victoria.

Farner, D.S., 1952. *Birds of Crater Lake National Park*. University of Kansas Press, Lawrence.

Gabrielson, I.N. and S.G. Jewett, 1940. *Birds of Oregon*. Oregon State College, Corvallis.

Godfrey, W.E., 1966. *The Birds of Canada*. National Museum of Canada, Ottawa.

Guiguet, C.J. *The Birds of British Columbia*, a series of handbooks. British Columbia Provincial Museum, Victoria.

Hoffmann, Ralph, 1927. *Birds of the Pacific States*. Houghton Mifflin Company, Boston.

Jewett, Stanley G., Walter P. Taylor, William T. Shaw, and John W. Aldrich, 1953. *Birds of Washington State*. University of Washington, Seattle.

Kitchin, Edward A., 1949. *Birds of the Olympic Peninsula*. Olympic Stationers, Port Angeles, Washington.

Larrison, Earl J., 1981. *Birds of the Pacific Northwest*. University Press of Idaho, Moscow.

Larrison, E.J. and K.G. Sonnenberg, 1968. *Washington Birds: Their Location and Identification*. Seattle Audubon Society, Seattle.

Mark, D.M., 1978. *Where to Find Birds in British Columbia*. Kestrel Press, New Westminster, British Columbia.

Milne, Robert C. and S.H. Matteson, 1965. *Checklist of Birds of Lassen Volcanic National Park, California.* Loomis Museum Association, Lassen Volcanic National Park, Mineral, California.

Nehls, Harry B. *Familiar Birds of the Northwest.* Portland Audubon Society, Portland, Oregon.

Peterson, Roger Tory, 1961. *A Field Guide to Western Birds.* Houghton Mifflin Company, Boston.

Pough, Richard H., 1957. *Audubon Western Bird Guide: Land, Water and Game Birds.* Doubleday and Company, Garden City, New York.

Ramsey, F.L., 1978. *Birding Oregon.* Audubon Society of Corvallis, Corvallis, Oregon.

Robbins, Chandler S., Betel Bruun, and Herbert S. Zim, 1966. *Birds of North America.* Golden Press, New York.

Small, Arnold, 1974. *The Birds of California.* Winchester Press, New York.

Stebbins, C.A. and R.C., 1953. *Birds of Lassen Volcanic National Park and Vicinity.* Loomis Museum Association, Lassen Volcanic National Park, Mineral, California.

Udvardy, M.D.F., 1977. *The Audubon Society Field Guide to North American Birds: Western Region.* Alfred A. Knopf, New York.

Wahl, Terence R. and Dennis R. Paulson, 1981. *A Guide to Bird Finding in Washington.* rev. ed. Terence Wahl, Bellingham, Washington.

Wilhelm, Eugene J., Jr., 1961. *Common Birds of Olympic National Park.* Olympic Natural History Association, Port Angeles, Washington.

MAMMALS

Bailey, Vernon, 1936. *The Mammals and Life Zones of Oregon.* USDA, Washington, D.C.

Banfield, Alexander W.F., 1974. *The Mammals of Canada.* University of Toronto Press, Toronto.

Burt, William H. and Richard P. Grossenheider, 1964. *A Field Guide to the Mammals,* 2nd ed. Houghton Mifflin Company, Boston.

Cowan, Ian McTaggart and Charles J. Guiguet, 1965. *The Mammals of British Columbia,* 3rd ed. British Columbia Provincial Museum, Victoria.

Dalquest, Walter W., 1948. *Mammals of Washington,* 2 vols. University of Kansas Publications, Museum of Natural History, Lawrence.

Ingles, Lloyd, 1965. *Mammals of the Pacific States.* Stanford University Press, Stanford, California.

Kritzman, Ellen B., 1977. *Little Mammals of the Pacific Northwest.* Pacific Search Press, Seattle.

Larrison, Earl J., 1976. *Mammals of the Northwest.* Seattle Audubon Society, Seattle.

————, 1970. *Washington Mammals: Their Habits, Identification and Distribution.* Seattle Audubon Society, Seattle.

Murie, Olaus J., 1974. *A Field Guide to Animal Tracks.* Houghton Mifflin Company, Boston.

Whitaker, John O., Jr., 1980. *The Audubon Society Field Guide to North American Mammals,* Alfred A. Knopf, New York.

INDEX

Plate references appear in parentheses and consist of a plate number – in boldface – followed by the page number for each plate.